THE SACK OF TROY.

Painted by Brygos early in the fifth century B. C.

Fig. 1.—The Acropolis of Athens, from the southwest.

THE LIFE OF THE
ANCIENT GREEKS

WITH SPECIAL REFERENCE TO ATHENS

BY

CHARLES BURTON GULICK, Ph. D.

ASSISTANT PROFESSOR OF GREEK IN HARVARD UNIVERSITY

ILLUSTRATED

COOPER SQUARE PUBLISHERS, INC.
NEW YORK
1973

TO

JOHN WILLIAMS WHITE

Originally Published 1902
Published 1973 by Cooper Square Publishers, Inc.
59 Fourth Avenue, New York, New York 10003
International Standard Book Number 0-8154-0456-5
Library of Congress Catalog Card Number 72-94074

Printed in the United States of America

PREFACE

THIS book aims to present the essential facts of daily life among the Greeks, particularly the Athenians, which experience has proved a boy or a girl may profitably learn while reading Greek authors or studying Greek history in preparation for college. The conjugation of λύω and the different forms of conditional sentences comprehend verities which must be thoroughly acquired and assimilated; but in the midst of them the pupil is apt to ask, " Who were the Greeks, after all, and how did they live? " " What did they wear, what did they eat, and what were their houses like? "

Such questions are pertinent and should be answered. I have therefore ventured to sift and reproduce in as untechnical a form as possible some of the settled knowledge about ancient life which affords useful lessons not only for the schoolboy but also for all educated persons to-day. In order to correlate the subject with the reading usually pursued in the schools, I have confined myself to a single period, the fifth and the fourth centuries, and have drawn frequently from the material which Xenophon's *Anabasis*, in spite of its well-known limitations, yet offers in abundance. The references to the *Anabasis*, however, are not

v

scattered throughout the pages of the text, where their constant interpolation would have been a source of irritation rather than a help, but have been gathered in two tables at pages 320–330.

Teachers generally concur in the opinion that foot-notes are distracting to the student, if not entirely neglected by him, and for this reason other authorities besides Xenophon are not cited, though I should have liked to acknowledge the source, ancient or modern, of some statements which may seem open to question. I have often felt that some of our best texts of the authors are overburdened with annotation. Perhaps a careful reading of such chapters in the present work as suit the teacher's purpose may do away with the necessity of requiring the pupil to study long notes in the text-books, which necessarily can offer but one or two points of view, and which usually conclude by referring the student to a dictionary of antiquities.

In order to render the pictures more useful, I have added an index of all the objects which they portray, by the use of which the teacher will gain much additional material, and may be able to assign subjects for short compositions on the externals of Greek life.

Though the book is intended primarily for students in our secondary schools and in the Freshman year at college, the general reader also, I hope, will find it adapted to his purpose. No knowledge of the Greek language is required, and though the citing of Greek terms could not be avoided, these have either been transliterated or so incorporated within the sentence that their meaning comes first, and the reader who has no acquaintance even with the Greek alphabet may calmly disregard them.

I fear that I may have offended many scholars by certain inconsistencies in spelling. The spelling of Greek names seems to be a matter of temperament; and whereas I cannot bring myself to give in Roman type the exact Greek forms of time-honoured names like *Aeschylus* and *Chirisophus*, I have found it equally impossible to Latinize such words as *Dipylon* and *lekythos*. In general, when a word has *ei* in the penult, it is so written in order to show the quantity and the modern pronunciation. An exception occurs in *Lycēum*, which, on account of its familiar occurrence in English, I have not altered, except to the extent of marking the quantity, as in *Peloponnēsus*. A Greek word quoted for the first time is put in italics, thereafter in Roman.

Most of the books mentioned in the bibliography have been my teachers, but I am indebted especially to Iwan von Müller's *Griechische Privataltertümer* (vol. iv, part 2, of his *Handbuch der klassischen Altertumswissenschaft*, 2d edition, 1892), and to the great *Dictionnaire* of Daremberg and Saglio, so far as it has appeared. My conviction that the Greek house of the fifth century had only one court was reached some years ago, but I am glad to acknowledge the help which I have derived from Professor Ernest Gardner's article on the Greek house in *The Journal of Hellenic Studies* for October, 1901.

It gives me pleasure to express my gratitude to Professor Clarence H. Young, of Columbia University, New York; to Rector W. H. Cushing, of the Westminster School, Simsbury, Conn.; to Dr. Theodore Woolsey Heermance, Secretary of the American School at Athens; and to Rector Charles Heald Weller, of the Hopkins Gram-

mar School, New Haven, for their generosity in allowing
me the use of photographs taken by them in Greece. My
thanks are also due to Mr. F. G. Kenyon, of the British
Museum, and to Mr. E. W. B. Nicholson, of the Bodleian
Library, for their kind permission to reproduce the papyrus
(Fig. 89) first published by Mr. Kenyon in his *Palaeography
of Greek Papyri*, Plate I ; and to the Council of the
Society for the Promotion of Hellenic Studies, for permission to copy Plate II in *The Journal of Hellenic Studies*,
1899, and a portion of Plate XII in the same journal, 1890.

To Professor Perrin and Professor Wright I am most
deeply indebted for their untiring zeal in reading manu-
script and proofs, and for the help and inspiration of their
scholarly criticism ; nor could I have undertaken and prose-
cuted the work without the sympathetic aid and encour-
agement of my wife.

HARVARD UNIVERSITY, *November 1, 1902*.

CONTENTS

THE LIFE OF THE ANCIENT GREEKS

THE LIFE OF THE ANCIENT GREEKS

CHAPTER I

GREECE, ATTICA, ATHENS

THREE great peninsulas—the Spanish, the Apennine, and the Balkan—extend from the European Continent into

Past and present.

the Mediterranean Sea. Of these, the last and most easterly is the smallest, and to-day perhaps the least important politically. The contrast between its present weakness and its past influence is great. The modern traveller, even with the plain record of history in his mind, and the evidence of splendid ruins before his eyes, finds it hard to connect in imagination the bare and rocky soil on which he stands with the life of a vigorous and intellectual people—a people who pointed out the way in poetry, art, science, and philosophy to their successors for all time.

If, however, the traveller climb even a moderate height in this little Greek peninsula, he will quickly discern some of the sources of inspiration to the people who have made

Nature of the country.

the land famous. They are the mountain and the sea, but especially the sea. These two, brought compactly and intimately together in alternating capes and gulfs, offer the utmost variety in physical environment, and are typical at once of the change and the stability, the versatility and the soberness, the rest and the unrest, that marked in turn the career of the people.

Greece—or Hellas, as the Greeks themselves called their home—lies in about the same latitude as Virginia; but the

1   1

proximity of hills and sea produces a remarkable effect, in that the climate and the vegetation of the temperate zone are brought within a few miles only of conditions of life that are almost tropical. None of the mountain tops, except Olympus on the northern border, are covered with snow throughout the year; and yet the snow does not disappear from Parnassus before one may pick and eat oranges and lemons in Sparta, hardly more than a hundred miles to the south. The pine and the fir grew but a few miles away from the fig and the olive; and even the palm was known on the island of Delos, and the date-palm on Naxos. The air is pure and mild, yet bracing enough in the old days to encourage the vigour and force that we see in the alert and enterprising Athenian and in the warlike, strenuous Spartan. The winds blew with a beneficent regularity which the early Greek mariner observed to his profit, and even in the wintry season they seldom rose to the force of a tropical hurricane. The winters were short, their severity lasting only from November to February. With the early spring came the " Etesian " winds, blowing regularly every morning from the Thracian north, and raising the sea in the narrow channels between the islands into a mighty swell; this, however, moves so evenly in its rise and fall that it is not dangerous, and the wind subsides entirely when the sun sets. With the evening a gentle breeze comes from the south, bringing with it a cooling, healthful breath which the ancient poets often extolled.

Climate.

The geological basis of the mountainous regions is chiefly limestone and a kind of tufa, called *poros*, which supplied serviceable building material for foundations and walls. The hills were pierced with numerous caves and grottos, which early imagination peopled with nymphs and other woodland divinities (Fig. 2). Often the limestone appears in the form of marble, as in the famous quarries of Attica, Euboea, and Paros. The larger rivers are found mostly in northern

The soil and the rivers.

and central Greece. The chief are the Aratthus in Epeirus, the Achelōus in Acarnania, and the Peneius, with its famous Vale of Tempé, in Thessaly. Others not so large, but important for the literary associations with which the poets have invested them, are the Asōpus in Boeotia, the Cephīsus in Attica, the Alpheius in Elis, the Eurōtas in Laconia, the Inachus in Argolis. Many streams are nothing but mountain torrents swelled by the melting snows in early spring

Fig. 2.—Caves of Pan and of Apollo on the Acropolis.

and entirely dry by the end of May. Some lose themselves through the porous soil in underground channels, to reappear elsewhere many miles distant. One of these streams is seen in Fig. 3. At the mouths of the rivers are alluvial deposits, usually of great fertility. In many districts, as at Cape Colias in Attica, were beds of white clay, excellent material for the potter; and coloured earths of metallic composition supplied the painter with his colours.

Wild animals were plentiful, notably the bear, the wolf,

the boar, and the deer.   Birds of all varieties found homes
in the thicker woods of the inland districts, in the reeds
that lined the beds of rivers like the Eurōtas,

Wild animals.

and even in the shrines and temples.   They
were carefully watched by the observant people, who gave them names from their ample vocabulary.
The migration of the cranes, the coming of the swallow in
the spring, the song of the nightingale—all were noted in
the life and poetry of the people.

The rivers and bays, too, supplied abundance of fish.
Sponges grew thickly in the waters by the coast, and were

FIG. 3.—Underground stream in Boeotia.

early used in the gymnasia and the baths (Fig. 119).   The
Phoenicians taught the Greeks how to obtain a rich dye-
ing material from the purpura, or purple fish.   The tortoise was a familiar object, and the song of the cicada was
so characteristic of the hot midsummer that this little
creature became the "chanticleer" (ἠχέτης) of the Greek

poets. Nature stood very close to the Greeks, and her influence on their lives was constantly recognized, often gratefully acknowledged.

So many kinds of folk were gathered under the single name of Hellēnes in this compact little country of Hellas, **Wide diver-** so diversified were their habits and feelings on **sity among** account of the variety of homes offered by **the Greeks.** mountain, seacoast, and river valley, that we must confine our attention mainly to one division of them. In Attica, in the most easterly portion of this easterly peninsula, in a space not quite two-thirds the area of Rhode Island, we find the forces of Hellenic genius at work most effectively in the fifth century B. C.; hence it is from Attica, as it appears during the period from the Persian Wars to the rise of Macedon, that we may derive the best illustrations of that genius as it showed itself in the manners and customs of ordinary life.

This limitation of our work, aside from the fact that Athens furnishes the most helpful lessons to be drawn from **Limitation of** ancient life in the Mediterranean basin, is ren- **the period** dered absolutely necessary when we consider **and the peo-** the long period of Hellenic existence, with its **ple to be** consequent change in modes of life from the **studied.** Mycenaean age (about 2000–1200 B. C.) down to the present, and, above all, when we face the fact, too often forgotten or neglected, that there were Greeks on the islands, Greeks in Africa and Sicily, Greeks in faraway Trapezus and in Massilia, at opposite ends of the world as then known to explorers. All these spoke languages necessarily affected by the tongues of the ruder peoples among whom they lived. Their modes of life, too, changed inevitably, if unconsciously, from those manners and customs which they brought at the beginning from their different homes on the Greek mainland.

CHAPTER II

ATHENS AND ITS ENVIRONS

A CHILD born in Athens when that city was at the height of its power grew up to find himself in a community full of political unrest and even anxiety, stirring with the eager, interesting life of an enterprising, enquiring, and socially gifted people, who had made their city " the hearthstone of Greece," " the council-chamber of Wisdom herself." Like **Athens the** most cities which had been founded in prehis- **centre of** toric times, Athens was a settlement grouped **Greek life.** round a steep and commanding hill. This hill, or Acropolis, rising out of the Attic plain four miles from the sea, stretches from east to west a distance of 1,000 feet or more, and is about 200 feet high. In remote times it had been the home of kings and the refuge of the villagers in the surrounding country from pirates by sea or from northern invaders by land; but it had become, in the Periclean age, the religious centre of the commonwealth. Here were the most ancient and most sacred shrines and altars; here the hearth of Hestia, goddess of home and communities, always remained, in spite of the growth of the city at the foot of the hill and the shifting of town life to lower ground. In the sixth century, to be sure, the Pisistratidae, like the kings long before, had occupied the Acropolis as a convenient centre of government and a means to maintain their power; but its defensive uses, though never quite forgotten, fell away after the Persian Wars, and the great statesmen of the fifth century devoted their energies and taste solely to its adornment.

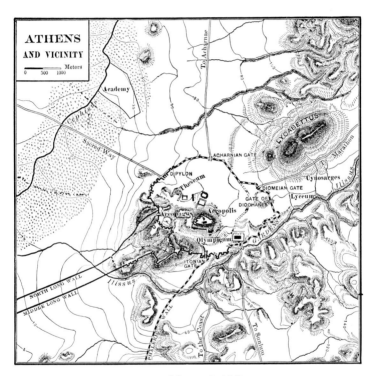

Fig. 4.—Athens and vicinity.

Toward the Acropolis converged roads from many directions. That from the Piraeus ran between the celebrated

Roads. Long Walls of Pericles, about two hundred and
fifty yards apart, affording safe communica-
tion with the harbour town at all times, in war or in peace.
Toward the northwest the Sacred Way guided the celebrants of the Mysteries through the beautiful Daphne pass
to Eleusis. Another road extended north to the collier

Fig. 5.—Mount Pentelicus as seen from the American School of Classical Studies.

town of Acharnae and to Deceleia. To the northeast, a road
passed the steep height of Lycabettus, and crossed or skirted
the hills into the plain of Marathon, with the marble quarries of Mount Pentelicus on the left; or it branched to the
right and led into the south of Attica, through the rich
midland plain, to the villages and towns of the eastern
coast. These roads were not paved, like the Roman military roads. Indeed, in the matter of building highways
the Greeks were far behind the Romans. The best of the

roads were merely smoothed of all impediments, and laid
evenly with sand or gravel or broken stone from the quarries.   Sometimes artificial ruts were cut in rocky portions
of the highways, two or three inches deep, with turnouts at
frequent intervals.   There was no side-path for persons on
foot, who therefore might be forced to stand aside, or climb
for safety on a wall, if they met a drove of asses or cattle.
Yet we are not to think of these roads as being thoroughly
bad.   Over the road from Sunium, thirty miles away, messengers could report at Athens the sighting of a vessel
bound for Piraeus several hours before it arrived.   All
roads in Greece used for festival processions, such as the
Sacred Way to Eleusis, were carefully kept in repair, and in
them the traveller on horseback, or the teamster carting
wares into the city, felt consciously the protection which
the religious sanctity of the road afforded him.   Here and
there, at the entrance to some large estate, the owner had
built a handsome gate of stone ; and as the road approached
Athens and entered the Cerameicus, or Potters' ward, it
was bordered by monuments to the dead so beautiful in
design and workmanship as to dispel any feeling of gloom
or sombreness.

The makers of these roads had not troubled themselves
to shorten distance and time by elaborate grading, and only
in places where the original ground was very
marshy was there a road-bed, banked by supporting walls.   The roads were useful chiefly
for heavy teaming : for the transportation of stone from the
quarries and ore from the mines, or for carrying the products
of the field to the morning market.   Most travellers, if not
burdened by luggage, could make better time by cutting
across hills and mountains through the numerous foot-paths.
But the highways offered every temptation to linger.   They
wound in and out between the hills, over streams, and past
neat farms, and presented a charming diversity.   Through
the plain, north and west of the city, flowed the Cephīsus,

Scenes on the roads.

on its way to the bay of Phalēron, its streams protected
from the warm sun by green groves of figs and olives, the
best in Greece. There were vineyards on the hill slopes,
the soil, rich enough though not deep, being carefully protected by intelligent terracing and irrigation. The Ilissus
flowed in a shady ravine at the east and south of the Acropolis. In the midland districts wheat and barley could be
raised in small quantities, and the mountainsides were protected from detrition by deep forests. Yet as early as the
fourth century B. C. the ruthless and short-sighted stripping

FIG. 6.—The spring Callirrhoë by the Ilissus.

of timber began, and in the Middle Ages desolation spread
through the carelessness of wandering shepherds, who, like
sportsmen and campers of to-day, frequently caused wast-
ing forest fires (cf. page 223).

The higher slopes were the home of sheep and goats.
In the heart of the hills there was building stone in abundance, and Pentelicus and Hymettus especially yielded
marble for the builder and the sculptor. Metals, too, were
found in the hills, and the silver-mines at Laurium, in the
south of Attica, are famous for the part they played in

transforming Athens into a sea power. Clay occurred near the city walls, favouring the growth of one of the most conspicuous industries of Athens—vase-making and vase-painting.

With all its diversity of soil and products, Attica was a snug little country, securely protected from the outside

Mountains of Attica. world by Parnes (4,200 feet), Pentelicus (3,300 feet), Hymettus (3,000 feet), and the sea. The Persians realized the danger of risking defeat in such a country, where escape was impossible except through narrow mountain passes. The compactness of the Attic territory is best appreciated from the summit of Lycabettus (the steep hill behind the Acropolis in Fig. 1), whence one may see the valleys of the Cephīsus and the Ilissus, the mountain walls around, the whole of the Gulf of Aegīna, and the coast of Peloponnēsus far to the south.

There is little wonder, then, that the Athenian took pride in his country, and contrasted his own history with that of other peoples—Thessalians, Boeotians, Argives, or Elēans—whose lands had been often overrun by foreign invaders. He alone, except the Arcadian, had always lived on his own soil. His was not a coast country exclusively, like that of Corinth or Milētus, nor yet an inland tract, hard to enter and impervious to progress, like Sparta and Thebes. The mountain, the shore, and the plain all furnished elements to form the Attic character; and as this diversity largely accounts for the early social and political history of Athens, so it explains too the later versatility and adaptability of Athenians generally. They were shepherds of the mountain, farmers of the plain, and seamen or fishers of the coast; and living as they did so close together, they entered into a thorough knowledge of one another's aims and modes of life.

The roads from the sea and the interior approached the city through suburbs (προάστεια), in which the houses were larger and finer than those in the city itself (ἄστυ). Here

and there were gardens planted round some sacred spring, notably those sacred to Aphrodīte in the Ilissus region. The most attractive suburb was the Outer Cerameicus, extending northwest to the Academy, which lay in a de-
Suburbs and parks of Athens. lightful grove of olives fostered and beautified by Cimon. But extensive parks, in the modern sense, were not laid out near Greek cities until much later, and then chiefly in Asia. The word *paradeisos* (παράδεισος), applied by the Greeks to the great game preserves of Eastern princes, is of Persian origin.

Fig. 7.--A portion of the Themistoclean wall.

Although the traveller journeying to ancient Athens would have seen in these suburbs a gradual transition from
The city wall. the lonely stretches of field and pasture to the noise and crowds of the city, he would have found himself confronted suddenly and abruptly by the great wall of Themistocles, which encircled the city with a protecting band nearly five miles in circum-

ference.   This was the wall built in eager haste by men, women, children, and slaves as a defense against Sparta and other jealous neighbours of Athens (Figs. 7, 233).   It was surmounted by towers at frequent intervals, and pierced

Fig. 8.—Wall of a tower in Messenia, with windows.

by gates ; some of these were of imposing architecture, like the great Thriasian gate, or Dipylon, at the northwest, which was the Athenian terminal of the Sacred Way. From them the streets (ὁδοί) converged to the agora (ἀγορά), which formed in every sense the centre of town life. Not all walls, of course, were built in such extraordinary haste, and there are many remains, in Athens and in other parts of Greece, of walls reared with great care and imposing strength. Such a wall, belonging to an ancient fortress in Messenia, is shown in Fig. 8. It is laid with regularly hewn blocks of stone that fit accurately one to another. Mortar was not used. Two windows are seen in the picture—narrow slits formed by cutting off the ends of the adjoining blocks at a sharp angle. A vase picture, copied in Fig. 16, which represents the wall of Troy and its gate guarded by Hector and Polītes, also shows the even succession of the stone courses.

The meaning of the word "agora" is explained only partially by our "market-place." In Homer it has its etymological sense of "meeting," "assembly," and Xenophon uses it with that meaning in one passage. After a time the name was transferred to the place of meeting, and in the towns it came to refer to the chief resort of the men. Thither they went not merely to do business with the tradespeople and artisans whose booths were there, but also to discuss politics or the news of the day with their associates while they sat under the shade of the plane-trees and poplars, or strolled in the porticoes which lined the whole "square."

The agora.

Fig. 9.—Roman gate of Athēna Archegetis.

The houses of the oldest families— the Eupatridae—remained near this centre until a late period, although the tradespeople finally usurped the agora itself, while the offices of the magistrates were removed, with a few exceptions, to other parts of the city. Gateways erected at various points presented dignified and imposing entrances to the agora. These, to be sure, were more numerous in Roman times, like the gate of Athēna Archegetis here figured (Fig. 9). Besides these, porticoes (στοαί),

which were narrow open structures with pillars supporting
a roof, served as a handsome setting to the statues, altars,

Fig. 10.—A paved way at Troy.

columns, and other decorations through which the daily
crowds made their way (cf. Figs. 31, 32).

The streets of Athens were notoriously narrow and
crooked, chiefly because the city was rebuilt in feverish
haste after the Persians destroyed it in 480
Streets. B. C. Like the country roads, they had no
pavement of regularly laid blocks of stone; nor had they
sidewalks. The ancient citadels, on the other hand, the
knowledge of which we owe to modern excavations, frequently show decided superiority in this respect. At Troy,
for instance, is a paved way which still exists in fairly good
preservation (Fig. 10). In wet weather, therefore, the mud
lay deep, and passing was difficult. These unpleasant conditions were aggravated by the unrestricted custom of
throwing refuse from the house at evening, and since the
streets were not lighted at night (page 140), people had to

pick their way through mud and filth. As a charm against disease, therefore, in those narrow alleys where light and warmth could not penetrate, it was customary to paint a picture of Apollo, the giver of health, on the walls of the

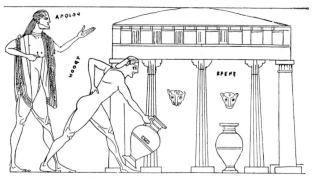

Fig. 11.—An ancient spring-house.

houses. The wider avenues ($\pi\lambda\alpha\tau\epsilon\hat{\imath}\alpha\iota\ \acute{o}\delta o\acute{\imath}$) were called later *plateiai* ($\pi\lambda\alpha\tau\epsilon\hat{\imath}\alpha\iota$), whence are derived " place " and " plaza." Some of these were dignified with names, such as " the Street of the Tripods," for example, which ran from the agora eastward and south below the Acropolis to the theatre.

In the harbour town, the Piraeus, the streets were not so bad. This port owed its origin virtually to the genius and foresight of Themistocles, and grew rapidly under the liberal policy of Pericles, who attracted thither many foreigners. Here, under the direction of Hippodamus of Milētus, the streets were laid out in regular lines, with spacious squares and abundant room for the active business plied there. Even in the upper city, the state did not wholly neglect the condition of the streets. A board of commissioners called *astynomoi* ($\dot{\alpha}\sigma\tau\upsilon\nu\acute{o}\mu o\iota$), five for Athens and five for the Piraeus, had, among other police duties, general oversight of the streets, and were charged not to allow the obstruction of them by barricades or by doors opening out-

ward from dwelling-houses. In particular, just before a
religious celebration at which there was to be a procession,
these officials were required to clean and level the streets
along the line of march. But we hear of no other provision
for the regular cleaning of the highways.

How refuse was removed from the streets we do not
know. The Athenians of the fifth century, at all events,
were not so scrupulous about the disposal of
sewage and the draining of waste water from
their houses as were the prehistoric inhabitants
of Mycēnae and Tiryns, where Dr. Schliemann found elaborate provision for carrying off water used in the bath.
But in Athens, as we have seen, the mud and filth in the
side alleys must have been intolerable, and until the fourth

Drainage and sewers.

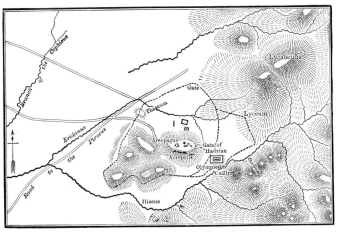

Fig. 12.—Plan of Athens, showing the watercourses.

century there was no restriction even against building
drains and gutters (ὀχετοί) from private houses into the street.
On the other hand, the stream called Eridanus on the map
(Fig. 12), which ran through the heart of the city from east
to west, became in course of time the regular receptacle for

2

waste matter. Accordingly, its bed was walled up and hidden by bridges and other structures. Air-shafts twenty feet deep were sunk here and there, showing that it was frequently inspected; and it debouched near the Dipylon, whence canals distributed its contents, for fertilizing purposes, over the plain between the Cephīsus and the Ilissus.

The houses of Athens were not supplied individually with running water, as a rule, and its people, as in other **Water.** Greek cities, were dependent on springs (κρῆναι) or artificial wells (φρέατα). A spring of fresh water, which the Greeks, like the Germans and the Portuguese, called "sweet" (ὕδωρ ἡδύ), was endowed with divine attributes in the popular fancy, and its protecting nymph or spirit was devoutly worshipped. The land round the Acropolis contained many such springs, and every house had also its cistern for the retention of rain-water. No

Fig. 13.—Women at the fountain.

springs were more famous than Callirrhoë (Fig. 6), in the Ilissus valley, or the Enneacrūnus, which Pisistratus furnished with pipes and with basins of sculptured marble. At the Dipylon, too, there was a magnificent fountain, and the growing needs of the city were further met by the building

of conduits which collected water from the brooks on Pentelicus, and led it to various fountains inside the walls, at the
corners of streets, or in the more open spaces (Figs. 11, 14).

In the matter of aqueducts, however, the Greeks could
never vie with Ro-
man engineering
skill. Nothing,
therefore, is more
characteristic of
Greek daily life
than the drawing
of water from
springs and wells
by women and girls
(ὑδροφόροι), who,
with water-jars
(ὑδρίαι, Fig. 13)
on their heads,
issued at early
morning in a long
procession to some
favourite spring,
often outside the
city walls. At a
well, by means of an
earthenware buck-

FIG. 14.—Remains of a street fountain at Priēne.

et (κάδος) attached to a rope (ἱμάς), they drew for themselves
the water required that day for household needs. The
Greeks under Xenophon and Chirisophus came upon
women performing this task outside an Armenian village.

We look in vain in Athens and in all Greece for anything that corresponds closely to the police force of a
Police. modern city. In general, a democratic state
like Athens relied upon its citizens, acting in
a private capacity, for the detection of crime, and in many
cases actually paid one-half of the fine imposed on a con-

victed person to his accuser. Any one who surprised another in the act of violating the law might hale him before a magistrate; or, if he felt unable to take such summary measures, he might lay information against the offender, whereupon the magistrate himself made the arrest. This system, while it tended to foster a vigorous personal responsibility to the law and a patriotic interest in the welfare of the state, nevertheless encouraged a grave evil in Athenian civilization, the practice of "sycophancy." The "sycophant" (συκοφάντης), in the Greek sense, was a man who got his living by threatening rich persons with legal process for real or alleged violation of the law, hoping thereby to extort money as the price of silence, or to gain part of the fine laid on his victim, should he be adjudged guilty.

We may perhaps discern the rudiments of a police board in the *astynomoi*, who, as we saw (page 16), enforced certain regulations regarding the care of the streets. In the market, too, a special commission, called *agoranomoi* (ἀγορανόμοι), were deputed to keep order. These two boards were attended by slaves belonging to the state, who were armed with bows, and therefore ordinarily called the Bowmen (τοξόται). Since they were of foreign origin, they were also named Scythians (Σκύθαι); or again *Peusinioi* (Πευσίνιοι), from a certain Peusin, otherwise unknown, who is said to have been the first to organize them. Similarly London policemen were called "Peelers," from Sir Robert Peel, who planned their organization. The Bowmen also acted as beadles in the courts and in the public assembly, to prevent undue noise and to eject obnoxious speakers or persons who interrupted the proceedings.

With all this, however, there was no regular patrol of the city streets in the interests of the personal safety of private citizens, and the dark alleys and the outskirts of the town were infested with footpads, who clubbed the belated citizen and robbed him of his mantle or purse.

CHAPTER III

DWELLING-HOUSES

THE Athenians as a rule enjoyed more space and greater comfort in their country houses than in those they occupied in the city. The mere fact that in the city houses were huddled closely together with party walls connecting them, shows at once the difference between them and the country houses, with more generous space, and a more rambling style, unrestrained by a neighbour's building. The foremost Athenian in town was no better off than his poorest neighbour in this regard. To our notions, houses in Athens were very small, grouped as they were to the number of 10,000 and more in a space limited by a city wall only five miles in circumference. Some rooms, from six to ten feet on a side, seem like mere cells. Even the richest men of the fifth century—excepting now and then a man with enormous wealth like Callias, or of extravagant tastes like Alcibiades—were averse to imitating the beauty and magnificence of temples and public buildings by rearing large dwellings. The ordinary Greek spent his whole day abroad with other men, and required shelter only for eating and sleeping. Conscious of his importance as the citizen of an imperial city, he found more satisfaction in the achievements—architectural as well as political—of that empire than in anything which he as a single individual could produce. Hence the mean appearance of the ordinary dwelling-houses, crowded among the narrow streets and alleys, became a subject of comment among the Greeks themselves. An old writer remarks that a stranger

External appearance of the houses.

21

entering the city would at first sight scarcely believe that this was really the great city of Athens. He would be re-assured, however, after a glimpse at the splendid temples, altars, gateways, and administrative buildings, on which

Inside.   Outside.

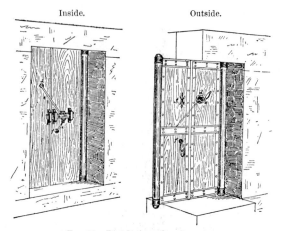

Fig. 15.—Restoration of a city gate.

the Athenians lavished the taste which they did not care to apply to the outward appearance of their private dwell-ings. But if Athens was deficient in this respect, Sparta lacked artistic decoration in a much greater degree. Thu-cydides says that if Sparta were razed to the ground, no student of history in later years could, from the ruins alone, conceive how great her political power had been.

The building materials in both town and country house were the same. The foundation was laid with rough stone, **Materials** not cut into rectangular blocks, but joined to-**of house-** gether in their natural state, with mud and **building.** smaller stones filling up the crevices. On this was reared the wooden frame of the house. The walls were made of mud squares or bricks (πλίνθοι) baked in the sun; for the Greeks at this time had not discovered the process of making kiln-dried bricks. When, therefore, a

Greek like Xenophon travelled in the Orient, he was struck
with admiration of the superior methods of the Babylonians
in this branch of building. In the *Anabasis* he particularly
mentions the fact that the "wall of Media" was built of
kiln-dried bricks laid in cement, and the foundation of the
wall of Mespila was of hewn stone, not rough stone loosely
fitted together.   These details must have attracted his
attention because they were not generally to be found in
Greek walls, whether of towns or of houses. So flimsy were
the latter, that burglars, instead of entering by a door, commonly dug their way through the wall, whence they were
called "wall-diggers" (τοιχωρύχοι). So the men of Plataea
made their way secretly, house by house, to a rendezvous in

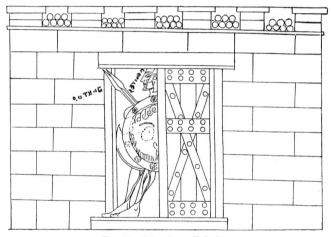

FIG. 16.—Gate of a walled city.

the city, digging through each party wall; and Xenophon's
men in a single night dug through the wall of a tower near
Pergamus which was eight plinths thick. This explains
why so few remains of Greek dwellings have been preserved.
Falling houses were not uncommon, and it would seem as
if the situation in Athens were scarcely better than in the

rude hamlets of Babylonia, where a foraging party sent
out by the Persians easily wrenched the timbers from the
houses.

Since the outer wall was extremely likely to crumble
away, it was protected in some degree by a kind of stucco

or plaster made of lime,
which was sometimes
painted in a single col-
our. The front of the
house, therefore, pre-
sented a perfectly bare
aspect to the street, re-
lieved on the ground
floor only by the door;
windows (θυρίδες), when

FIG. 17.—Double window.

there were any, were either in the second story, or set so
high—nine or ten feet from the ground—that they seemed
from the outside to belong to the upper rooms.

City roofs were regularly flat, whereas the thatch roofs
of the country were sloping. Hence in town the roof might
become a pleasant resort for the family on warm nights.
From it, too, the women raised their lament for Adōnis
when the annual festival in his honour came round. Clay
tiles protected the roof from rain. These sometimes proved to be a convenient and dangerous
weapon against an invader who penetrated too incautiously
into a narrow street. One such tile, flung by a woman from
the roof of a house in Argos, cost Pyrrhus his life. Sometimes the roof was lined with a row of large clay pots
(χύτραι), set up in the curious belief that they would
frighten away the birds. The commonest of these were
the owls, which became symbolic of Athens and Athēna,
being regularly figured on the coins of the city (Fig. 199).
The proverb "owls to Athens" passed current in antiquity as the equivalent of the modern "coals to New-
castle."

The roof.

Such, in general, was the external appearance of a house inhabited by the ordinary citizen. Houses were not numbered, and even the streets, as we saw, did not always bear fixed names. A man must go himself, or send a slave, to find out the residence of any one whom he sought. The state, to be sure, kept track of a citizen's family and ward in the register of his deme (page 89). In practical life his house was described as being near some well-known temple, fountain, wall, or gate. Moving was not uncommon among the middle and the lower classes, though always recognized as troublesome and undesirable. The favourite quarter for residences was the deme Collytus (Κολλυτός), just north of the Acropolis. Here, unfortunately, the modern city was built in 1834; for it has rendered excavation next to impossible, and greatly restricted our opportunities for learning about the construction and arrangement of houses.

If, now, we try to gain an idea of the inner arrangement, we find ourselves embarrassed by the meagreness of our information. Excavations in various parts of Greece, Italy, and Asia Minor, while they have yielded immense additions to our knowledge of the architecture of temple and theatre, have, as yet, brought to light very few examples of a Greek house of the fifth century. We must therefore fall back on **Internal arrangements of the house.** what we can gather from ancient writers; and since their evidence is never given in formal description, but has to be deduced from mere allusions, often scant enough, the result can be accepted only as uncertain and provisional. We must remember, too, that not all houses were built exactly alike, any more than they are to-day. We may assume the greatest variety in number and arrangement of rooms, according to the location of the house and the means of the owner. The accompanying diagram, therefore, is designed to show only a possible arrangement of the town house, assuming that it contained most of the rooms and appurtenances mentioned by Greek writers.

We enter at *A* a door which opens into a passage called the *thyron* (θυρών, *B*). This leads into a court (*D*) open to the sky. The court, or *aulé* (αὐλή), was the central and essential feature of the city house, since it formed the principal means of admitting light and air. In the country house the position of the court was quite dif-

The court.

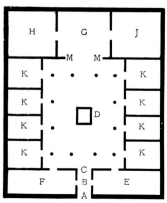

FIG. 18.—Theoretical plan of a city house.

ferent. There, it stood in front of the edifice, and was not, strictly speaking, a structural part of it. This made it a survival of the old Homeric arrangement, in which the yard fronting the house was surrounded by a wall on three sides, with the façade of the building completing the fourth.

Since the front door (*A*) of many houses was visible from the court (*D*) and led almost directly into it, this door was called the " court door " (ἡ αὔλειος θύρα). In many houses it might be set in a little from the street, so that the recess thus formed made a kind of vestibule (τὰ πρόθυρα) open to the street. In a rich man's house this might also be extended outward into the street by means of supporting columns, which formed a small porch (see Fig. 96). In this area often stood a little shrine to Hecaté and a symbolic representation of Apollo Agyieus—guardian of the streets—in the shape of a pointed column (page 262). Next it an altar may have stood. So also, to invite the protection of Apollo, laurel or bay trees were sometimes set out before the front door; and there was, further, the inscription above the door, μηδὲν εἰσίτω κακόν (*Let no harm enter*). One of the household slaves sat in a small room on one side of the entry (*F*) to act as porter (θυρωρός) and answer (ὑπα-

The entrance.

κούω) a visitor's knock. For this there was a metal knocker (ῥόπτρον) ; or the person desiring entrance beat on the door and called " παῖ, παῖ " (*Slave!*) ! Often the porter was a surly

fellow whose wrath was easily roused, especially when a visitor pounded too vio‐ lently with his fists, or kicked in ill-bred fashion with his foot. The door opened in‐ ward, by a handle or ring called the ἐπι‐ σπαστήρ (Fig. 95).

FIG. 19.—Door of a house.

Opposite the por‐ ter's room in many houses were stalls for horses (*E*) ; for the Greeks, like some villagers in Europe to-day, had no **The rooms.** scruples at housing animals under the same roof with themselves. So chickens and other birds, especially quails and jackdaws, were often kept in the court (Fig. 94). When Xenophon comes upon Arme‐ nians living in underground houses, in which were also gathered their sheep, goats, cattle, and fowl, he is struck

FIG. 20.—Greek keys.

not so much by the miscellaneous char‐ acter of the inmates as by the unusual construction of the dwellings below the ground.

In many houses, doubtless those nearest the market‐ place, the rooms just mentioned served as the workshop (ἐργαστήριον) and salesroom (πωλητήριον) of artisans and tradesmen ; or physicians had their offices (ἰατρεῖα) here.

If they had hired their quarters, these were of course entirely shut off from the rest of the house.

Even the modest house of Socrates had its court (*D*). Such courts were always rectangular, though the rectangle

was not necessarily symmetrical (see Figs. 26 and 30). In the better houses it was bounded by a columned portico or peristyle. On one side of the court, usually the north, since that was open to the sun's rays, was a hall or living-room (*G*) called the *pastas* (παστάς or παραστάς).

Fig. 21.—Door opening into a sleeping-room.

This seems to have derived its name from two engaged columns or pilasters (*M, M*), called παραστάδες, which marked the entrance from the court into this hall; hence

it was not divided by a door from the court, but formed a recess or alcove to it. Here, or in the court if the house were too small to contain a pastas, the daily life of the women and children took its course (see Figs. 94, 95); from here they retired to the rooms adjoining the pastas or in the upper story if the masculine members of the family came home with friends who were not kindred.

Fig. 22.—Door of a storeroom.

Round the court were grouped the rooms (δωμάτια, οἰκήματα, *K*), which, of course, varied in number and position with each house (contrast Fig. 26 with Fig. 28). Some-

times only two sides of the court were thus surrounded,
the third being bound by the wall of the house (Figs. 26,
28, 29). Some rooms were sleeping-rooms (κοιτῶνες, also
δωμάτια) ; some, guest-cham-
bers (ξενῶνες) ; some, store
closets (ταμιεῖα). At best
they were mere cells, with no
other opening than the door-
ways connecting with the
court. These were hung with
curtains or *portières* (παρα-
πετάσματα) or furnished with
regular doors.

These doors were either
single or double. A single
door opening into a bedcham-
ber is seen in Fig. 21, with

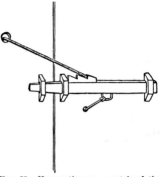

Fig. 23.—Key resting on a notch of the
bolt inside a door.

an ornamented handle at the top. In Fig. 22

**Doors and
locks.**

a maid is carrying her mistress's jewel-casket
back to its place in the storeroom, the door of
which is double. She inserts a large key
(κλής), which is simply a metal bar bent twice
at right angles (see Fig. 20). This she works
until its inner end catches against a knob
or notch on the bolt inside (Fig. 23), when
it becomes easy to thrust the bolt to one
side. The key is then pulled out and the
door opens by means of the handle, seen
in Figs. 21, 22. In locking, it was necessary merely to pull the bolt in place by a
strap which hung through a hole on the
outside of the door (Figs. 15, 22, 23). The
strap was then taken off and carried away

Fig. 24. — Priestess
with a key.

or thrust back into the hole. A good deal of noise, caused
both by the bolts (often in a city gate these were double)
and also by the hinges, attended the opening of a door.

There was another kind of key, more like our own, shown in Fig. 24. This was inserted in a slit in the door, such as may be seen at the left in the door of Fig. 95. The hook at the end of the key exactly fitted a hollow in the bolt, and accordingly, when turned to right or left, effected the locking or unlocking of the door. A "Laconian" key with three teeth is mentioned; but the construction of the lock was complicated and is not entirely certain.

In the middle of the court stood the altar of *Zeus Herkeios* (Ζεὺς Ἑρκεῖος), on which the father of the family, as its priest, offered sacrifice to Zeus, protector of the family circle. Here, too, were statues of Zeus and of Apollo Patrōos, the family god of all Ionians.

At home the master and his friends had their banquets and symposia in the hall of the men, the *andron* (ἀνδρών), which we may place at *H*. In its relative size, being larger than most of the other rooms, and in its importance as the scene of indoor life and the daily occupations of the family group, it corresponded to the great hall (μέγαρον) of the Homeric house. As far as this room, and no farther, strangers might penetrate, and then only if the master of the house was present. The whole of this part of the house, or that to which the andron stood as the centre, was from it termed the *andronĭtis* (ἀνδρωνῖτις). But when the adult males were abroad, as they generally were by day, the wife, children, and slaves might gather round the circular hearth (ἑστία) for the business and pleasure of the day, which was either in this room or in the pastas (*G*). This hearth, the real centre of domestic life, was the scene of many solemn and important religious ceremonies that affected the welfare of the family. In the houses of the poor it also served as the ordinary cooking hearth.

Every dwelling, however, provided special quarters for the women and the girls, to which no man outside the immediate circle of relatives might have entrance; and since

The men's quarters.

all the rooms just mentioned were in plain sight of the court, through which visitors must pass in order to reach the andron, an entirely separate suite was reserved for the

The women's quarters.

women. To this they were not, of course, obliged to confine themselves except when the male inmates had callers. This suite, like the other rooms we have just seen, may have opened on the court; in this case a strong door divided it from the court. Such quarters may possibly be recognized in J (Figs. 26 and 27), with its adjoining inner room, K, both of which, though connecting directly with the court, have no connection with the large reception-rooms or *andrōnes* recognizable in H. In some houses the women's quarters must have been in the second story, as in the houses of Figs. 28 and 29. The name applied generally to the women's quarters was *gynai-konītis* (γυναικωνῖτις), and it naturally embraced a larger number of rooms than the andronītis, since at home, during the master's absence, the women had free range of the house. One of the rooms of the gynaikonītis was the bedroom of the master and the mistress (J in Fig. 18); even in prose this retained its ancient and revered name of *thalamos* (θάλαμος). Here the head of the house kept his strong box and his valuables. Here, too, were little images of the patron gods of marriage—the θεοὶ γαμήλιοι and γενέθλιοι.

In many, and probably in most, houses there was a separate room used as kitchen (ὀπτάνιον), although among the

The kitchen.

poor, whose space was cramped, cooking was done also at the hearth in the andron or the pastas. In Fig. 27 the room marked K^2 at the left of the entrance A^2 seems to have been the kitchen; in Fig. 28, K^1, at the right of the entrance A^1, may perhaps have been the kitchen. The absence of any fireplace in the ruins of these houses may be accounted for by supposing that the inhabitants used portable ovens or braziers, like those shown in Figs. 126 and 129.

In the earlier ages, and even later in rural districts, an

open fire was made for cooking on the family hearth
(ἑστία). Later an earthenware oven (κρίβανος, κάμινος, or
ἱπνός) kept the fire within bounds. A board or shelf pro-

The fire-place.
jected over the oven. On it could be ranged
dishes, cups, and other utensils (ἐργαλεῖα) for
cooking; also the crane which held the cal-
dron, flesh-hooks (κρεάγραι, Fig. 127) for pulling meat out of
the pot, and the like. The smoke of the fire rose through
an opening in the wall or the roof; but since it was not
conducted through a pipe, it must also have blown about
until it found its way through doors, chinks, and crevices.
The hole in the roof (καπνοδόκη) could be closed with a
board or trap-door (τηλία).

We have thus traversed the whole of the first floor, according to the plan given in Fig. 18. A solid wall, which
might mark the beginning of another house, terminates
the rooms at the back. Such party walls may be seen in
Fig. 25, showing the plan of a
block of four houses discovered a
few years ago in Priēne, near Milētus. Some houses had more than
one entrance, and were accordingly said to be ἀμφίθυροι (see Figs.
27 and 28). The second entrance
might be at the back or at the side,
opening on an adjoining alley.

The second story was absolutely necessary in most Greek cities.
Even the large and conveniently
arranged house of Fig. 28 had
an upper floor, reached by stairs

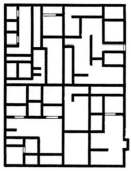

FIG. 25.—Plan of a block of four
houses at Priēne.

(κλίμακες) made of wood. The second story either covered
the whole of the lower portion—except of course the court,
which was open to the sky—or else extended over a portion of it only. In the former case the house was an
οἰκίδιον διπλοῦν; in the latter, the upper floor, usually called

ὑπερῷον, suggested rather a tower, and was consequently called πύργος. Sometimes it projected a foot or two over the street, resembling old houses in Europe to-day. From it windows (θυρίδες) looked into the street. The upper story was reached by a stairway inside, unless it was let to strangers, in which case steps from the street on the out-side led directly to it, thus avoiding any disturbance of the inmates below. Houses thus let were called *synoikiai*, " flats " (συνοικίαι), in contrast to *oikiai* (οἰκίαι), which were designed for a single tenant. They sometimes had balconies (περίδρομοι). Although we hear of such tenements mostly in the fourth century, they must have been a profitable in-vestment for citizens in the latter half of the fifth as well, because the state did not allow the numerous foreigners then settling in Attica to own houses. If the upper story were not let out, or used in general as the gynaikonītis, it was devoted to the female slaves. In the *Anabasis* we read of a loft (ἀνώγεων) where nuts were drying.

Some houses, further, had cellars for storing wine in huge jars and casks (πίθοι, κέραμοι), like those seen in Fig.
Cisterns. 107 ; and most had cisterns (λάκκοι) for catch-ing rain-water. This was especially true in places like Delos, a small island where wells and springs were scarce. But we have already seen that, in the fifth century at least, water was not carried by mains under the streets to the houses, and for good drinking water slaves had to be sent to the springs and fountains (Figs. 11 and 13).

There were no appliances for maintaining an even heat throughout the house. In the low-lying districts of Greece
Heating. near the sea the climate demanded none. In very severe weather, or on the upper levels, portable braziers (ἐσχάραι, πύραυνοι, see Figs. 126 and 129) supported on tripods, or basins filled with glowing char-coal, could be carried from one room to another at pleas-ure ; and the hearth in the andron could be used for a bon-fire in winter. Curiously enough, conflagrations—except,

3

of course, in war—seem to have been infrequent. The walls of mud or broken stone, perishable as they were otherwise, at least tended to restrict the spread of fire. There was no fire-brigade at Athens; if a fire occurred, the market commissioners (ἀγορανόμοι), and later the astynomoi (see page 16), probably rendered what aid they could. Arson (πυρκαϊά, ἐμπρησμός) was punishable with death, being regarded as an attack on life.

The court furnished most of the light to the rooms. Those on the second floor derived a scanty addition of

Lighting. light from the small windows which looked into the street. Houses which faced the south were preferred when they were obtainable, since the light and heat of the sun in their courts were greater. At night oil lamps were used; at the entrance of some houses was a niche to hold a lamp at night. Such niches were found in the houses of Figs. 26 and 28.

We must next see how far the plan of a house sketched above (Fig. 18) on the basis of information given to us by

Houses on the island of Delos. ancient Greeks agrees with what archaeologists have discovered in our day among the ruins. In the island of Delos the foundations and

parts of walls have been laid bare belonging to houses that date from the second century B. C. The ground-plans of some of the houses appear in Figs. 26, 27, 28, and 29. They are not, to be sure, free from some Roman features, such as the handsome mosaic which paves the courts (αὐλαί) of the houses in Figs. 27 and 29; but they are thoroughly Greek in all essential features. In Fig. 26 we see a house very symmetrically built, forming nearly an exact square, which meas-

Fig. 26.—House on the hill (Delos).

ured about fifty feet on each side. The entrance is at A, where the door-posts of marble still stand. In the use of this material the house probably shows an advance on the poorer constructions of rough stone and mud bricks that were erected in the fifth century. At the right of the entrance is a niche raised to the level of a man's head, for receiving a lamp at night. We pass through the entry ($\theta\nu\rho\dot{\omega}\nu$) B, and a second door, C, into the court ($a\dot{\nu}\lambda\dot{\eta}$) D. The shape of this is peculiar, since it opens out on the north side of the house into a long space extending through the entire depth of the house. There was no porter's room. The peristyle in the court had eight columns of the Doric order. The large room, H, was probably a reception-room, which we may call the andron, while J and K may have been apartments for the women exclusively. They also had rooms upstairs, for at O was a stairway. Most, if not all, the rooms had windows, but so highly placed—in some

cases ten feet above the ground — that it was impossible to see through them. They were designed to give light only.

In Fig. 27 we see a house of a wholly irregular shape; it proves how the nature of the ground and the space at the disposal of the builder determined the arrangement of each dwelling. This house had two entrances, the

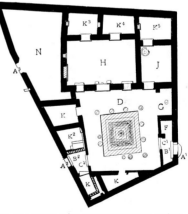

FIG. 27.—House north of the sacred lake (Delos).

principal one being at the corner ($A^1\ B^1\ C^1$). At the left, as the visitor entered A^1, he found in the angle a small stone bench on which he could sit and wait until the porter admitted him. The porter's lodge was at *F*, on the right. Twelve solid Ionic columns formed the peristyle. In the court (*D*) were a cistern and a well. The men's hall seems to have been at *H*, adjoining which were smaller rooms (*K*³ *K*⁴), which may have been men's sleeping-apartments. Perhaps the separate women's quarters were at *J* and *K*⁵. The circle in *J* marks the position of a large wash-basin (λουτήρ, see page 138). At *G* was the pastas (probably), convenient in its proximity to the women's rooms. The kitchen, however, seems to have been far removed from them, being at *K*², at the left of the second entrance (*A*² *B*² *C*²); it is to be remembered that hot dishes were perhaps not so much in demand as in our northern climate, so that the carrying of food across the court to the andron at *H* produced no inconvenience. What the large room *N* was for we do not know. It originally connected with *H*, but was later separated entirely from the rest of the house, and given an entrance (*A*³) of its own. It may therefore have been let out as a shop. It, too, had a cistern.

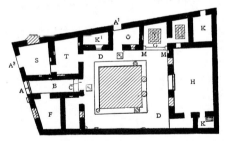

FIG. 28.—House in the Street of the Theatre (Delos).

The house in Fig. 28 is perhaps the most interesting of all. The porter's lodge is at the right (*F*), and the entrance is relatively long. There were twelve Doric columns forming the peristyle, beyond which was the fine large reception-room *H*. The pastas at *G* had a floor paved with mosaic, in the Roman fashion. The rooms *S* and *T* seem to have been a shop, owned and managed by the owner of the house, since it communicates at the rear with the court. It has, of course, its own entrance from the street (*A*²). At *O* was a stairway, and it is likely that the women's sleeping-rooms were upstairs.

In Fig. 29 we have a house of simpler construction. The number of rooms is so small that there must have been a second story, reached probably from some part of the room *J*. We come first upon an entry over six feet wide, to the left of which was probably the porter's room (*F*). On the right (*E*) were probably the accommodations needed for horses and other animals. At the end of the passage is a second door a little wider than the first, which opened directly on the spacious court (*D*), about forty-two by thirty-four feet. The twelve columns forming the peristyle are clearly made out. They were of white marble, with Doric capitals, and nearly ten feet

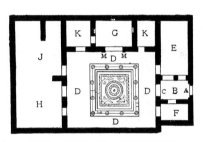

Fig. 29.—House on the Inopus (Delos).

high. In the open space bounded by the columns the floor was paved with a handsome mosaic, a mark of that later Hellenistic luxury which we can not assume for an earlier period. For in the fifth century, and even later, the floors were at best nothing but pebble surfaces stamped and beaten smooth. One side of the court is bounded immediately by the house wall. The large space in the rear was probably the site of the andron. The explorers recovered smaller columns which must have supported the second peristyle, belonging to the upper story.

Houses in Priēne. The houses unearthed by German excavators at Priēne may also be safely used to illustrate the main features of an Athenian house, although they date from the third century B. C., and bear many signs of a luxury which belongs only to the period of Greek history after Alexander the Great. Each house is a rectangle, as shown in the diagram (Fig. 25), about fifty-four by seventy-two feet. The area covered by each differs therefore only a little from the area of the house at Delos represented in Fig. 29. These houses had only one door each, and this opened on the side street. It led directly into the court, without any connecting passage. The walls inside had a coating of marble, therein differing greatly from the ordinary house at Athens two centuries before; for there the walls of mud or rubble were covered simply with whitewash or stucco. Alcibiades went to the very verge of rash extravagance, it was thought, when he had his walls decorated with paintings. Other traces of advanced interior decoration were found at Priēne, such as handsome cornices and mouldings in marble, Ionic half-columns, triglyphs painted in different colours, and other ornamental devices—e. g., a satyr's head in stucco, painted bright red. Little figures of Eros (Love) appeared, perhaps originally hung from the ceiling. We know nothing about the ceilings of a house of the classical period. In the better class of houses they may have been panelled, like the ceilings of temples.

FIG. 30.—House in Dystus.

The only remains known of houses belonging to the fifth century have still more recently been found in

House in Dystus.

Dystus, an ancient city of Euboea. The houses here were mostly two-storied, and had walls of rough stone laid one on the other much in the fashion of the stone fences in rural New England, with smaller stones fitted into the crevices. A plan of one of these houses is given in Fig. 30. The front door (*A*) is at the end of a long, descending passageway. On passing the second door (*C*) the visitor finds himself in a long entry which widens out beyond the room *F*, probably the porter's lodge, into a spacious apartment (D^2) large enough to be a court (αὐλή). In it was a fountain. The real court, however, is seen in D^1, which is surrounded by the rooms *K*, perhaps sleeping-rooms, and *G*, perhaps the pastas. The small room *M*, which could be securely locked, was probably the storeroom. The passage D^2 divided the house into two nearly equal parts. Opposite the part just described was a large room, doubtless the andron, behind which were two other rooms (*K*, *K*). It is likely that all that portion of which D^1 is the centre was the gynaikonītis. whereas *H* and the rooms behind were devoted to the men.

The contrast between the ancient house, so well adapted to the simpler needs of a people living in a warmer climate than ours, and the ordinary house of northern Europe or America, is seen to be great. The Greek house, depending for light mainly on the court, necessarily included that inside its walls, whereas the modern house, deriving its light from more numerous windows, or from halls and corridors, has its court or garden or lawn, as the case may be, outside. Though, as we have seen, two-storied houses were common, the stairs, which are so prominent to-day, were an unimportant feature of the ancient edifice.

CHAPTER IV

THE OUTWARD SURROUNDINGS OF ATHENIAN LIFE

LIFE at Athens in the fifth century was so predominantly public in its nature that in the case of the men it is
The outdoor almost misleading to speak of their "home
life of the life." A change, to be sure, came later, when,
men. from the middle of the fourth century, the
history of society throughout Greece becomes a history of the gradual shifting of men's interests from public to private matters, from political questions to social and domestic concerns; and, on the intellectual side, we see a change from the vigorous production of great literary works, often offered in public competition, to the quiet and secluded study of them by scholars and critics. We, however, are concerned mainly with the fifth century, the age at once of hope and of accomplishment, and no survey of life at this period can be complete without a glance at the public buildings and other edifices with which men had to do.

The agora, as we saw, was daily crowded with men. Of course, too great devotion to the market and to the gossips
that gathered there was not regarded as wholly
Boundaries of respectable. A man who had no other pursuit
the agora. than to lounge there all day was thought to be
a hoodlum, and the word *agoraios* (ἀγοραῖος), was used by more circumspect persons to denote a street idler. Like all idlers in commercial cities, these *agoraioi* were ready to join every street brawl, to maltreat a foreign peddler, or to molest a schoolboy. Yet for all that, eminently respectable citizens resorted daily to the agora as the social centre.

40

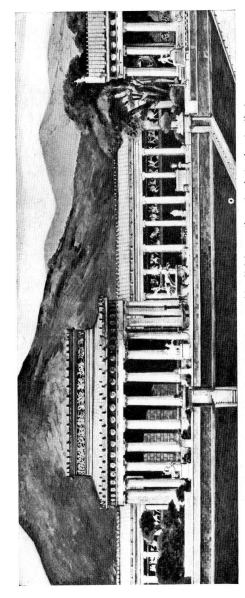

FIG. 31.—The so-called *Tholos* at Epidaurus, with adjoining porticoes (conjectural restoration).

At Athens the agora lay in the hollow north of the Areopagus and the Acropolis, in the ward or deme called Cerameicus.   A part of the western side was bounded by a
gentle elevation called "Market Hill," the Colōnos Agoraios, at the foot of which stood one of the chief buildings
of this district, the King's Portico, στοὰ βασί-
Public buildings. λειος, the corridor in which the archon called
"the King" had his office.   Here also the
Court of the Areopagus
held their sittings. Hither came Socrates to ap-
pear before the archon
at the summons of his
accusers; and here, five
centuries later, St. Paul
addressed the Athenians,
who then, as they had
done before, made this
their favourite resort.
Farther south stood a
group of buildings like-
wise dear to the hearts
of democratic citizens.
The first was a precinct
and sanctuary dedicated
to the Mother of the
Gods, and called the
Metrōon. Here the state

FIG. 32.—The double portico (*stoa*) at Pergamus, restored.

archives were kept.   The second was the chamber in which
the Council of Five Hundred (βουλή) held meetings.

The third edifice was devoted to a committee of the
Council called the Prytanes (see page 207), who attended to
the routine business of the Council, and offered sacrifice for
the weal of the state in the "Rotunda" or *Tholos* (Θόλος), a
structure so called on account of its circular form; it enclosed the sacred hearth of Hestia, a symbol of the depend-

ence of the state upon the family. The general appearance of the Tholos may be fairly conjectured by a comparison with a similar though handsomer structure built in the fourth century at Epidaurus (Fig. 31). A priest was in attendance to conduct the rites necessary as a preliminary to all public and private business; and a public slave acted as sacristan and attendant of the Prytanes, who also dined here. Situated near the heart of trade, it was a convenient repository for the official weights and measures. The other magistrates—for example, the chief Archon, the Polemarch, and the six Thesmothetae—must have occu-

Porticoes. pied offices near here. There were, further,

other porticoes (στοαί) besides that of the King (βασίλειος) : one was the stoa of Zeus Eleutherios; another was a special portico for the sale of grain, the στοὰ ἀλφιτόπω-λις; again there was the famous "Painted Porch,"

Fig. 33.—Detail of balustrade in the portico at Pergamus.

στοὰ ποικίλη, which Cimon's brother-in-law Peisianax had reared. Its walls were covered with historical paintings by Polygnōtus and Micon.

This gives but a partial idea of the varied scene. There were besides countless altars (Fig. 34; see also Figs. 242, 243) and shrines, statues, and especially stēlai—i. e., slabs of marble or other stone on which were inscribed public and private memorials of all sorts. Here was also the famous row of Hermai (οἱ Ἑρμαῖ) guarding the agora, as the Herm before each house door guarded the family (Fig. 35). Many of these Hermae were very old, dating back to the archaic period of art, and all were held in veneration. At their bases offerings, including even money, were

laid, and secrets were confided to their ears. The statues of Harmodius and Aristogeiton stood opposite the Metrōon, a daily reminder of the struggle that ended in the establishment of democratic institutions in Athens (cf. Fig. 138).

While, therefore, this part of the city could not compete with the citadel in the well-ordered and artistic grouping of buildings, it derived an interest from the very irregularity in which its works of art had been reared ; for they pictured in historic sequence the tastes and needs of the people at different times throughout a period extending from Pisistra-

FIG. 34.—Altar of Dionysus.

tus to Pericles. One temple, commonly called the Theseium, still stands on Colōnos Agoraios, and is the best

Temples. preserved of all Greek temples (Fig. 36). To understand its construction, we must examine some features that constantly recur in Greek temple architecture. The principle was simple. The sanctuary (ναός, *cella*) was a space enclosed by solid walls and columns supporting a dead weight of entablature and roof, without the later Roman device of dis-

FIG. 35.—An archaic Herm.

tributing the thrust by means of arches. In the earliest construction, which was of wood, we should have seen only a frame of uprights on which the cross-beams were laid. The roof sloped on both sides, meeting at the top in a ridge-pole, and projecting eaves shielded the sides. The ends formed a gable. This shape was retained down to the latest times, after stone had taken the place of wood

Fig. 36.—The "Theseium," from the northwest.

as a material for building; and so conservative is man in all that concerns his religion, that many details of the original wooden structures were reproduced in conventional form, as, for instance, the nail-heads at the bottom of the triglyphs on the entablature (Fig. 37).

In the space thus enclosed the divinity to whom it was consecrated was supposed to dwell. His presence was usually made real to the worshipper by some object—at first

by a mere stone, or roughly hewn pillar of stone or of
wood; then by some representation of the god, wooden
images more or less crude; and finally by the

Ritual statues. statues in marble and other
material wrought by the
masters of sculpture (see
Fig. 253). Sometimes, however, the image was lack-
ing, and the priests usually
could narrate some legend
to account for its absence.

While the *naos* (*cella*)
was the essential feature,
it was usually entered by
a kind of vestibule, called,
naturally enough, the *pronaos* (πρόναος).

Construction of temples. This, in its
simplest con-

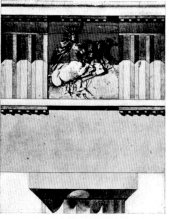

Fig. 37.—Architectural detail from the temple of Athēna at Ilium.

struction, was formed by prolonging the side walls of the
naos, which then terminated in an engaged pillar, or pilas-
ter. Between these, and directly opposite the door of the

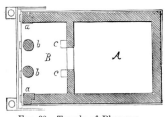

Fig. 38.—Temple of Rhamnus.

naos, were placed two free
columns, to aid in supporting the roof of the pronaos.
This construction (Fig. 38)
is seen in the plan of the
little temple of Themis at
Rhamnus, in the northeast-
ern part of Attica: *A* is
the naos; *B* is the pronaos
ending in the piers *a a*. These were called *parastades*, in
Latin *antae* (cf. the parastas of the private dwelling, page
28). Thus this kind of temple was regularly designated by
the Romans a *templum in antis*. A chamber exactly corre-

sponding to the pronaos might also be built at the rear of
the naos; and a further step was reached when columns
were set entirely round the three parts thus formed. The
temple is then "peripteral," and this result is achieved in
the temple on Colōnos Agoraios, from which we started, and
to the plan of which we now return (Fig. 39). In this, the
naos (*A*) remains the most secluded portion of the edifice;
B is the pronaos; *C* the chamber behind the naos (ὀπισθόδο-
μος). This temple is built of Pentelic marble, and is forty-
four feet wide and one hundred and four feet long. It rests

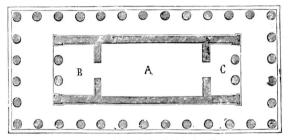

Fig. 39.—Plan of the "Theseium."

on an elevation, technically called stylobate, reached by three
steps, the undermost being a common limestone found abundantly in the Piraeus. The columns, which are of the Doric
order, number six at the front and the rear, and thirteen
(counting those at the corners twice) on the sides. Above
the columns we can recognize three distinct architectural
elements (cf. Fig. 37). First comes the solid, substantial
architrave, presenting a perfectly plain outer surface. Above
it alternate in regular order triglyphs and metopes, beginning with the former. Last is the triangular gable, or pediment. At both ends, east and west, the pediments in this
temple were filled with sculptured groups, of which no ves-
tige remains. The metopes, which are the rectangular spaces
between the triglyphs, extended like them entirely round
the temple, to the number of sixty-eight. Of these, eighteen

were adorned with reliefs; the rest may have contained
paintings. The metopes of the east front represented some
of the Labours of Heracles. On the sides adjoining the
east front were figured the exploits of Theseus, in eight
metopes, four on each side.

We do not know the year when this temple was built,
or the god to whom it was sacred. According to a recent
theory, it was a temple of Hephaestus, built just before
the outbreak of the Peloponnesian War. Hephaestus and
Athēna were patrons of the potters, who plied their craft
in the Cerameicus, of which the hill on which the temple
stands was a part.

There were numerous other temples in this neighbourhood; but in no part of the city had their construction
been planned so systematically, and with re-
The
Acropolis.   sults so beautiful and imposing, as on the
Acropolis. This was itself a sanctuary, consecrated chiefly to Athēna. Artemis, to be sure, enjoyed a
share of the adoration there paid to the gods, and her
priests were powerful enough to prevent the building of
that portion of the grand gateway to the citadel which
trenched on her precincts. Yet Athēna reigned, on the
whole, supreme; almost all the edifices—temples, statues,
altars, treasure-houses—which stood on the citadel belonged
to her worship, or to the worship of divine and heroic be-
ings connected with her in ritual and in legend.

From the market the Acropolis could be approached
either by a steep path between it and the Areopagus, which,
however, was impassable for wagons, or by a
Approach
to the
Acropolis.   longer, gentler rise on a road which wound
round the western and southern slopes of the
Areopagus. Near the summit the visitor came upon a wide
staircase ascending to the gateway, or Propylaea (Fig. 41),
built at the instance of Pericles by the architect Mnesicles,
who began his work in 437 B. C. Six impressive Doric columns stand at the entrance to a hall which is divided into

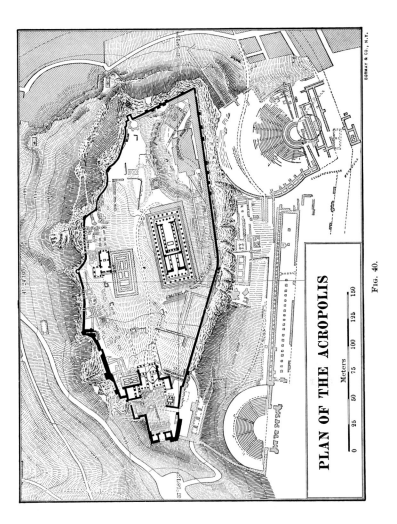

PLAN OF THE ACROPOLIS

Meters

0   25   50   75   100   125   150

Fig. 40.

4

three aisles by Ionic columns (for the style of which cf. Fig.
46), three in each row. Passing between them, or through
the middle aisle, we reach some steps which lead to five
doors in a row piercing a wall—the real gate. From these
we enter a rear portico, which, like that in the front, had
six Doric columns facing the Acropolis plateau. At each
side of the entrance halls are wings. That on the left was a
picture *salon* or *pinakothēkē* (πινακοθήκη). Behind this was

FIG. 41.—A portion of the Propylaea.

a spacious hall. The wing on the right is much smaller
than the pinakothēkē opposite, and the hall behind it was
never finished, because it would have encroached on the
domain of Artemis.

The summit of the Acropolis. The number of splendid objects that once
met the visitor's gaze as he emerged from the
Propylaea is too great to admit of detailed
mention, much less description. Only a few of the most
prominent can be noticed here. Directly in front stood

the great bronze image of Athēna made by Phidias. It portrayed the goddess in her martial character, as indicated in

Statue of Athena.

the title Promachos, or Champion, given to the statue in later times. It stood so high that the tip of the spear and crest of the helmet were visible above the roof of the Propylaea to passengers on board ships entering the Saronic Gulf. She bore a shield richly adorned with figures added by an artist after Phidias's day. She wore a helmet and carried a spear. Some notion of Athēna as a warrior goddess may be gained from Fig. 42 and also Fig. 67. On the visitor's right was the precinct of the Brauronian Artemis, who was worshipped in a very ancient ritual celebrated by Euripides in the *Iphigeneia among the Taurians.*

FIG. 42.
Athēna Promachos.

But the most conspicuous edifice of all was the Parthenon, known to Athenians in

The Parthenon.

the days of Pericles as the temple of Athēna Polias, "guardian of the state." Beneath the foundations may be clearly distinguished the beginnings of a great temple of Athēna projected by Cimon, the predecessor of Pericles. The Parthenon, as we all know, however, was the work of Phidias, begun in 447, and finished shortly after 432, by the architect Ictīnus. Its ground-plan may be seen in Fig. 40, and a view of the ruins from the west is given in Fig. 43. It is a Doric peripteral structure, with eight columns at the ends and seventeen on each side. The entrance was at the east end, thereby affording abundant room for the great processions at the Panathenaea (page 274), which would thus be obliged to traverse the length of the temple before the head of the column turned and disappeared in the pronaos from the sight of those in the rear. The number of steps ascending to the stylobate of the temple was, as

Fig. 43.—The Parthenon as it appears to-day.

usual, uneven, in order that the worshipper might begin
the ascent and enter the pronaos with the right foot.   This
temple, unlike the so-called Theseium, was prostyle; i. e.,
instead of pilasters, it had six free columns both before
and behind the naos.   Within the naos were two parallel
rows of columns, ten in each row,
connected at the inner end by five
other columns.   In the space thus
marked off stood the magnificent
gold and ivory statue of Athēna,
also the work of Phidias.   Even
the late copy of it, the statuette
here figured (Fig. 44), which is
practically all we have to judge
of the work, is enough to show
the richness of Phidias's work.
The goddess stood erect, her tunic reaching to the feet.   On her
breast was a head of Medūsa; on
her head she wore a helmet adorned
with griffins on each side and bearing a sphinx at the top (cf. Fig.
141). In one hand she held a spear,
in the other a Victory, Niké.   At
her left rested a huge shield, and
near the butt of the spear a snake

Fig. 44 —Athēna Parthenos.

was figured. Almost every free sur-
face, down to the edges of the soles of the sandals on the goddess's feet, was covered with rich and varied sculptured reliefs.

Behind the naos, i. e., to the west of it, was the *opisthodomos*, in which, probably, were stored state treasure and
the more valuable offerings entrusted to the goddess for
safekeeping; more particularly special temple property and
vessels used in the processions were kept here.

Both pediments were ornamented with striking scenes
in sculpture.   The east pediment represented the birth of

Athēna; the west, her contest with Poseidon for supremacy over Attica. All the metopes were filled with reliefs, a
Sculptures fact which illustrates the lavish way in which
of the the artistic and the financial resources of the
Parthenon. state were employed in this supreme crea-
tion. They contained scenes from the battles of the Cen-
taurs and the Lapithae—a favourite theme with the Athenian sculptors of the time. All this adornment was seen
from the outside, without entering the temple. Round the
building formed by pronaos, naos, and opisthodomos—to
which the columns served as a shell—extended in superb
array the celebrated Panathenaic frieze, gracing the outside
wall of the naos near the top. To see it one had to enter
the portion of the temple covered by the outer columns.
It is generally believed that this represents the elaborate
procession which formed part of the Panathenaic festival
held every four years in honour of Athēna. At this a saffron-
coloured robe (*peplos*), specially woven and embroidered
with scenes portraying the exploits of the goddess in battle
against the giants, was dedicated with solemn ritual (see
page 274).

The roof of the temple was covered with tiles, and surmounted at the top and lower corners by *acroteria*—ornaments (cf. Fig. 249) in terra-cotta bearing conventional designs. Rain-water was conducted from the roof by leaders
which terminated in lions' heads, from whose mouths the
water spouted free of the sides below. The Pentelic marble
of which the temple was built was hidden by paint, blues,
reds, and gilt or orange predominating. The background
of the metopes seems to have been red, the channels of the
triglyphs deep blue.

The altar. A little north of the east front was the great
altar to Athēna; for it must not be supposed
that animals were sacrificed inside a temple. In most sanc-
tuaries there were, of course, tables made of silver or gold
placed near the cult statue—idol, as the Christian Fathers

would call it—to receive the daily gifts of worshippers. These consisted of simple unburnt offerings, such as fruit, flowers, vessels in metal or pottery, cakes, birds, and the like.

FIG. 45.—The Erechtheium, with the Porch of the Maidens.

The northern half of the Acropolis was occupied by the most ancient, and therefore the holiest, precinct of all. Here stands a building, or rather a group of buildings, in **The Erechtheium.** honour of Athēna, with whom were associated Poseidon, Hephaestus, and the hero Erechtheus. This edifice, the Erechtheium (Fig. 45), is of superlative beauty. It contains the famous Porch of the Maidens (often called Caryatides), and the often-copied door of the north porch.

Another exquisite structure rises at the extreme south-western corner of the Acropolis, and commands a wide view of the western part of the city and the Piraeus. It is **Temple of Athēna Niké.** the little Ionic temple to Athēna Niké, better known as the temple of the Wingless Victory (Fig. 46). From an inscription, of which a portion is given in Fig. 192, we know that it was built shortly after the middle of the fifth century. It is amphiprostyle,

but has no outer columns surrounding it. A frieze runs
entirely round the wall on the outside, presenting on three
sides battle scenes, on the fourth an assembly of the gods.

Besides many altars—one, for example, in front of this
temple of Niké—statues and votive offerings everywhere,
set up by grateful devotees in the *pronaoi* or in the inter-
columniations of the temples, crowded the citadel on every

Fig. 46.—The Temple of Athēna Niké.

side.   These offerings (ἀναθήματα) were of many kinds.
One large class of them consisted of little images, in metal
or in clay, dedicated by persons who had recovered from
some illness.   Often a limb or other part of the body was
represented, according to the nature of the disease.   This
custom, like that of weaving the peplos for the goddess, is
kept up in many churches in Greece to-day.

Though Athens is to us the type of a Greek city, we must not imagine that the splendours of her Acropolis could

Superior conditions of life at Athens.
be equalled in any other Greek city, say Thebes, or Sparta, or Syracuse. To that extent, therefore, the daily life of her citizens was different from that of other Greeks; for their interest and wonder must have been constantly excited, and their imaginations inspired by what they saw about them. On the other hand, the Acropolis had not always presented the rich and varied array which we have just seen, all of which belongs to the latter days of Pericles. The old precinct sacred to Athēna and Erechtheus had, to be sure, existed as an object of love and veneration since the days of Homer. Closely connected with it was the ancient temple of Athēna Polias, that stood in the middle of the Acropolis in the sixth century. This the Persians ruthlessly destroyed, but its ruins were perhaps visible in Xenophon's day, being kept as a perpetual reminder of the impiety of the barbarians.

In a later age, when independent Greece had passed away, and princes with authority derived from Alexander spent their wealth in keeping alive the ancient art, cities like Pergamus, Antioch, and Alexandreia became noted for the splendour of their public buildings. The Acropolis of

Pergamus.
Pergamus (see Fig. 47) in the days of its prosperity almost rivalled that of Athens in magnificence. An agora with spacious porticoes, a splendid temple to Athēna, a library (Fig. 90) which vied with that of learned Alexandreia, and, above all, the matchless altar to Zeus the Saviour (Ζεὺς Σωτήρ), itself a temple on a grand and novel plan (Fig. 238), are some of the chief features in the surroundings of regal Pergamus.

As for Athens, there remain many structures in the lower town which we shall notice later. Thus, at the southern foot of the Acropolis lay the precinct of Dionȳsus, with its little temple *in antis*, later obscured by an elaborate

Fig. 47.—The Acropolis of Pergamus (restoration).

portico belonging to the Dionysiac theatre, and superseded
by a newer and larger temple a few steps farther south.
The agora, also, which on the south was probably prolonged
to a considerable distance west of the Areopagus, was filled
in this vicinity also with many buildings, such as store-
houses for temple and state property ($\theta\eta\sigma\alpha\nu\rho\omicron\iota$). From
here one reached the Pnyx, the hill where the people met
in full assembly (page 209). Near the sacred groves—the
Academy, the Lycēum, and Cynosarges—were gymnasia
and palaestrae. Everywhere the eye rested on rich and
diversified adornment. The wonder is that Athenian writers of the classical period should have regarded them so
much as a matter of course, of every-day experience; for information about them in the literature remains scanty to a
tantalizing degree.

CHAPTER V

THE population of Athens and Attica comprised three classes—citizens, aliens, and slaves—and in the fifth century amounted to at least a quarter of a million,

Classes of inhabitants. probably many more. The citizens were such adult males as enjoyed full political rights, and their families; the term *astoi* (ἀστοί) included them all, whereas *politai* (πολῖται) was applied only to the enfranchised males. The number of the latter before the Peloponnesian War was over 35,000—perhaps nearer 40,000; with their families, the number of free inhabitants must have reached 100,000 or over. Most of them lived in the country, visiting Athens only for business or in the exercise of political duties. These formed the sturdy productive portion of the citizens, who felt most keenly the irksome restraint of the city when Pericles compelled them to move into town on account of Spartan invasions. During the Peloponnesian War, therefore, their numbers fell off at a dangerous rate. The great plague, at the very beginning, carried away almost a fourth of the inhabitants of all classes; the terrible defeat in Sicily still further diminished the population; and by the end of the war, in 404 B. C., there were scarcely more than 20,000 male citizens left.

Citizenship. The three classes were kept distinct, at least in their political relation; only now and then a special vote of the people granted the status of citizen to a foreigner or (most rarely) to a slave for conspicuous patriotism. According to a law of Pericles, only those persons

60

who were born of citizens on both the father's and the mother's side were accorded the full rights of citizenship. The enforcement of this law was somewhat lax during the war, when radical tendencies in the republic predominated; and Aristophanes—like many other comic poets, a conservative—bitterly ridicules certain foreigners who managed to wriggle into citizenship. The law was enforced anew in 403, when a soberer democracy was restored after the deposition of the Thirty Tyrants; but, in obedience to the forgiving spirit of the time, it was not applied to persons born before that year. Further, there were so many foreigners in Athens, and relations with her allies were so intimate, that intermarriages were frequent, and it was inevitable that many children should be enrolled as future citizens who could not fulfil the law's requirement. We hear of several revisions of the citizen list in Athenian history. The people, however, might vote to confer citizenship upon a foreigner or an Athenian only one of whose parents was of citizen birth, as a reward for distinguished services to the state in peace or in war. The balloting was secret.

Foreigners living in Athens.

A man in the full possession of all the rights (τιμαί) of citizenship was said to be *epitimos* (ἐπίτιμος). Various offenses against the state, such as the bribery of officials, embezzlement of public funds, cowardice in battle, false witness, neglect of filial duties—for here the state too was concerned—were punished by a diminution or total abrogation of citizen's rights, called *atimia* (ἀτιμία). Complete atimia involved the loss of all political privileges and legal redress; and the exclusion from temples, markets, and other places where citizens congregated.

Civil rights.

All citizens of the three upper divisions as rated by Solon—*Pentekosiomedimnoi, Hippeis, Zeugitae*—were liable to special taxes in time of war (εἰσφοραί). The lowest class, or *Thētes*, were exempt. Further, those whose property amounted to more than two talents

State income.

performed in regular turn certain special services (λῃτουργίαι, cf. "liturgy") which required considerable outlay. The chief and most expensive was the equipment of a chorus for a lyrical or dramatic performance. The citizen charged

with this duty (chorēgus, χορηγός) had to collect the members of the chorus, pay for their training in music, the dance, and the words they were to sing, provide them with costumes and masks, and pay for their keep during their period of training. A generous chorēgus might in this way win lasting renown, for his munificence contributed largely to the winning of the prize coveted by competing choruses; and the victory was recorded on tablets of marble or bronze erected in conspicuous places, and also, at least in the case of lyric performances, commemorated by the presentation of a tripod to the victorious chorēgus, who dedicated it to Dionȳsus, and set it up in the Street of the Tripods, leading to the theatre (see page 16). The gymnasiarchia was another form of public service, in which the citizen was obliged to pay for the services and the training of those who took part in the torch-races at the Panathenaea and other celebrations.

FIG. 48.—The chorēgic monument of Lysicrates.

Still another form of liturgia was the holiday dinner (ἑστίασις), at which a citizen entertained the members of his tribe (φυλή) at the Dionysiac and Panathenaic festivals. Finally, the manning and equipping of a trireme (τριηραρχία) was a very common mode of liturgia, in which, on account of the great expense, two or more citizens were usually associated. The state furnished the hull and the mast, and the trierarchs—for such they were called while performing this service—supplied the rigging, the provisions, the crew, and their pay (see page 199). Sometimes rich citizens made voluntary donations (ἐπιδόσεις) to individuals who they saw were in need of supplies for a military campaign.

Rewards for public service were often bestowed by the Council or the popular assembly, such as exemption from taxes; a front seat in public gatherings, espe-
Public rewards. cially at the theatre (προεδρία); a crown, originally of olive or laurel, later of gold (Fig. 194); and maintenance at public expense in the chamber where

the Prytanes dined (σίτησις ἐν πρυτανείῳ). Thus the descendants of Harmodius and Aristogeiton, and winners at the Olympic games, were honoured in the last - mentioned way; and Socrates, in all seriousness, claimed the same reward for his lifelong endeavours to rouse his people to uprightness and true knowledge. Crowning became especially frequent in the fourth century. The proposal to

Fig. 49.—Marble seat of the priest of Dionȳsus in the theatre.

reward Demosthenes in this way, and the opposition called out from Aeschines, his rival, occasioned the best known and most perfect production of Greek oratory—the oration *On the Crown*. Citizens were sometimes rewarded also by

the honorary title of " Benefactor," εὐεργέτης. This appellation was sometimes conferred by one state on the citizen of
another, as Cimon was called the εὐεργέτης of Sparta. In
some cases he represented that state in all transactions with
his own people, and entertained and aided all citizens who
came from it to visit his own. In this capacity, which
was partly official, partly friendly, he was called *proxenos*
(πρόξενος), an office which figures conspicuously in the international history of Greek states (see page 253).

In external appearance there was little to distinguish
the citizen from the free foreign resident, except that
individuals among the latter class might retain here and
there the dress and bearing peculiar to their home country.
The Athenian citizen generally bore himself like a free
man, with perhaps a tendency toward arrogance, but with
less regard for dignity and composure in gait and attitude
than the Roman maintained.

The resident foreigners, or metics (μέτοικοι), formed a
class by themselves, since naturalization was not so easy a
process as it is to-day. They made their home
in Athens or the Piraeus, attracted thither by
the commercial and social advantages which
the city afforded. It was part of Pericles's wise policy to
invite such men to leave the country of their birth and
settle in the state which he was building up. Herein the
liberal spirit of Athenian institutions is strongly contrasted
with the narrow and suspicious attitude of Sparta, whose
policy of exclusion (ξενηλασία) was almost as rigid as that
of China. A well-known example of the wisdom of Pericles
in this regard is furnished by Cephalus, a Sicilian, whose
son Lysias became the first really eminent orator of Attica.
Cephalus passed thirty useful and honourable years in
Athens, and was a man whom Socrates was glad to visit and
engage in conversation. At the beginning of the Peloponnesian War there were at least 10,000 metics in Attica,
most of them living in the Piraeus; including their fami-

The
foreigners.

lies, perhaps 45,000. While few of these, doubtless, possessed the integrity and the dignity of Cephalus, still they were on the whole industrious and enterprising, and contributed largely to the wealth of the state. This was especially true in ancient communities whose citizens despised trade and manual labor. As a class, however, they were held in dislike by the ordinary citizen, and their relation

Disabilities of foreigners. to the natives was somewhat similar to that which the Jew holds in Continental Europe to-day. Race prejudice was of course much stronger in antiquity. The indignation with which Apollonides is expelled from the company of Cyrus's surviving captains, not only because of his bad advice but also because he was a foreigner, is evidence of this. And so the metics were among the first to fall victims to the cupidity of the Thirty Tyrants. Often, no doubt, some of them placed private gain above the interests of the state, and certainly they were frequently charged with forming " corners " in the market and arbitrarily raising the price of staples in daily use.

In deference, therefore, to popular opinion, many restrictions were laid upon metics. After a certain period of residence, every foreigner was required to select a citizen to represent him in all dealings with the state ; for a metic, having no political rights, could not, among other things, conduct a case at law. This citizen, called his προστάτης, seems to have been responsible in a certain degree for the good behaviour of the metic. If a metic failed to choose his representative within the prescribed time, he was liable to prosecution (γραφὴ ἀπροστασίου) before the archon-polemarch, who presided over all cases that affected foreigners. The whole proceeding is analogous to the requirement of a passport in some European cities of all foreigners who purpose to stay longer than a few days.

Metics were also obliged to pay a special poll-tax (μετοί-κιον) not exacted from citizens, and when a special war-tax (εἰσφορά) was levied, they paid a higher rate than the citizens. Their other liabilities were the same as those of citizens. In war they served as hoplites (page 194), but could not be admitted to the ranks of the cavalry, whose members were an aristocratic body of young men with de-

FIG. 50.—A citizen with his two sons; the elder is on the point of joining the cavalry.

cidedly exclusive tendencies. Rich metics were bound to perform the regular liturgies, like rich citizens; and frequently they acquitted themselves of this obligation as loyally and generously as any citizen. In the great festivals, where sacrifice was offered by and for the state, they were allowed a share of the burnt offerings. Conspicuous worth and loyalty were sometimes rewarded, at least in certain periods of democratic reaction, by citizenship. Citizenship was certainly more easily obtained by foreigners in Athens than anywhere else in Greece. Ordinarily, however, the reward was limited to requiring the metic to pay no more taxes than the citizen; to making him, as the phrase was, ἰσοτελής. Sometimes, too, metics were allowed to own houses—Lysias and his brother owned three—or to march in the same ranks with citizens, and not in a special division by themselves.

There was no period in the history of Greece when society was not affected by the presence within it of large numbers of slaves (δοῦλοι, οἰκέται). At Athens almost every family owned at least one, and in the whole state there must have been in all considerably over 150,000. Hipponīcus, one of the richest men of Greece, owned 600; Lysias's family, who possessed an armour fac-

Slaves.

tory, kept 120 in the workshop; the general Nicias employed
1,000 in the mines. But fifty was ordinarily considered a
large number for one person to possess. Slaves were usually acquired by purchase, though a few also were born and
reared in the master's house. Some were actually Greeks,
sold into captivity at the sacking of their native city, as
when the Lacedaemonians captured Plataea in 427 B. C., or
when the Athenians took Sciōne and Torōne five years later.

In the retreat of the Ten Thousand under Xenophon,
many inhabitants of the interior were kidnapped by the
Greeks, for it was a rule, universally recognized, that the
conquered became the possession of the conqueror, except
Origin. by special stipulation; as where Tissaphernes
exempted from slavery the natives in the villages of Parysatis, which he allowed the Greeks to plunder;
and Syennesis managed to have returned all Cilician captives. The terrible suffering of the enslaved Athenians
in the quarries of Syracuse after the disastrous end of the
Sicilian expedition in 413 B. C. is the most awful example
of this custom. Sometimes the great numbers of captives
designed for the slave market so impeded the march that
their captors were forced to let them go. Traders imported
them into Athens from Thrace, Phrygia, Lydia, Paphlagonia, Syria, and the countries round Pontus. There was a
peltast in Xenophon's army who had been a slave kidnapped from Pontus, and who, when the Greeks reached
the country of the Macrōnes, was able to act as interpreter.
"For," said he, half pathetically, "I believe this is my
native country."

Slaves were employed in every conceivable way. As
house servants, they tended the door (as θυρωρός, see page
26), fetched water from a spring or street
Employ-
ments. fountain, washed clothing, waited at the table,
prepared food, and made clothes for the family.
Boys going to school were attended by slaves or "pedagogues" (παιδαγωγοί), and the nurses of young children

were commonly slave women. The mistress (called δέσποινα)
usually had a special slave to assist her at her toilet, and
the master (δεσπότης) when he went out was attended by
slaves who acted as body-servants (θεράποντες, ἀκόλουθοι) and
messengers. The Athenian, however, rarely made a vulgar
display with a large retinue of servants when he went
abroad, as the Roman or the Persian did. Outside of
purely domestic uses, slaves were employed as miners,

FIG. 51.—The American School of Classical Studies, on the site of the Lycēum.

especially in the silver-mines at Laurium, and as agricul-
turists and herders; also as stevedores, boatmen, overseers,
and business managers. Many of them often got permission to go out to work for pay, giving a percentage of
their earnings to their masters. In this way they actually
became well to do, and might subsequently purchase freedom. Investors frequently bought large numbers of slaves
and let them out for hire.

The state owned many slaves (δημόσιοι), who served it in

various occupations deemed too menial for citizens. Such
were the Scythians (Σκύθαι), armed with the bow, who kept
order in public places (page 20). State ac-
State slaves. countants and secretaries were mostly slaves
or freedmen. Public slaves were also employed in the
mint, in public works, such as the making and improve-
ment of roads, and as executioners and torturers. Even in
battle, when the need was pressing, they were sometimes
induced to risk their lives by the promise of freedom.
Many served in the battle of Arginūsae (406 B. C.), and became later the envy of their associates.

As a rule, the treatment of slaves in Athens was not
severe, although it depended entirely on the character of
the master, who had unrestricted control over their lives.
He might not kill a slave wilfully, however, since that
involved the pollution of blood-guiltiness, for which he
must atone by some act of expiation to the gods of the
state. The law technically shielded the slave against excessive physical maltreatment, but since the slave had no
political status, it is not easy to see how he could bring an
action against a cruel master. Religion protected him
better, for he could fly for asylum to the shrine of Theseus
in the agora or of the Dread Goddesses (αἱ Σεμναί) on the
Areopagus. The worst that could befall a faithful slave
was to be examined under torture if his master were prose-
cuted in a legal action (see page 212). On the other hand,
the master was sometimes restrained from violence by the
fear that his slave might concoct some charge against him
for the benefit of his enemies, since, unfortunately, many a
family had an ancestral feud with some other; and in
time of war, by the fear that the slave would run off to the
enemy. Kindly feelings of humanity also played their
part, especially among the more enlightened Athenians.
A newly purchased slave was welcomed to the hearth with a
shower of confetti (καταχύσματα). Slaves also had access
to the feasts and celebrations in which the whole state

took part; the only exception was the Thesmophoria, a
festival of the women from which all men were excluded.
During the three days of the Anthesteria they were allowed
to come and go with no restraint whatever. It is noteworthy that no uprising of slaves took place in Athens
until after the Roman conquest, though 20,000 ran away
to the Spartans while they occupied Deceleia. The same
fidelity was displayed in even a greater degree by slaves in
the South during our Civil War.

Freedom was the reward, as we saw, of service rendered
in battle. It was bestowed either by the master, or by a decree of the people, in which case the master was reimbursed
for the loss of his property. Slaves who turned state's evidence (μηνυταί) were sometimes thus rewarded. The freed-
man (ἀπελεύθερος) passed to the condition of metic, and his
former master became his patron (προστάτης, page 65).

These, then, were the people that filled the streets and
the agora. The women who were also to be seen in the
crowds were chiefly those of the lower classes,
Street scenes. whose poverty compelled them to throw aside
the conventional Athenian modesty, so far as it related to
women, and to mingle with men in their daily occupations
in the market or at the fountains. A busy crowd of
hucksters vending all kinds of wares filled the larger
streets. Here and there a drover, clad in skins, and with
his legs wound round with woollen bands in lieu of stock-
ings, would be driving in from the hills a flock of sheep
or goats. Or a farmer from the plain would be urging
on his pack-ass or his mule which drew a creaking cart
with solid wheels, laden with wood or market produce (cf.
Fig. 285). A modern would have missed the pleasure driving to be seen in a city to-day. It was unseemly for a man
to ride in a carriage, at least in the town; and any one who
drove his racing chariot to a banquet, as Themistocles is said
to have done when he was a young man, was thought to have
attained the extreme of extravagance and presumption.

CHAPTER VI

CHILDHOOD

WE have now noted some of the external conditions that surrounded a child born at Athens in the middle of the fifth century. Much had been done for **The child and the state.** his comfort by long centuries of growth, during which the Greeks had come to be distinguished from the rest of the world as a Hellenic nation; years in which this nation, favoured by the climate, the land, and in Attica especially by the sea, had steadily increased in power and promise, learning lessons from the people of Egypt and the East; until Athens, after her final struggle with the Persians, began her own independent career, and her people, gifted with native genius and the teachings of their fathers, had made a powerful state and a tolerably comfortable city to live in.

Fig. 52.—Peasant's child with goat.

A boy born at this time was, as everywhere, the object of his mother's devotion; but, more than that, he was, in a sense scarcely appreciable to-day, his father's pride. For the **Pride in boys.** father felt assured that through the boy his old age would be cared for; that the family name and the worship of family gods and ancestors would be perpetu-

71

ated after his own death; that the state would have another citizen to take his place when he had gone or was too
old to remain actively in her service. To have no children,
especially male children, was one of the most serious calam-
ities that could befall a Greek; and the state had an interest in the matter as well, because it was thought that
childlessness tended to loosen the ties between citizen and
commonwealth. Hence a man, in making a promise on
oath, could attest his sincerity no more solemnly than by
calling down destruction upon himself and his children in
case he should prove to be a perjurer (page 282).

Greek education (παιδεία) began deliberately at birth,
where it should always begin. The aim was to make the
boy in the image of his father—to conform to
**Aim of Greek
education.** the type of manhood and citizenship which
each Greek state held as its own ideal; to be
a gentleman, καλὸς κἀγαθός, really a *man*, worthy of the freedom which the men of Marathon and Salamis had won.
Discipline, and not the mere acquirement of knowledge,
was always the object. Far back in Homeric times the
father took an active interest in the nurture of his child,
and the loss of this oversight in the case of an orphan was
felt most keenly.

The birth of a boy was announced by an olive-branch
hung on the doorpost; if the baby was a girl, tufts of wool
**Customs
when a child
was born.** were displayed. The first bath was given by
dipping the child in lukewarm water and oil
—a custom surviving in modern Greek bap-
tisms. In Sparta, where special measures were taken to
make children hardy, the
water was tempered with
wine, which was thought
to impart vigour. In most

FIG. 53.—Infant in swaddling bands.

places except Sparta, the baby was tightly wrapped, like
an Indian pappoose, in a narrow woollen band (σπάργανα),

twisted round and round from the neck to the feet (Fig. 53). The cradle (λίκνον) or basket was so made that it could be suspended like a swing, or might be rocked on the floor.

Artemis and other divinities were invoked to protect the child, and special precautions were taken against the "evil eye" and malignant spirits which might bewitch and harm it. Two family festivals celebrated the birth, both of very ancient sanctity.

Fig. 54.—Child in cradle.

The first was religious in character, and usually took place five days after birth. The nurse, or some woman of the family, with the child in her arms, ran round the hearth in the andron, followed by the members of the household. This ceremony—the ἀμφιδρόμια—was designed to place the child forever under the care of the family gods. It was followed by a feast, at which shell-fish were always eaten. The second festival was the "name-day," in some parts of Europe (e. g., Russia, Finland, Sweden) held perhaps of greater importance than the birthday. Certainly among the Greeks it was indispensable, for it was then that the father, in the presence of guests, formally recognized the child as his own, committed himself to its upbringing and education, and gave it a name. The naming was celebrated on the tenth day (δεκάτη) with great conviviality and mirth; the guests brought presents (γενέθλιαι δόσεις), a sacrifice was offered to the family gods, and an abundant feast followed. The child received but one name. Very commonly a boy took his grandfather's name, sometimes his father's, in a slightly altered form. Sometimes a diminutive or shortened form of the grandfather's name was given; the orator Lysias, son of Cephalus, was named for his grandfather Lysanias. Or the boy might be named from an intimate friend, or from some god—as Theodotus, Apollodōrus—or from some noteworthy experience in his father's life. Later in life a nickname derived

Greek names.

from some personal peculiarity or association might usurp the place of his real name.   Two famous instances are the poet Stesichorus, so-called from his achievements in marshalling lyric choruses, though his real name was Teisias ; and the philosopher Plato, who was first named for his grandfather Aristocles, but who is said to have been dubbed Plato by his teacher in gymnastics, because of his broad shoulders.   In every case the father and mother, after careful and some-times even heated discussion, selected a name derived from some word of good omen.   On the tenth day, then, the child was presented to its nearest relatives and the most intimate friends of the family ; its right to life and to a name was form-ally recognized by the father, for, unhappily, the exposure of infants, especially of girls, was common in antiquity. Parents, by no means always poor, who wished to relieve themselves of the care and expense of rearing their chil-dren, sometimes placed them in baskets (Fig. 54) or earthen-ware vessels (χύτραι, page 136), and set them secretly in some temple, in the hope that some kind-hearted person might take pity on the little unfortunate and bring it up.   Or, when more brutal feelings prevailed, they carried the child to some bleak mountainside to die of exposure or by wild beasts.

There remained still another ceremony, by which the position of the child as future citizen was also recognized. State recog-nition of the child. This was at the Apaturia (page 281), an old Ionic family festival held in the late autumn. On the last of the three days of this festival—called the κουρεῶτις—the child born during the preceding year was presented to his father's clansmen, or phratry (φρατρία), after the sacrifice of a sheep offered by the father. Following it, the brethren of the phratry(φράτερες) decided by a vote whether or not the boy or girl was the lawful and legitimate offspring of Athenian parents.   If the legiti-macy of the child was established, the name was enrolled on the register of the phratry (τὸ φρατερικὸν γραμματεῖον). If not, the child was held to be a bastard (νόθος) before the law, and could not aspire to inheritance or to citizen's rights.

The mother, of course, exercised a general oversight over all her children up to their eighth year; but every household not too poor had its **Care of the child.** nurse (τροφός), either a slave woman or a foreigner, who performed all the common duties of her office. Spartan nurses seem to have been sought after, much as French or German nurses are among us. The nurse prepared the baby's food, often mingling honey with it; in the case of a child still toothless, she chewed the food first herself. She sung the baby to sleep with ancient lullabies, some of which the great tragic and lyric poets have reproduced or imitated. **Nursery tales.** When the child grew to some understanding, the nurse told stories out of the great wealth of Greek mythology and Aesopian beast fables which circulated among the Greeks from the earliest times; also ghost stories, chiefly to frighten and subdue the rebellious: about the horrible bugaboo called Mormo; about Acco, who carried off bad children in a huge sack; or Lamia, once a princess, who ate her own and others' children; or Empūsa, a hobgoblin that took any shape it pleased. If these stories failed to restrain the naughty child, then the sandal was vigorously applied. The methods of discipline were crude,

Fig. 55.—Grave monument to a nurse.

but not more so than most in vogue to-day, and only philosophers like Plato and Aristotle objected to the homely
training of these slave nurses. Their charges grew up to
love and honour them. Eurycleia, in the *Odyssey*, is a good
example of the revered nurse; and monuments placed over

nurses' graves still
remain to testify to
the gratitude felt for
their labour and care
(see Fig. 55).

Children's toys
and games are much
the same the world
over. So the Greek
baby had his rattle
(πλαταγή), the little

Fig. 56.—Toy cart and pet dog.

**Toys and
games.**

girl had her pets, and her doll (κόρη) made of
painted clay or wax, often with movable hands
and feet (see Fig. 231). Baby-houses, toy
dishes, tables, wagons, and animals were as interesting then
as now. Sometimes the older boys made their own carts
(ἁμαξίδες), and hitched to them dogs or goats. For older
children, too, there were the swing (αἰώρα), the ball (σφαῖ-
ρα), the whipping-top (βέμβιξ, ῥόμβος), the hoop (τροχός).

Fig. 57.—The swing.

Many games resem-
bled those played to-
day: hide-and-seek
(κρυπτίνδα), tug of war
(ἑλκυστίνδα), ducks
and drakes (ἐποστρα-
κισμός), and blind
man's buff, or the
"bronze fly" (χαλκῆ
μυῖα), in which the boy who was "it" was struck with whips
by the others until he caught one of them. Another
amusement among the street gamins, not so innocent, was

to catch a beetle (μηλολόνθη), tie a string to it, and so control
its flight. Jackstones, played with knuckle bones (ἀστράγα-
λοι, Fig. 230), "pitching pennies," played with bronze coins
(χαλκίζειν), and hopping with one foot on a greased wine-
skin (ἀσκωλιασμός), were other favourites, the last being a
sport indulged in by grown people at the Dionysiac festival
of the Anthesteria.

Boys and girls
grew up together
under the sole
charge of mother
and nurse until
they were seven
years old. From
this point, so far as
his education was

FIG. 58.—Children playing with cart and doll.

**Early
education.**

concerned, the boy parted from his sister, who
remained in careful seclusion in the house, and
got what little knowledge her mother could
impart, depending on her father or brothers for knowledge
of what was going on in the world. The boy, on the other
hand, was placed under the special charge of a slave (παιδα-
γωγός), whose business it was to follow him everywhere—to
school and back, in his sports, and in the house. Only in
the constant presence of an elder, it was thought, could a
boy learn proper modesty and reverence (αἰδώς), polite bearing, and self-restraint in all things (σωφροσύνη), the last
being the ideal of Greek ethics. On the same principle,
the sons of Persian nobles were educated at court, that
they might see nothing of a contaminating and debasing
character. The guardian slave, to be sure, was often an
illiterate person of foreign origin, and was never a teacher
in the strict sense. But he was assumed to be competent
to teach the boy manners, the proper way to eat, walk, sit,
and dress, and could see to it that the boy fell into no bad
companionships. Such a tutelage had as much influence

for good as that of the old-fashioned Southern "mammy,"
except in the case of very old and weak slaves, such as
the pedagogue whom Pericles assigned to Alcibiades in his

Fig. 59.—Playing ball.

school-days. The sympathetic pedagogue is seen in Fig.
318. The slave had power to enforce his direction by corporal punishment applied with the rattan (νάρθηξ) or the
strap (ἱμάς). From him they learned to rise, stand, and be
silent in the presence of their elders; and to wear their
mantles carefully folded about them when they went into
the street (see the younger lad in Fig. 50).

CHAPTER VII

SCHOOL TRAINING

THE Greeks took a broad view of the meaning of education (παιδεία), and made it include all that the boy received

Object of Greek education.
from his elders, before he became of age, in the training of his body, mind, and morals. When the little boy (παῖς) had grown into a lad (μειράκιον), he was introduced to three main branches of discipline; and no matter how poor his parents were, every Greek boy gained some knowledge in all these three. The object,

FIG. 60.—A boxing lesson.

it should always be remembered, was the physical and moral development of the citizen, and not the acquisition of expert knowledge. These branches were gymnastic (ἡ γυ-

Main branches of education.
μναστική, *sc.* τέχνη), music (ἡ μουσική), and reading and writing (γράμματα). The last two—i. e., music and letters—were sometimes embraced

under the single term "music" (μουσική), which in classical Greek implies more than the narrower modern term

79

music, being made to include the words and thoughts of a poet as well as the musical strain to which they were adapted.

Instruction in gymnastic was given in the palaestrae (literally " wrestling-grounds," from πάλη, " wrestling "), of which there were several in Athens (cf. Fig. 72). These were laid out in a free and open space, therefore mostly in the outskirts of the city, and not too shaded from the sun. In accordance with the Greek idea that boys require the constant supervision of older persons even in their sports —an idea far removed from English and American theory **Gymnastics.** and practice—a private teacher, called παιδοτρί- βης (Figs. 60, 61, 74), gave systematic lessons in wrestling (πάλη), boxing (πυγμή), running (δρόμος), the broad jump (ἄλμα), throwing the discus (δισκοβολία), and casting the spear (ἀκόν- τισις). All these were taught so universally that it was easy to im- provise " track meet- ings " (ἀγῶνες γυμνικοί) on almost any occasion. Such are frequently mentioned, therefore, by Xenophon, as held in connection with

FIG. 61.—Practising the broad jump.

some religious festival; as when Xenias the Arcadian cele- brates in distant Asia his native festival, the Lycaea, with games, for which the prizes were gold flesh-scrapers or stri- gils (στλεγγίδες χρυσαῖ); or again, when the Greeks, on their safe arrival at the Black Sea, render thanks to Heracles and proceed to hold games, with the Spartan Dracontius as referee. Greek literature everywhere, from Homer to St. Paul's epistles, contains many references to the games and metaphors derived from them; as when Xenophon speaks of the gods as the umpires (ἀγωνοθέται) of the uneven strug- gle between the Greeks and the Persians—and not merely

are those games meant in which professional athletes figured, but also the simple contests of ordinary citizens
trained in their youth to understand and enjoy them.

These exercises were practised naked, the body being
first anointed
with oil. This,
with the dust
and sweat, was
scraped off at
the close of
the contest by

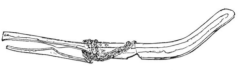

FIG. 62.—Flesh-scraper (strigil).

a kind of comb (στλεγγίς, called by the Romans *strigilis*,
Figs. 62, 63), after which the boys took a cold plunge; for the
palaestra was often near a stream. In this way boys added
Swimming. a knowledge of swimming and diving to their
other accomplishments, a knowledge assumed as
general in Homer and Xenophon. The diver is mentioned
in the *Iliad*, and some of the soldiers at one point during
Xenophon's march to the sea took off their tunics and
swam across a stream; a few only did not know how to swim.

**Military
training.** Boys of aristocratic birth were trained in
the use of arms and in military tactics (τὰ ἀμφὶ
τάξεις καὶ ὁπλομαχία). In the palaestra were also
practised punching the bag, or σκιαμαχία, ball playing, tug

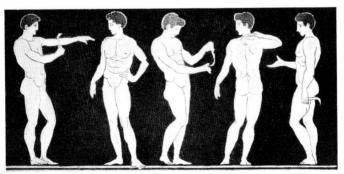

FIG. 63.—The use of the strigil.

of war, and other games begun in childhood. At the yearly
festival in honour of Hermes the boys had an opportunity to
display their progress; and at the national games—Olympic, Pythian, Nemean, and Isthmian—boys were frequently
entered as contestants, and their victories as well as those
of professional adult athletes were celebrated by the lyric
poets—Pindar, Simonides, Bacchylides, and others.

In music, taught by a master of the lyre (κιθαριστής),
the pupil learned to play on the lyre and to sing (Fig. 64)

Music.   to his own accompaniment. The lyre, called in
Homer φόρμιγξ, later κιθάρα, κιθαρίς, or λύρα, was
the ancient national instrument of Hellas, always associated
with the Hellenic god Apollo.   There were many varieties
of form, and the *kithara*, in
the strict sense, seems to have
had greater resonance than
the *lyra*. In principle, however, they were the same. In
the lyre the complete shell of
a tortoise was used as a sound-
ing-board. Into the natural
openings at either end were
fixed goat's horns, which were
connected near the tips by
a cross-piece or yoke (ζυγόν).
The strings were drawn tightly from this yoke to the shell

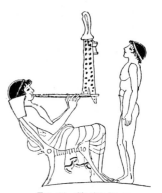

Fig. 64.—Singing lesson.

below, which constituted the base of the instrument, and
there were fastened by a bridge (ὑπογύριον).   The sounding-
box of the kithara was made of thin wood, metal, or ivory,
and might be either rectangular or semi-oval in shape.
The arms also were of wood or metal instead of horn, and
might form one piece with the box (Fig. 66).   Some forms
of it greatly resembled the modern zither (cf. Fig. 95).

The flute (αὐλός) belonged originally in Asia Minor, and
though flute-playing was regularly taught, it became less

popular in the latter part of the fifth century among Athenian gentlemen, after the fastidious Alcibiades set the example of discarding it because it distorted the face. It was played like the clarinet rather than like the modern flute, the mouthpiece being at the end of the pipe or cylinder, not at the side. Originally the pipe had only three or four stops. To increase the range, therefore, it was more common, especially at public entertainments, for the player to use two pipes, which had either a single mouthpiece in common or might have each its own. For convenience in holding they were fastened to the player's mouth by leather bands passing

The lyre and the flute.

Fig. 65.—Use of the double flute at the public games.

round the neck and head, as in Fig. 65. Among the Greeks, therefore, the flute remained as a rule the national instrument of the Boeotians only, or was confined to professionals who played it chiefly to accompany dancing, or in marching to battle.

The superiority of the lyre in polite society is typified by the story of Apollo's contest with the Phrygian Marsyas (Fig. 66); and in Homer, it is the Trojans, never the Greeks, who use the flute. All Greeks, but especially Athenians, laid stress on some musical attainment, even though great technical skill was not desired; for when a man entered society he must be able to sing to his own accom-

paniment the lyrics and glees that everybody knew.   The
Greeks also felt profoundly the moral influence that certain musical strains can exert, and the old-fashioned looked

with disfavour on
the artificial varia-
tions and wonderful
trills which virtuosi
began to introduce
toward the close of
the fifth century.
Besides the flute,
used for marching,
the army also de-
pended on the trum-
pet (σάλπιγξ) for
signals, for which

FIG. 66.—Musical contest between Apollo and
Marsyas.

the Thracians used a horn. "In peace," so ran the famous saying, "sleepers are waked by cocks; in war, by
trumpets."

Dancing was not one of the subjects taught in the regular
curriculum at Athens in its flourishing period, though boys

Dancing.

of promise, like Sophocles, for instance, were
often singled out for special instruction in it,
that they might appear in the choruses of boys which com-
peted at the festivals.   But in Crete and Sparta every one
could dance, especially in the *pyrriché* (πυρρίχη), a panto-
mimic war-dance in which young men wearing helmets
clashed swords and shields together.   Byron in *The Isles
of Greece* and many other writers in England to-day incor-
rectly associate the pyrriché (not *pyrrhic*) with Pyrrhus and
the Pyrrhic phalanx.   In Xenophon's account of its performance in the *Anabasis* it is noteworthy that this and
other mimetic dances, or ballets, are not danced by the
Athenian soldiers, but by a professional dancing-girl (ὀρχη-
στρίς), by a Mysian, and by some Thessalians.   Still, the
pyrriché was early imported into Athens, and became by

the beginning of the fourth century a regular feature of
the Panathenaic festival (page 274).

The third branch of education, γράμματα (also μουσική in
the wider sense), comprised reading and writing, for which

Reading and writing.
the boy attended the school (διδασκαλεῖον) of
the *grammatistes* (γραμματιστής). In reading,
the pupil learned the names, forms, and values
of the letters, whence he proceeded to the study of sylla-
bles and of whole words, with their
changes of inflection. In writing,
the teacher wrote a copy and
drew lines for the scholar, who,
with his hand guided by the teacher's, tried to imitate the model. The
writing was done on wooden tablets

Materials for writing.
(δελτοί, Fig. 67) covered
with wax; the instru-
ment was an iron graver
with a sharp point (γραφίς, Lat. *stilus*). To write, then, was properly
to scratch (χαράττειν), whence letters were called "characters" (χαρα-
κτῆρες). Pupils who had attained
proficiency enough to warrant the
use of more expensive material
wrote on paper, made from the
stem of the papyrus plant (βίβλος),
which grew chiefly in Egypt (page

FIG. 67.—Athēna with writing-tablets and a writing-
point.

108). With this they used a reed pen (κάλαμος) and ink
(μέλαν, cf. *atramentum* from *ater*), made of lampblack and
gum which had been pounded together in a mortar. School-
rooms could not boast of a desk, and in schools which were
held in the open air, the scholar was lucky if he had a
bench (βάθρον) to sit on.

The authors read and studied were the epic poets, especially Homer (*Iliad* and *Odyssey*), Hesiod, Aesop, and the

moralists, like Theognis and Solon. The verses were learned by heart, so that their influence on the character and on the whole attitude of the Greek toward life **Authors studied.** was strong and persistent. The lessons were learned at school, not at home, the pupil re-peating the words aloud after the master, or writ-ing them at his dictation. Not a few Greeks, espe-cially Athenians, learned in this way to recite the whole *Iliad* and *Odyssey*, and were noted for their ex-cellent memory (μνημονικοί).

Fig. 68.—Boy's handwriting on the wall of a house.

Although most Greeks were far from illiterate, and set a high value on a knowl-edge of the national literature—it was only **Teachers.** at Sparta that a large number of persons were ignorant of reading and writing—still the profession of teacher (γραμματιστής) was in low repute. The teachers were freedmen, or citizens who had lost means and social posi-tion, and they depended on the voluntary donations of parents, often rendered in kind instead of in cash, on the last day of the month. Thus the teacher was often at the mercy of a stingy parent, one of whom is related to have deducted a por-tion of the fee because his son was sick one day. The school-

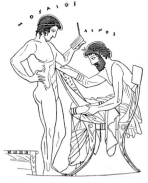

Fig. 69.—A lesson in the poets.

rooms—when school was not held in the open air—were ill furnished, with none of the apparatus for comfort and instruction demanded to-day.

It was only after the fifth century that subjects less ethical than reading were added to the course, such as geometry, astronomy, and arithmetic. The Greeks as a rule were not skilful calculators, and the grown man regularly counted with his fingers (ἐπὶ δακτύλων συμβάλλεσθαι, πεμπάζειν, cf. πέντε) ; or else, in more important financial problems, he used a counting-board (ἀβάκιον).

Mathematics.

In the fourth century, when the Athenians began to wake to a conscious appreciation of the works of art about them, drawing (γραφική) was introduced into the school course as necessary to the proper understanding of sculpture and painting.

Fig. 70.—Counting-board.

Thus, under a well-ordered scheme of work and play, citizens' and metics' sons passed their early years.

Illiteracy.

Of course there were street gamins, like the one who grew up to be a sausage-seller, described in a play of Aristophanes, who wandered about the streets and in the agora at will, stealing wares, chiefly food, and acquiring a mere smattering of reading, with little writing, and no gymnastic or music. But illiteracy in Athens was extremely rare. Even girls must have gained some knowledge of reading, and often of writing, according to the ability and willingness of their mothers or nurses to impart instruction to them. In the simpler branches of housekeeping, however, girls of the middle and lower classes were more systematically taught; while the richest learned at least how to spin, weave, sew, and embroider. (Compare also pages 108 ff., on books and reading.)

Training of girls.

In ordinary cases, the life of a lad during this early period of training was happy and interesting, with abundant variety in town and in the country, in school and palaestra, and at the family and state sacrifices. His sports kept him in the open air; his studies were few enough to admit thorough mastery of them. He learned no languages other than his own; no history, except what his father told him of their ancestors' exploits, or as he imbibed it incidentally when the teacher commented on the poets; no geography, though maps were coming into use among scientific men; no botany, zoology, or algebra. Though, like a modern boy, he played ball and marbles, and flew kites, he could not skate or coast—snow and ice do not linger in Greece, except in the mountainous portions—and he had no hockey, golf, or tennis.

A boy's interests.

The relations between teacher and pupil were not friendly. The Greek believed in the efficacy of corporal punishment—" he that is not flogged can not be taught," said a poet—and scholars lived in constant dread of the schoolmaster (cf. Fig. 60). Xenophon, evidently out of his own experience, well illustrates this when he says that Clearchus's soldiers felt toward Clearchus as boys feel toward a teacher; and Xenophon no more questions the right of teachers to use the rod for the good of their pupils than he questions the similar right of parents. The bitterest lot that could fall to children was, on the death of their father, to be handed over to a cruel or avaricious guardian. The state, however, through its chief archon, exercised a certain control over guardians (ἐπίτροποι), who, if information of maladministration of property came to the archon, might be required to render an account of the treatment they had bestowed on their wards (ὀρφανοί, ἐπίκληροι). Institutions for the care of waifs at public expense, such as orphan asylums, did not exist; but the state looked after the orphans of distinguished soldiers who had fallen in battle.

Relations between teacher and pupil.

At eighteen, a boy reached his majority, and was once more presented by his father or guardian to the members of his father's phratry. The father or guardian on this occasion offered a special sacrifice —*koureion*, κούρειον (page 74)—the meat of which was distributed to the members. The priest of the phratry also received certain perquisites, such as a cake, two quarts of wine, and a drachma (page 246) in money. Further, the boy had to be enrolled in his father's deme; for every citizen, after Cleisthenes had systematized the democratic constitution at the close of the sixth century, was a member of one of a hundred or more demes (δῆμοι) or districts spread over Attica. Originally, the deme was a local, territorial division, according to which the demesmen (δημόται) were actual neighbours, and united by a common local interest. But if a man moved away, he still remained a member of his original deme, and into this his sons, too, were enrolled. If the demesmen accepted the youth as properly qualified for citizenship by reason of age and legitimate birth, his name was inscribed in the deme register (ληξιαρχικὸν γραμματεῖον), whereupon he became entitled to citizen's rights and liable (theoretically) to citizen's duties; he could inherit property and exercise independent control of it, and he might perform priestly functions, if any such belonged to his family.

The margin notes: **The age of majority.** / **The demes of Attica.**

The change from boyhood to manhood was marked by a symbolical act, performed just before the introduction to the phratry. The young man invited friends of his own age to a drinking bout (οἰνιστήρια). After a libation to Heracles, his hair, which during childhood had been allowed to grow long, was cut off and dedicated to some river-god. In fact, this ceremony was so typical of the passing from boyhood to man's estate that it gave its name to the sacrifice, koureion, offered at the time; this word and the words for "cutting the hair" (κείρω) and for "barber" (κουρεύς)

are all related.   The young man, however, did not enter
immediately upon the duties of citizen.   After taking oath
in the temple of Aglaurus that he would be a loyal citizen
all his life, he, with other young men of his age (*ephēbi*,

The ephebi.   ἔφηβοι), was placed under the charge of a " mod-
erator " (σωφρονιστής), a middle-aged man who
saw to it that the youth had instruction and drill in military tactics, while performing light garrison duty in the

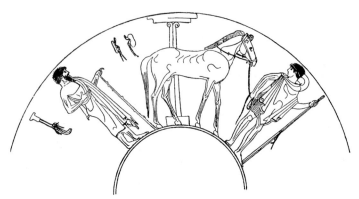

FIG. 71.—Ephēbus receiving parting instructions.

Piraeus (cf. Fig. 71).   At the end of a year the ephēbi were
marshalled before the whole body of the people, to whom they
exhibited their skill in tactics and warlike accomplishments,
such as archery, spear-casting, and fighting in heavy armour.
The state then presented each with a shield and spear, and
for another year the young man was assigned to garrison
duty on the frontiers of Attica.   Many of the richer young
men then joined the ranks of the permanent cavalry (ἱππεῖς),
on passing an examination instituted by the Council, which
affirmed their rank, their property qualification, their horse-
manship, and the good condition of their horses (page 194).

CHAPTER VIII

THE OCCUPATIONS OF YOUNG MEN

THE young man of twenty who did not belong to the lowest social class, and who consequently was not obliged to follow any trade, found himself in times of peace free to enjoy many sports and avocations. On the athletic side, the gymnasia were at his disposal—originally "exercising-grounds," situated outside the city walls, where they were afforded the shelter of shade-trees and were adjacent to some stream. The chief of these were the Academy ('Ακαδήμεια) and the Lycēum (Λύκειον), which grew to such importance in the lives of the

FIG. 72.—Scene in the palaestra.

people that they were later adorned with buildings, porticoes, statues, and seats for non-contestants, and laid out with pleasant paths which became the favourite resorts of strollers. All classes of men thronged hither during the

91

day, but chiefly in the afternoons; and the philosophers especially found the places so much to their taste, and so suited to their needs in the conversational style in which they carried on their researches, that they have given over the words "Academy" and "Lycēum" to modern languages as

denoting, not places where bodily training may be had, but centres and sources of mental cultivation.

We get a good notion of the elaborate arrangements for gymnasium and palaestra which were in vogue in later times from a view of the excavations at Olympia. The chief feature of the palaestra was the portico (στοά), a whole stadium in extent, from which several rooms branched out, suit-

FIG. 73.—Niche and statue in the portico at Pergamus.

able for bathing and exercises of all kinds. That such were adorned with sculptures and wall paintings in most cases is clear from Xenophon, who tells us that in Athens the Lycēum, really a precinct sacred to Apollo Lyceius, contained paintings by one Cleagoras.

Here the open-air palaestra kept the young man's body exposed to the sun, and made it brown and ruddy with health. Two kinds of wrestling were distinguished. In the "upright" or "face-to-face" wrestling (πάλη ὀρθή), the contestants stood upright, and tried, by lifting their opponent from the ground, to throw him. Three throws decided the contest. In the other, called "rolling" (ἀλίνδησις), the struggle continued on the ground, the two rolling over and over until

Wrestling and boxing.

one acknowledged himself beaten. In the stadion, also, the youth practised sprinting, either for a 200-yard dash

Fig. 74.—Wrestling; marking out a course.

down one side of the course (δρόμος, στάδιον) or for a longer distance. In the latter case he might double the post at the end of the course, and finish at the start-

Running. ing-point; this made a *diaulos* (δίαυλος, literally "double flute"; cf. page 83). Or the course might be covered six, twelve, twenty, or twenty-four times, in what was the most strenuous running exercise of all, the *dolichos* (δόλιχος).

Fig. 75.—The *dromos* or *stadion* (200-yard dash).

Another game of the palaestra which was thought becoming a free-born youth was javelin throwing, in which the Persian Cyrus also excelled. A rifled motion was given to the javelin by winding a thong (ἀγκύλη) tightly round the

shaft. The thong was held fast when the spear was thrown, so that it was sent off with a rotary motion (Figs. 76, 65). The young man also learned discus throwing and leaping. The throwing of the discus, extraordinarily popular in antiquity from the earliest times, has become better understood in recent years since the modern "Olympic games" were instituted in 1896. The adjoining cut (Fig. 77), which is composed of figures derived from vase-paintings (a, b, c), from a coin (d), and from a statue (e), shows the successive positions assumed by the thrower when hurling in proper

FIG. 76.—Spear with thong (ἀγκύλη).

"form." Figs. 65 and 78 also show the first position, while the contestant is sighting the course; the second position is also given in Fig. 79. In the broad jump, the contestant held in each hand a weight (ἁλτῆρες), shaped

FIG. 77.—Five positions in throwing the discus.

like a dumb-bell, by which he gave himself a greater impetus (Figs. 61, 79). These three sports, when given at a public festival, were run off to the accompaniment of flute music. They belonged to the so-called *pentathlon* (πέν-ταθλον), which also included in its five events running and wrestling. The pentath-

The pentathlon.

lon is a collective name for what, in the regular public contests, was an event by itself, the several sports in it being of the nature of heats. Just what the order of procedure was we do not know, but victory in three out of the five seems to have decided the whole.

FIG. 78.—Measuring the course just before the throw.

Boxing (πυγμή) was practised in such a rough and brutal fashion that it prop-erly belonged only to pro-

Boxing.

fessional athletes. In con-junction with wrestling, it formed the most severe of all physical exercises, the so-called *pankration* (παγκράτιον), which demanded the use of all the powers of the combatants. In simple box-ing, the knuckles were often reen-forced by leather straps which were distinguished as "soft" and "hard"; these, in the latter part of the fourth century, had also nails or bosses of lead fixed in them. The result of a contest fought to a finish with such weapons must have

FIG. 79.—Discus throwing and jumping.

been extremely repulsive even when the consequences were not fatal. For this reason, as well as for others, gentlemen's

sons did not go in for this sport. To be sure, it came to
be recognized with the others as one of the regular events

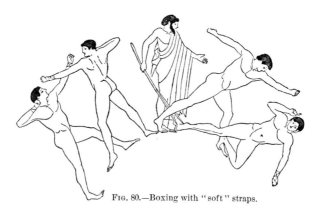

Fig. 80.—Boxing with "soft" straps.

at the national festivals, to be expected with eagerness and
applauded with enthusiasm. But the contestants themselves were usually looked upon as bul-
lies, like the Thessalian professional Bo-
ïscus, who is mentioned with repugnance
in the *Anabasis,* and the Spartan government prohibited the sport altogether.
This was not, however, because of its
roughness, but because the contest could
not end until one competitor had acknowledged himself beaten; and that
no Spartan would do. That he did not
mind mere brutality in wrestling Xenophon shows in his account of the games
improvised at Trapezus. Some one had
objected to the spot chosen by the Spartan director of the games. "How," said
he, "are they going to wrestle on such rough and bushy
ground?" "All the better," replied the director; "the
man who is thrown will be hurt all the more."

Fig. 81.—Boxer with
"hard" straps.

The most aristocratic amusement, begun and pursued in
early manhood, was riding (ἱππική), although the Athenians

Riding.
were not especially good horsemen. In Homer,
riding is scarcely known; war-horses are driven
to the chariot. Not until the middle of the seventh century B. C. was horse racing—i. e., a jockey riding on a single
horse (κέλης)—introduced at the Olympic games (see Fig.
87; cf. page 103). In some parts of Hellas—wherever the
land was flat, as in Thessaly and Boeotia, in Sicily and
southern Italy, Cyrēne, and Ionia—there were skilful riders.
But in Sparta riding was long neglected, and in Athens,

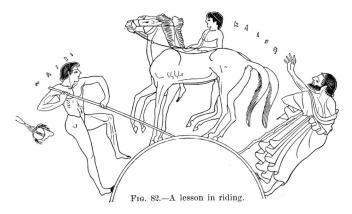

FIG. 82.—A lesson in riding.

although the cavalry (ἱππεῖς) were an ancient body, it was
not until after the Persian wars that riding came into
much fashion. Then the state required its richer citizens
to keep a horse for field service (see page 194). The Persians, like their modern successors the Turks, were expert
riders. Cyrus was conspicuous for his love of horses and
for his skill in using them.

In spite of deficiencies which would to us seem ridicu-
lous in a rider, the young men of the smart set, like Alcibiades, made the keeping of horses (ἱπποτροφία) fashionable,
and many a father, we are told, was ruined by his son's ex-

7

travagance in this regard. Most young men preferred to
drive their animals to a chariot (ἅρμα, δίφρος, δίφρισκος),

Chariot driving.
leaving riding to their jockeys. Chariots were
not used by the later Greeks in war, as they
had been in Homer; their use in classical
times was confined to the hippodrome. The best breeds of
horses were branded with the obsolete letters koppa and
san, ♀, ⋗, whence they were called respectively *koppatias*
(κοππατίας) and *samphoras* (σαμφόρας). A mark which looks
like a brand is seen on the horse in Fig. 243. The price of
a good horse was ordinarily ten or twelve minae (about
$200); this was very high, when we remember that the
purchasing power of money was perhaps three or four

times greater than
it is to-day. Xeno-
phon, who at the
end of his wander-
ings owned an ex-
cellent horse of
which he was very
fond, was obliged
through lack of
means to sell it.
He received fifty
darics (page 246)

FIG. 83.—Young man with a hare.

for it. It is a pleasure to read that some friends of his
arrived later, who bought the horse and returned it to him,
refusing any recompense.

Hunting was another favourite sport, by no means confined to the rich. The farmer had to hunt noxious animals,

Hunting.
especially the fox and the hare, for which
traps were set. A young man returning home
with his hound and a hare he has thus caught is shown in
Fig. 83. In Homer, it is the lion, more than the wolf,
which is the pest of the sheepfold and cow-pen, but other
animals of the chase are well known in Homer. They are

the wild boar, the leopard, the wolf, the hare, deer, and wild goats or chamois. In the fifth century the lion survived only in the mountain wildernesses of Macedonia and Epeirus. Dogs (αἱ κύνες) were so essential to the hunter that

Dogs. they gave their name to the sport (κυνηγετική) when it developed into an art. A work on the art of hunting still survives among Xenophon's writings. The choicest breeds were the great Molossian hounds of

Fig. 84.—Home from the chase.

northern Greece, the Laconian fox-hounds, and the fierce mountain dogs of Arcadia. The woods and hills of Attica, Peloponnēsus, and central and northern Greece abounded in game, particularly deer, foxes, hare, birds, and even bears and wolves. Game preserves like that of Cyrus at Celaenae were not owned by Greeks until after the time of Alexander the Great. The weapons in commonest use were the javelin (ἀκόντιον), the spear (δόρυ, λόγχη), the sling

Weapons. (σφενδόνη), and sometimes, as in the heroic age, the bow (τόξον). But a special club with a curved end was used for throwing at hare. Birds were not hunted, properly speaking, but were lured to sticks smeared with birdlime, or to nets and snares. Traps (νεφέλαι) were set also for wild boar and hare. The hunter usually wore a special costume, of which the most conspicuous features

were his broad-brimmed hat (πέτασος, page 166) and his
boots, whereas neither hat nor boots were worn in ordinary

Attire.

life. The latter were necessary to protect his
legs from brambles, for hunting on foot was
almost exclusively the rule among the Greeks. The Persians used horses, a fact which, Xenophon thinks, requires
special mention. At the end of his day's sport, the hunter
offered a portion of
his catch to Arte-
mis, dedicating the
skin at some tree or
altar in the forest.

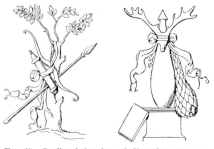

Fishing in the
eyes of the Greeks
was not a sport,
though it was occa-
sionally included by
them in the occu-
pation of hunting.

Fig. 85.—Spoils of the chase dedicated to Artemis.

Fishing.

Deep-sea fishing was a profitable profession,
especially in the harbours of Piraeus and Phalēron and at Byzantium, where fishermen's boats (ἁλιευτικὰ
πλοῖα) were always in the harbour.

Most of the sports and athletic exercises just described
were included in the entertainments of the great national

**The national
festivals.**

festivals. Here they formed a part of the
honour paid to the gods, and were glorified and
even sanctified in a way hardly comprehensible
to-day. Besides numerous local festivals belonging to the
different cities, such as the Panathenaea at Athens, or the
Carneia at Sparta, there were four great occasions of national, Pan-Hellenic interest. These were the Olympia in
honour of Zeus, held every four years in Elis; the Pythia,
held in honour of Apollo, at Crissa, near Delphi, also every
four years; the Nemea, another Zeus festival, in Nemea
(Argos), every two years; and the Isthmia, in honour of

Poseidon, held every two years at Corinth. At the Pythia
musical contests, as most pleasing to Apollo, were the chief
features, but running, wrestling, horse and chariot racing,
and all the rest, were events as eagerly watched here as elsewhere. This festival was held in the winter, in the third
year of every Olympiad. At the Nemean and the Pythian

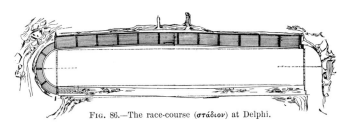

Fig. 86.—The race-course (στάδιον) at Delphi.

games, also, contests in flute and lyre playing, and in singing to their accompaniment, were included with the others.
The Nemea came in the second and fourth years of every
Olympiad, alternately in winter and in summer. The
Isthmia similarly alternated between spring and summer,
in the first and third years of each Olympiad. In this way
the national festivals never conflicted with one another,
and at the Olympia, especially, the whole world of Greeks,
from one end of the Mediterranean basin to the other, gave
themselves up to the joyful service of the god. A cessation

The Olympia. of hostilities (ἐκεχειρία, " a staying of hands "),
sanctified by all the instincts of religion, al-
lowed the travellers from distant homes to journey undis-
turbed to the place of celebration. A motley crowd it was—
men of all countries, ranks, and ages. Thus the priest of
the Ephesian Artemis, Xenophon tells us, made the long
journey to Olympia to attend the spectacle; but no women
were allowed at Olympia. The visitors (θεωροί) brought
their slaves, who could not be spectators, but who carried
tents, bedding, and all that was needed for living. Olympia was not a town, in the strict sense, and even if it had

been, the inns would not have sufficed to accommodate the immense number of worshippers.

The contest earliest instituted in the history of Olympia, the one with which every Olympic celebration opened and which conferred the greatest renown upon the victor, was

Contests at Olympia. the short-distance foot-race (στάδιον, 600 Greek feet; Fig. 75, cf. page 243). Then came the other running events, the *diaulos* and the *dolichos* (see page 93). Wrestling, the pentathlon, and boxing were added in later years. For a hundred years these were all the competitions that were open at Olympia. Then, in

Fig. 87.—Entering for the horse-race and the chariot-race.

the seventh century, chariot racing was introduced, and from this time on the older simplicity became lost in the lavish display and reckless extravagance of princes and tyrants and private individuals, among whom Dionysius of Syracuse and Alcibiades of Athens made themselves conspicuous. Here the requirements of the competitors were not so much speed on the part of their horses, as coolness and judgment on their own part, and dexterity in rounding the dangerous post at the end of the stadion (Fig. 86). Xenophon speaks of the bewilderment and confusion which sometimes came upon one in the hippodrome. The result would inevitably be the destruction of the chariot, and perhaps the death of the horses and the driver. Although each driver was supposed to keep to his own part of the course, the struggle to reach the inside at the turning-point was very eager, and it frequently happened that one rival disabled another by crashing into his chariot and taking off a wheel.

In the middle of the seventh century the horse-race (page 97) and the pankration were introduced, both of which tended to foster professional jockeyism and pugilism. Not long after, contests of boys were established in running and wrestling. Other modifications and additions came slowly, the most interesting and useful of which was the running in heavy armour (ὁπλίτης δρόμος, also called δίαυ-

FIG. 88.—Racing in armour.

λος, Fig. 88). At Olympia there were no musical or literary contests, unless we except a competition between trumpeters and between heralds, which was inaugurated in the fourth century; but a poet or singer might often seize the opportunity to attract a group of listeners and make known his works to them.

Prizes. The official prizes (ἆθλα) bestowed at the national festivals were not valuable in themselves. They were mere wreaths, "crowns" (cf. 1 Corinth., ix, 25). At Olympia it was a crown of wild olive; at the Pythia, of bay or laurel; at Nemea and the Isthmia, a

wreath of parsley. As a badge or token of his success, the
victor also received a palm-branch, and was bedecked with
ribbons and streamers. But though the prize was incon-
siderable in itself, it was perhaps more coveted than any
other honour a Greek could gain. To win it he surrendered
himself to long months of practice. For the Olympia, he

Training for the games. had to certify that he had been in training
for ten months preceding the festival; and
thirty days before it occurred he had to repair
to Olympia and exercise under the special supervision of
the authorities of Elis. None but Greeks were eligible to
compete. When, for a single event, the number of candi-
dates was too large, the contest was divided into heats. In
wrestling and boxing, if an uneven number of applicants
were entered for the sport, of course one lucky person would
draw a bye. He would then sit at one side (hence he was
called the ἔφεδρος) and enjoy a considerable advantage when
he finally entered the ring against the tired-out victor of
the preceding round. Besides the banquet with which the
victor was entertained at Elis, and the privilege of having

The victor. a conspicuous share in the sacrifice and merry-
making amid which the festival ended, his re-
turn home was made a triumphal procession, almost a royal
progress, by his countrymen. Poets of high renown were
hired to compose odes in honour of his victory (ἐπινίκια). All
the poems of Pindar which we possess to-day, and almost
all by Bacchylides, are of this sort. That the returning
hero might not enter his native town by the vulgar path,
we are told that a part of the wall was sometimes torn
down for his entry. More material rewards were given
at local games, e. g., the Panathenaea; so also at games instituted by private persons (see page 80). The Athenians
granted an Olympic victor (Ὀλυμπιονίκης) the privilege of
dining at public expense in the Prytaneium (page 63).
Artists were hired to make bronze statues of him, which
were set up either at home or at the scene of his victory.

His name was often used in determining the date of an historical event. Thus Thucydides speaks familiarly of the Olympic festival at which Androsthenes of Arcadia won his first victory in the pankration, as an occasion which would be readily recalled by all his readers. The custom of dating by Olympiads, however, which is practised so largely in Greek histories to-day, was not adopted by historians until a century after Thucydides and Xenophon, when it became an official mode of reckoning time. Still, among the people it was enough to mention the name of a victorious runner at Olympia, or a winning horse at Delphi, to fix the year in popular chronology (see page 242).

In spite of the harmful tendencies, which finally culminated two centuries before Christ in the introduction of the pankration for boys, the games had a distinctly educative value, not the least part of which was due to the opportunities for travel which they afforded. Very few Greeks did not, at least once in their lives, go to one of these festivals. Socrates speaks of himself as an exception in this regard; he was an incorrigible stay-at-home.

Influence of the games.

On the side of mental culture, which began in the schools with the elements of reading and the study of the poets, there came a new and momentous influence into the lives of the young men of Athens when, in 427 B. C., Gorgias, the distinguished rhetorician and sophist, came to Athens on an embassy from Leontīni, in Sicily. His grace of style, his flowing periods, and his brilliant utterance gave a fresh stimulus to the cultivation of that natural eloquence which was latent in all Greeks, and which finds its illustration as early as Homer. The Athenians, especially, were ever lovers of talk (φιλόλογοι) and of debate, and disposed to hear all sides of a question. Never, perhaps, has there lived a people with greater mental curiosity, so eager to hear and learn novelties, as that which

Higher mental education.

Oratory.

thronged every morning in the Athenian agora. " For all
the Athenians and strangers which were there spent their
time in nothing else, but either to tell or to hear some new
thing " (*Acts*, xvii, 21). Their city, since the rule of the
Pisistratidae in the sixth century, had been the chief centre
of literary effort, the source of all intellectual inspiration,
in Greece. When, therefore, the new rhetoric was introduced among them, they took it up with enthusiasm, and
its professors, the sophists, became from that time on the
chief educators in Athens, and, in fact, everywhere throughout Hellas. Men like Gorgias of Leontīni, Protagoras of
Abdēra, Hippias of Elis, and Prodicus of Ceos, were fol-
The sophists. lowed, in all the cities which they visited, except Sparta, by bands of young admirers, who
paid them high fees for their instruction in the art ($\tau \acute{\epsilon} \chi \nu \eta$)
of public speaking. A typical example is Proxenus, Xeno-
phon's friend, who attached himself to Gorgias because he
aspired to a distinguished career ($\tau \grave{\alpha}\ \mu \epsilon \gamma \acute{\alpha} \lambda \alpha\ \pi \rho \acute{\alpha} \tau \tau \epsilon \iota \nu$), and
left his teacher only when he felt that he had learned how
to govern and to carry himself as an equal of the great.
The effects of this new and " higher " education were mani-
fold and far-reaching. On its worst side, it tended to make
Faults of the young men less attentive to substance than to
sophistic form; it emphasized victory, the winning of
training. one's case, over the love of truth and fair play.
The teachers themselves held opposing doctrines, which
they often urged with acrimony against their rivals. So
that, seeming to be contentious themselves, they fostered
consciously or unconsciously that spirit of litigation for
which Athens was blamed by her neighbours. Some young
men, doubtless, developed a fondness for mere disputation
without results, a sham brilliancy and show of knowledge,
a " smartness " not based on real wit—in short, the qualities of mind and the methods of reasoning which are to-
day called " sophistical." Men like Gorgias certainly had
no conscious intention of injuring the young whom they

influenced. This is seen in the case of Proxenus again, who was a soldier of sweet and noble bearing, even if he lacked force in administering discipline; very different from Menon, the uncouth Thessalian in the *Anabasis*, who thought that a man who was not a rascal must belong to the uneducated class.

The training derived from the sophists was in no case so harmful as the lack of it would have been. Without this **Merits of the** new interest inspired by them, most young men **sophistic** would have had more time to spend in gambling **training.** at the low drinking shops ($\kappa a\pi\eta\lambda\epsilon\hat{\imath}a$) of the city and the Piraeus, or in betting on cock and quail fights. On its best side, the sophistic training offered an education beyond the mere school rudiments. It opened the way to the study of law, of practical politics, of ethical questions, of the natural sciences, and of the Greek language itself. For with his new training, for the first time, the speaker came to recognize consciously the wonderful richness and flexibility of his mother tongue, and its surpassing power in description, narrative, argument, invective, and appeal. The sophists at least created an atmosphere in which alone could be kindled an interest in the deeper moral questions propounded by Socrates and Plato. Neither of these would have got an audience had it not been for the preliminary schooling which young men acquired through the new rhetoric. It made possible the work not only of great orators like Lysias, Demosthenes, Aeschines, and the Romans Hortensius and Cicero, but also of historians like Thucydides and Xenophon, and philosophers like Plato, Aristotle, and Epicūrus.

Recitations The rhapsodes, also, reciters of epic poetry, **of epic** contributed not a little to the intellectual en- **poetry.** tertainment and instruction of the people. Crowned with a wreath and carrying a staff as the badge of their office, they were received with honour in all the large cities, especially on the occasion of some religious festi-

val. In Athens, at the Greater Panathenaea held every four
years, their recitations of Homer formed a conspicuous and
time-honoured part of the festival. This part
The
rhapsodes.
of it was held in the Odeium, the "Academy of
Music" built by Pericles. Here, standing before
eager listeners, they stirred by their sympathetic and often
dramatic declamation the feelings of thousands of people,
moving them to delight, to tears, or to anger, according to
the mood of the story. In Sparta, too, there were contests
between these declaimers. Other poets besides Homer were
represented, but the chief class remained the Homeridae
(Ὁμηρίδαι), who, claiming to be descendants of the great
poet, faithfully kept up the tradition of his poems and
spread a knowledge of them throughout Greece long before
they were committed to writing, and even afterward.

Besides all these sources of intelligence and knowledge
of the world of men and things, the Athenians, and many
Books and
general
reading.
other Greeks as well, gleaned much from books.
Reading was far more general in the Periclean
age than is commonly supposed. A popular
play of Euripides was immediately published and widely
circulated. The same was true of the works of the comic
poets. Men as different in character as Euripides the
dramatist and Eucleides the archon owned libraries; and of
course the schoolmasters (γραμματισταί), poor as they were,
owned the works of the poets whom they taught. We hear
of reading by lamplight, and this in spite of the physical
difficulties in the way. For books were reproduced by
handwriting on papyrus (see page 85), an exceedingly light
and perishable material derived from the *biblos*. This is a
large reed or sedge that grew profusely in shallow waters
in Egypt. There it was used by the poorest classes in a
variety of ways: for mats, baskets, fuel, the
Papyrus.
joints of boats, and even for food. Although
it had to be transported from Egypt to Attica, the material itself could not have been very costly; and some of

the poorer grades of the manufactured "paper" (χάρτης, χαρτίον) need not have been expensive. It was prepared by carefully unrolling the inner portion of the stem with a sharp knife. This brought to hand a thin and delicate

FIG. 89.—An official letter on a papyrus of the third century B. C.

strip or narrow sheet, which had to be reënforced by placing on it, transversely, another similar strip. The two were then pressed tightly together. If the juice of the plant was insufficient to make them join, a little paste was added. The surface was then made smooth and even, and bleached in the sun. Sheets of this kind were then pasted together at their edges to make long rolls. The whole of the *Odyssey* could be contained in a roll of ordinary width 150 feet long. The Greeks of the fifth and fourth centuries endured the inconvenience of very long rolls. Each roll was called a *biblion* (βιβλίον). The whole of Thucydides, the whole of the *Anabasis*, or of the *Hellenica*, circulated in their authors' lifetime each in a single roll, undivided into "books." The inconvenience of this was appreciated in the third century by the great librarian Callimachus of Alexandreia, who used to say that a long roll (μέγα βιβλίον) was a big nuisance (μέγα

Division into books.

κακόν). Following his example, the scholars of a later day began to divide the works of classical authors into the "books" with which we are now familiar. These signify the portion of the work contained in a single roll. The *Anabasis* was at first divided among six rolls, and still later among seven, the number which survives to-day.

All this convenience of division was unknown in the classical period. Homer, not being as yet divided into

Fig. 90.—Ruins of the great library at Pergamus.

"books," was cited by recalling a scene from the poems: thus, "From the Exploits of Diomēdes" (ἐκ τῆς Διομήδεος ἀριστηίης) is Herodotus's way of citing *Iliad*, 6, 289 ff.; or again, "The Transmission of the Sceptre" (ἐκ τῆς τοῦ σκήπτρου παραδόσεως), is Thucydides's citation of *Iliad*, 2, 108.

Other impediments to reading arose from the **Difficulties of reading.** fact that words were not separated, but run together. There was no punctuation or accentuation; in prose, no paragraphing, or numbering of lines. A tag, containing a superscription (ἐπίγραμμα) which gave

the author's name and a rough title to the work, aided the
reader in selecting the roll he wanted. He sat as he read,
rolling up one end as he unrolled the other (Fig. 69). Books
were kept in cylindrical cases (τεύχη) which were open at the
top, and they not infrequently, therefore, suffered from mice.

There was an active trade in books (βίβλοι γεγραμμέναι)
in the fifth century, of which Athens was the chief centre;
it was long before she yielded her supremacy to Alexandreia
and afterward Rome in this matter. A section of her market, called the *biblia* (cf. page 238), was devoted to the sale
of books, which were reproduced and circulated by men
called *bibliographoi* or *bibliopōlai* (βιβλιογράφοι, βιβλιοπῶλαι).
No better evidence of the extent of this trade is given than
by Xenophon, who, speaking of the large number of shipwrecks in the Pontus on the Thracian coast, mentions
books along with beds and chests and other common objects as cast up by the sea. The rolls which contained a
single author's works were tied together in separate bundles
(δέσμαι) and shipped in wooden cases. If books were so
widely distributed, they must have been widely read.

While the material derived from papyrus was sometimes
used even for letters, accounts, and other business, both
public and private, tablets (δέλτοι) were perhaps more common for such purposes. These
were made of some hard wood, such as box;
they were covered with a thin layer of wax, sometimes
gypsum, and the writing was done by a graver or *stilus*
(γραφίς; see Fig. 67). Several of these tablets could be
joined together like the leaves in a book, and, in fact, it is
from them that the modern book form is derived. To prevent the wax or gypsum of one from rubbing against another, each tablet had raised edges. Temporary notices,
such as those summoning the citizens to military service,
were posted, in a similar manner, on boards (πίνακες, πινάκια)
covered with gypsum. Warrants and summonses issued by
the courts were set down on wax tablets. From such mate-

**Writing
tablets.**

rials the writing could be easily erased, and they never were
used for permanent documents. These were entrusted to
the stone-cutter and the engraver, who inscribed them on
marble or bronze.

Finally, the theatre exercised an absorbing influence in
forming the lives and characters of Athenians. Its educative power was greater than can be measured
to-day, for it sprang from the popular religion.

The theatre.

Both religion and the state, therefore—the two were virtually one in antiquity—united in its support, and every
performance in the theatre recalled to the citizen his
dependence upon both, his obligation to both. Attendance

Fig. 91.—The theatre at Athens, in its present condition.

at the dramatic contests was the duty and the privilege of
all citizens, even the poorest; for these a fund (θεωρικόν)
was provided by the state in the last years of the fifth century, which insured them not only a free ticket, but also
spending money for the holiday.

The performance of a play was not an every-day occurrence. In Athens it was confined to two festivals held
every year in honour of Dionȳsus. Just as the
The festivals of Dionȳsus. national contests in athletic sports crowned
and embodied the gymnastic training of Greek
youth, so also the Dionysiac festivals, with their performances in the theatre, strengthened and glorified their
education on the mental side. These festivals were the
Lenaea and the *Greater Dionysia* (see page 274). The
Lenaea was the older of the two festivals, and closer to the
hearts of the common people. It was held in mid-winter,
and comedy was the chief feature. The Great Dionysia,
held in the spring, was the occasion of display and magnificence before Athens' guests, for the city began, at this time
of the year, to fill with strangers—merchants, or travellers,
or politicians. Tragedy, on account of its dignity, held the
principal place in this festival.

The sacred precinct of Dionȳsus, at the foot of the
Acropolis on the southeast, was the spot where most of
the great dramatists exhibited their works for the first
time (Figs. 40, 91). They were often repeated in other
towns of Greece where theatres had been erected.

In the precinct was the circular dancing ground, or
orchestra (ὀρχήστρα), all that was really essential to the production of a piece. It was marked off by a
The dancing ring. periphery of stone, and in its centre stood the
altar to the god. The ground was not paved,
but beaten hard by the tramp of many feet in the dance.
For the chorus, which had been developed by slow stages,
lasting many years, out of the rude bands of masqueraders
who celebrated the god with mirth and jesting
The chorus. at the time of the vintage and harvest, was still
felt to be the most important part of the Dionysiac festivities, and retained its prominence until the fourth century.

The orchestra was large; at Athens it was over ninety
feet in diameter. Such a space could easily afford ample

8

freedom of movement to the fifty men or boys who sang
hymns to the gods, particularly Dionȳsus, in the "dithyram-

Number of chorus and of actors. bic" contests (page 275). Fifteen men composed the chorus of tragedy, and twenty-four
of comedy, and again, though they danced as
well as sang, there was room for the free play of both actor
and chorus therein. In tragedy and in comedy the number
of actors was usually limited to three. They were therefore obliged to assume different rôles, the same actor appearing at one time as a messenger, at another as a maiden,
or again as a king. The audience (οἱ θεώμενοι) in the fifth
century sat on wooden benches rising on tiers on the adjacent hillside. About the middle of the fourth century

Accommoda- tions for the audience. the orator Lycurgus caused the erection of a
permanent stone auditorium, the remains of
which are still to be seen. The word "theatre"
(θέατρον) was originally used only of this part of the building—the part occupied by the spectators. The actors, in
the early days of the drama, changed their costumes in a
tent or booth, in Greek, *skené*. This word has survived and
expanded in a wealth of varied associations, in all European
languages. At first, however, there was absolutely no

Absence of elaborate scenery. scenery. The progress of the story, the careful
and often brilliant descriptions of the poet,
made it clear to the spectators whence the
hero had come and whither he was going. Gradually, as
poets came to attach less importance to the chorus, and as
the actors achieved greater prominence in the piece and
came to demand more "setting" and background, the idea
was conceived of utilizing one wall of the *skené* as a "scene."
It was painted as occasion demanded, to represent the
façade of a temple or of a palace, the wall of a citizen's
house, or the rocks and sands of a desert. With such limitations as to scenery, every Athenian, no matter how dull,
was obliged to rely on his own imagination to picture for
him the setting, in a degree unknown in modern times;

for to-day "spectacular effects" are lavishly provided to
make up for the demerits of a play or the spectator's lack
of imaginative power. If, to the modern taste, the scenery
of a Greek play was deficient, this was counter-
balanced by the elaborate costumes, and by the
skilful technique of actors and chorus. Extraordinary care was devoted to the training of the voice. The
actor must be able to sing as well as to declaim ; and the
chorus, also, must be trained to sing as one man, and, in

Training of actors.

Fig. 92.—Masks used in tragedy.

addition, learned the dance figures necessary for the proper
representation of feelings in pantomime. In tragedy the
costumes were ordinarily rich and dignified, as befitted the
gods and the heroes of mythical times who were brought

Fig. 93.—Masks used in comedy.

on the scene. In comedy there was every variety of grotesque and comic device, especially when the chorus mas-
queraded as birds, or wasps, or clouds, or irate old men, as
frequently happened. Masks were always used,
in tragedy and in comedy, by both actors and
chorus. Hearing was more important than seeing in the
vast space occupied by the theatre ; it has been estimated
that 17,000 people could find places here. While, therefore,

Masks.

the modern theatre-goer would have missed the facial expression, the play of features, by which an accomplished actor can convey so much, he would still have felt a compensation in the ease with which the well-trained voice carried through the clear Attic air.

The literary quality of the pieces, produced as they were for the god, and, as it was believed, with his sanction, was so high that it has never been surpassed.

Dramatic contests. Not all the poets, of course, were equally good, and some were positively bad; yet a high standard was maintained, partly by the fact that dramatic performances, like all other public exhibitions in Greece, took on the form and spirit of contests between choruses or between poets. They were *agōnes*—competitions for a prize —exactly comparable to the severest events in the athletic meetings. These contests lasted throughout three days of the festival, beginning early in the morning and ending at sunset. In their turn also they contributed to inspire that love of agonistic display, whether in athletics, or in public debate, or in court-room speeches, or in rhapsodic recitations, which distinguishes the Athenian of the fifth and fourth centuries above all other men before or since his time. They

Popular dramatic taste. formed and educated in him a power of acute observation, of sane literary judgment, founded on a knowledge of the principles underlying all true poetry which he had learned in school. Coming at such long intervals, in an age when the memory was not spoiled and the attention distracted by the hasty reading of newspapers and magazines, a dramatic performance left an extraordinarily deep and lasting impression. In the fifth

Old plays reproduced. century plays of Aeschylus and Sophocles seem to have been reproduced; and as the century drew to a close the habit of reading them and producing them for a reading, as well as a listening, public, became more and more common. Relying on these factors, but especially on the good memories of their au-

dience, the comic poets were able to ridicule what they
thought were defects in tragedy by quoting with mock
seriousness verses from the tragedians or ap-
Comic burlesques. plying them in inappropriate situations to
give the effect of burlesque.

Another factor in maintaining a relatively high standard of literary merit was the archon, or chief magistrate
Administra- of the state, to whom the poet who proposed
tion of the to compete must first submit his play. The
festivals. " King " (ὁ βασιλεύς) had charge of the Lenaea;
the Chief Archon (ὁ ἄρχων *par excellence*) managed the
Greater Dionysia. We do not know what means these officials employed in approving or rejecting a poet's application.
Being, however, responsible magistrates, with the care of
august religious ceremonies laid on them, it seems clear
that they did not often " grant a chorus," as the phrase
was, to an utterly trivial and unworthy production.

It is to be remembered, however, that taste in regard to
literature, manners, and morals is constantly changing.
What we should reject to-day as weak or vain or false in a
poet's sentiments might often commend itself to an ancient
judge because of its simplicity, or patriotism, or rhetorical
skill.   Hence many poets who are now almost forgotten
and whose works are entirely lost were successful competitors
against the four dramatists, Aeschylus, Sophocles, Euripides,
and Aristophanes, whom we to-day regard as having attained
perfection in their several ways, and who in their own day
were the most talked of men of their profession. Yet Euripides, in his long and distinguished career of fifty years, is
said to have won only five first prizes.

Thus we have reviewed the circumstances and influences which affected the lives of men in their young manhood with a more or less educative force. What has been
said about the literary and dramatic contests, however, and
about books and reading, would apply as well to the older
men, and also to women; for though women might not at-

tend the Olympic games, the festivals of their own country were in the main open to them, and they were permitted to attend the performances of tragedy, if not of comedy. These educating influences, of course, were strongest in the latter half of the fifth century, when Pericles was in power. Art, letters, and politics, claimed the interest of the ordinary citizen far more than they do to-day, because it was the policy of Pericles to render the democracy of Athens a leisure class, supported by their slaves and the revenues of the empire.

CHAPTER IX

MARRIAGE AND HOME

A YOUNG man in Attica did not, as a rule, marry immediately on coming of age. Frequently he waited until he
was thirty or over. Association with other men
The marrying of his age, his comrades (ἡλικιῶται) in gymnas-
age. tic and other sports, and military service as
well, kept him from making a union which to many Greeks
was distasteful; for girls of even good family were known
to be often ill educated, without any positive attraction
other than modesty and good character. They were strictly
guarded by their parents within doors, so that their knowledge of the world was extremely limited and their range of
interests narrow. Except at the greater state festivals, when
girls sometimes were allowed certain duties, or through a
chance glimpse at a window in the upper story, the young
Restrictions man might never see his future wife until the
laid on wedding-day. Love-matches, therefore, were
women. very rare, and marriage (γάμος) in general was
the result of a prearranged contract between the parents
of the bride and the groom, whose wishes were seldom consulted as a matter of right.

In restricting women as they did, the Athenians, like
all the Ionians, differed widely from other Greeks. People
Women in in other states, such as Lesbos or Sparta, still
other parts retained to a great degree the customs of the
of Greece. Homeric age, which were simpler and franker
in this regard. In Homer women and girls move more
freely in men's society; they enjoy greater reverence, as

wives and mothers, than we see paid to them by the later
Athenians, and they exercise greater influence over the
conduct of husbands and sons. In the Homeric age a wife
could be obtained only by bringing, in rivalry with other
lovers, rich presents to her father (πορὼν ἀπερείσια ἔδνα),

FIG. 94.—Women at home.

and the suitor must prove himself to be a young man of
physical and mental distinction ; whereas in Athens, at the
later time, the wife's parents offered a dowry as an induce-
ment to marriage. The young man's father bore the chief
part in the selection of a wife, and chose for his son some
daughter of a friend whom he deemed his equal in rank
and property. It was the father who arranged with the
bride's father or guardian (κύριος) all the preliminaries, such
Dowry.   as the kind and the amount of the dowry (προίξ,
              φερνή), the value and extent of the trousseau
and other personal belongings she was to bring with her,
and other matters, all of a strictly business nature. The
arrangement was looked upon as a contract, with sureties
Betrothal.   given, and as such the betrothal was called
              ἐγγύη or ἐγγύησις—" the act of giving security "
—for which the presence of witnesses, but not of the be-
trothed, was necessary. The bride's guardian had complete control over her fate ; he was said " to give her
away," and thus the expression " given away " (ἐκδιδομένη) is

used of a married woman in the *Anabasis*. Legally, the
bride was a mere chattel, passively submitting to the disposition of her friends. Of her the verb γαμῶ, "marry," is
always used in the passive.

**Lack of ro-
mantic ele-
ment in Greek
marriage.** This system, prosaic and unromantic as it seems, in
which pecuniary and social advantage was considered above
the personal inclination of the parties most
concerned, was designed to be an aid to the
growth and power of the state. Marriage was
entered into in order that a new family circle
might be formed to perpetuate the worship of the gods of
home and state, and that the ties between citizens and commonwealth might be strengthened through well-trained and
loyal children. The system produced many happy unions,
and not infrequently furnished inspiring examples of devotion between husband and wife or parents and children.
The marriage of Cimon's sister Elpinīce to Callias is perhaps the most conspicuous love-match of the fifth century,
and its effects were far-reaching. To prove his love, Callias is said to have paid the fine of fifty talents which Cimon
owed the state, and thus restored him to a long career of
eminent public service; and years later, through Elpinīce's
good offices, Cimon and Pericles were able to come to an
understanding on important matters of state policy.

**The wedding-
month.** Weddings ordinarily were celebrated in the winter; one
of the winter months, *Gamelion* (Γαμηλιών, page 241), was
sacred to Hera as goddess of marriage (Ἥρα
γαμήλιος). The time of the full moon was preferred, the days of the waning moon avoided,
though in general the Greeks were not so fastidious about
lucky and unlucky days as were the Romans. The several
acts of the ceremony, however, were performed with a scrupulous care which attested the importance attached to marriage, and the desire that it should be brought to pass in a
way to propitiate the favour of the gods. As her wedding-
day approached, the bride (νύμφη) was called upon to perform

little offices of devotion to the protecting divinities of her community.   Some were pathetically significant of the new life she was to lead.   Young as she might be—for girls were sometimes married at fifteen, or younger—she must hence-

Fig. 95.—Women at home.

forth consider herself a woman.   She was to pass entirely from the care of kindred—father, brother, grandfather, or uncle—to the guardianship of an unknown husband (ἀνήρ).

Dedication to the gods.   As a token of farewell to the old life, she would dedicate her girdle, or the toys she had played with as a child, or a lock of her hair, to some divinity, either to a local nymph, or to Artemis.   To Artemis all girls in Attica were consecrated when they were ten years old (page 276).

On the wedding-day the bride and the bridegroom bathed in water brought from some spring of special sanctity by boys or girls belonging to their families.   This **The sacred bath.** bath, which had almost the importance of a sacrament in the eyes of a Greek, was called the *loutra* (λουτρά) ; the water-carriers specially chosen were the *loutrophoroi* (λουτροφόροι).   The bride was dressed in some light colour and crowned with a wreath by her brides-maid (νυμφεύτρια).   The groom, also dressed in **The dress.** holiday attire, and with a wreath on his head, went with his parents to the bride's house, where the invited guests were assembled, and the chief act of the ceremony began.   As the guests entered, each received a cake called *sesamé* (σησαμῆ), made of sesame seeds pounded and roasted and mixed with honey, the prototype of the modern fruit-cake used at weddings. No wedding was complete without it. The bride's father then offered sacrifice, called

The sacrifice. in this case τὰ προγάμια or τὰ προτέλεια, to the gods of marriage (θεοὶ γαμήλιοι). Care was taken to remove the gall of the victim, as a sign that no bitterness was to enter into the lives of the married pair. After the sacrifice came the banquet, at which, in addition

The banquet. to the animal just roasted on the altar, the guests partook of a large flat cake, also made of sesame. The women were allowed to be present, contrary to the usual custom at banquets, though they sat at separate tables, the bride among them, with her veil closely wrapped round her face. The meal ended with a libation and ceremonious wishes for the happiness of the couple. As evening came on, the bride was given over to the groom by her mother, whereupon he led her to the bridal chariot

The procession. which was to take them to his home. The bride sat on a bench (κλινίς), while the groom and his best man (the πάροχος or παράνυμφος) stood near. The wagon was surrounded by the relatives and guests, who formed a procession singing the wedding song to Hymenaeus, accompanied by flute or lyre players.

The song and the torch. Behind the chariot followed the mother of the bride, holding the nuptial torches. These were carried also by other members of the procession. It sometimes happened that the groom lived in a distant city, making a long journey necessary. In this case, of course, the procession would disband at the city gates. A bridal party of this character was met by Xenophon's troops in the road from Babylon when they came upon a certain Orontas who had married the king's daughter.

Arrival at the groom's house. Arrived at the door of her new home, the bride found it specially decorated in her honour, and the couple were showered with confetti (καταχύσματα) by the groom's mother. After eating a quince at the threshold, the bride was led into the bridal chamber (θάλαμος), while outside the door the friends sang more wedding-hymns (ἐπιθαλάμια, *epithalamia*) and devised jokes, both practical and verbal, at the expense of the door-

Fig. 96.—The bridal party arriving at the groom's house.

keeper. On the next day, or soon after, the couple "received" their family and friends, before whom the bride stood unveiled for the first time. Presents were brought, which from this circumstance were called δῶρα ἀνακαλυπτήρια, or simply ἀνακαλυπτήρια (from ἀνακαλύπτω, *unveil*). Another sacrifice and another banquet ended the festivities, and the bride's name was then entered on the roll of the phratry to which her husband belonged.

Presents.

Once settled in her new home, she possessed a liberty somewhat greater than that allowed to her as a girl (κόρη, παρθένος); still her interests and pleasures, if she belonged to the upper class, were bound by the walls of her house, which she might not leave without the special permission of her husband. Even then a slave must go with her. Custom excluded her from the banquets and symposia given by her husband in the house. His friends were at most only speaking acquaintances of hers, whom she seldom saw except in his presence. Only at the festivals could she appear in public as a matter of right. No wonder that her mental horizon was narrow,

The wife in the new home.

and her body often injured by her sedentary life, so that
she sometimes resorted to the tasteless practice of using cos-
metics to correct the paleness caused from such conditions.

Further, the wife enjoyed no legal status. Her hus-
band, as her guardian ($\kappa\acute{\upsilon}\rho\iota o\varsigma$), became her representative
before the law, but only in a limited way was
he responsible to the state for her well-being.
Divorce for the husband was much easier than
for the wife. He might simply " dismiss " her, in the presence of witnesses, provided he returned her dowry to her
former guardian, who might also require him to furnish
alimony or maintenance ($\sigma\hat{\iota}\tau o\varsigma$), so long as she remained
unmarried. In case of divorce the children remained with
their father. The wife, on the other hand, found divorce
from a cruel or unfaithful husband very difficult. She
must submit in person a written complaint before the
archon, and from this the mere physical power of her husband might prevent her.

*Legal dis-
qualifications
of women.*

Still, in families where the sturdy morality of the old
Attic period had not been affected by the degeneracy that
set in during the Peloponnesian War, we are
not to assume that the life of a young wife
was always unhappy. In spite of the restrictions placed on her coming and going, she,
with the help of her slaves, soon became adjusted to her
new surroundings and absorbed in the duties of the home.
These comprised, above all, the care of her husband, sick or
well, and the nursing of sick slaves ($\theta\epsilon\rho\alpha\pi\epsilon\acute{\iota}\alpha$); the dispens-
ing of household stores ($\tau\alpha\mu\iota\epsilon\acute{\iota}\alpha$), in which she was assisted
by an elderly slave-woman chosen to be stewardess ($\tau\alpha\mu\acute{\iota}\alpha$);
general oversight over the household property; and the
making of clothes in all its processes—spinning, weaving,
sewing, and embroidering. An embroidery frame is pictured in Figs. 97 and 99; and a girl, with her spinning and
basket for holding the yarn, is shown in Fig. 98; cf. Fig. 97.
A capable wife was always entrusted with her husband's

*The wife as
manager of
the house-
hold.*

money, though generally he controlled the family purse. Finally, the nurture of her children in their infancy and early youth gave her a moral, if not a social, pre-eminence

Fig. 97.—The occupations of women.

in the home, and attached to her their love and respect and the sympathy of her husband. The slaves, too, were apt to become as much devoted to their mistress (δέσποινα) as to their master (δεσπότης), and through her tact the do-

Fig. 98.—Girl spinning.

mestic circle (οἱ οἰκεῖοι) felt a sense of unity which the more restless father, with his many duties abroad, could not give. It must have been in rare cases only that young men ran away from their fathers and mothers, like some of the soldiers who joined Cyrus's army. On the contrary, the Greeks generally had a strong feeling for home and kindred, and they were acutely sensitive to the disgrace arising from family quarrels. Twice in the *Anabasis* the term " brothers " (ἀδελφοί) is used as a synonym for the nearest and dearest tie existing among men, while " father " (πατήρ) is used of any benefactor or patron.

CHAPTER X

FURNITURE AND UTENSILS OF THE HOUSE

THE smallness of the rooms in an ordinary city house and the open-air life of the men deterred the inventive
Limited variety of furniture. faculty of ancient artisans from devising the many kinds of household furniture which modern life and a colder northern air demand for the comfort of indoor life. Elaborate cupboards, sideboards, wardrobes, fireplaces, and settles were not needed, and therefore were unknown. While, however, modern civilization has the advantage in the multiplicity of articles of furniture, it has never attained, except here and there in copies of ancient models, to the number, variety, and beauty we see in the articles which belong in the few classes of furnishings that were absolutely necessary. Taking, for example, the class of drinking vessels by itself, we come on
Multitudi- nous patterns of furniture of a given kind. scores of names for the articles in that class, all of which differed in slight ways now quite unknown. Long lists of confiscated chattels ($ἔπιπλα$ $δημιόπρατα$) found on official records attest the inventiveness of the potter, the smith, and the cabinet-maker, and their eagerness to gain variety within the narrow circle which simple tastes marked out for them.

The couch or bed ($κλίνη$) was perhaps the most important of all the household furniture, on account of the many ways in which it was used in the classical period. In Homer (where it is called either $λέχος$ or $δέμνια$) we find it used only for sleeping. In later times it was employed not only

127

for rest at night, but also at meals, or as a sofa whereon
one might recline while reading or writing, or finally as a

Beds.

bier at the burial of the dead. The couch was
made of four strips of wood fitting into each
other and supported by four posts. The whole frame was
strengthened by ropes; it was therefore not unlike an

Fig. 99.—Bed, chair, footstools.

old-fashioned "four-poster." Sometimes the head, and
even the foot, had an incline upward, and some couches
had backs, thus shaping them much like a modern sofa.
The more luxurious beds were inlaid with gold or ivory, or
covered with ornamentations in silver or gold. In Armenia
the soldiers under Xenophon found bedsteads with silver legs
at the headquarters of a Persian commander. The plainness
of an ordinary couch was commonly hidden by the abundant
coverings, often of rich material. Sometimes a piece of
tapestry, permanently attached to the frame, surrounded
the four sides like an old-fashioned valance. The mattress,

**Bed cover-
ings.**

used in later times, was made of linen or woollen cloth stuffed sometimes with the soft pods
of certain plants, sometimes with tufts of wool;
feathers were used in later times. Over the mattress were
laid rugs or other soft coverings (τάπητες, στρώματα). The

sleeper's comfort was increased by cushions and pillows (προσκεφάλαια) stuffed with feathers or wool. At night he kept on his tunic or *chiton* (page 154), since a special night-dress came into use only in later times; and he covered himself with large robes or mantles (χλαῖναι), or, if the nights were cold, with the skins of sheep or goats (κώδια, σισύραι), which he wrapped round himself like an army blanket. The poor used a mere pallet of straw; this was all the sol-dier had when sleeping in barracks or in a permanent camp. Travellers and soldiers on the march lay on the bare ground wrapped in their cloaks or *stromata* (στρώ-ματα); the lat-ter were car-ried in linen

FIG. 100.—Couch with cushions and valance.

bags called *stromatodesmoi* (στρωματόδεσμοι). At a banquet improvised while on the march, at which Xenophon's men entertained the Paphlagonian Korylas, the guests had noth-ing better to recline on than these pallets (σκίμποδες).

The bareness of the earth floor was relieved in richer houses by rugs (τάπιδες), usually imported from Asia Minor or from Carthage. Some of these were as ex-pensive as the costliest " Orientals " imported to-day. In the *Anabasis* a rug worth ten minae (more than $180) was given as a present to the Thracian prince Seuthes. Rush mats (φορμοί, ψίαθοι) were used by poorer people, even to sleep on.

Rugs.

Among chairs the *thronos* (θρόνος) was chief. It had de-scended from Homeric times, when we see it occupied by

the king, or the master or mistress of a family, or tendered
to guests to whom special honour was shown. In classical

Chairs. times it became more and more the seat of honour for judges, presiding officers, umpires at the
national games, and other officials; in the temples it stood
ready to be occupied by the god whose presence was believed to be near. It is mentioned in the *Anabasis* as the
symbol of kingly power. The *thronos* had arms and a back
and straight legs, and stood so high that a footstool, sometimes permanently attached to it, was necessary. In daily

life the *diphros* (δίφρος) was
more useful. In shape it resembled not the *thronos*, but
the *thrēnys* (θρῆνυς) of the Homeric poems. This was a stool
without either back or arms.
It is often figured in vase pic-

FIG. 101.—A diphros of bronze (votive offering) found at Athens.

tures, where a cushion sometimes appears on it. A special
kind (called ὀκλαδίας δίφρος) was something like our camp-
stool, in that it could be folded. The legs of the diphros
might be either straight (Fig. 99) or curved (Fig. 101).
Even those which did not fold were frequently carried
about to the public assemblies and elsewhere. An easy-
chair (κλισμός) with a back is shown in Figs. 95 and 97.

In the house, tables (τράπεζαι), which ordinarily stood
much lower than ours, were used only at meals, and never for

Tables. such purposes as writing, for instance; hence the
word *trapeza* is frequently the symbol of hospitality. In the market-place they were set in the booths of
tradesmen, artisans, and especially money-changers or bankers. The surface, which was commonly oval or rectangular,
rested on three or on four legs (τρίποδες, τετράποδες). It was
with such tripods or three-legged tables set before them that
Xenophon and his friends were entertained at dinner by
Seuthes. The legs were curved or straight, with every va-

riety of tasteful ornament (Fig. 102; cf. Figs. 130 and 131, where their relatively small size is shown).

FIG. 102.—Greek tables.

In lieu of wardrobes the Greeks had chests, which, like all other objects in the house, afforded opportunity for ornamentation and display.   These chests, or trunks
Chests.
(κιβωτοί, κιβώτια), were needed for storing clothing, records, money, and other valuables.   They were secured by seals, by locks, or by ropes intricately knotted.   Their importance in the household and the fact that they formed a staple of commerce are seen from a passage in the *Anabasis*, where we read of beds and chests being frequently

FIG. 103.—Chest and footstool.

cast up from shipwrecks on the Thracian coast.   There were other wooden boxes or crates employed in shipping merchandise (ξύλινα τεύχη).   Besides these larger chests, no household was complete without smaller caskets or cases

for ornaments and jewels (Figs. 22, 95, 136).   A beautiful
specimen of cabinet work is shown in Fig. 104, being a chest
two metres long, and
the oldest example of
Greek woodenware in
existence.

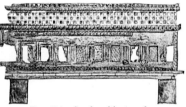

With this seeming-
ly meagre equipment—
beds, chairs, tables, and

Mirrors. c h e s t s —
the house-

FIG. 104.—Greek cabinet-work.

hold furnishings in wood were complete.   There were no
large wall-mirrors or cheval-glasses.   Hand-mirrors, made
of polished bronze, silver, and even gold, and having richly
ornamented backs and handles, were carefully kept in spe-

FIG. 105.—Bronze mirror.   FIG. 106.—Top of a mirror case of bronze.

cial boxes (λοφεῖα, Fig. 106) to prevent scratching and tarnishing.   Glass mirrors were not known to the Greeks of
the classical period, and no mirror of any kind is mentioned in Homer.

It is in the multitude and variety of vessels (ἀγγεῖα) made of clay, metal, stone, and wicker that the inventive and artistic genius of the Greeks, as applied to the small details of daily life, is most strikingly shown. Vessels of bronze, silver, and gold were set up in the houses of the rich as ornaments or bric-à-brac, or were dedicated in the temples as offerings in fulfilment of vows to the gods. For domestic needs those in clay, being cheaper, answered all purposes where to-day glass, wood, or tin is employed. Xenophon mentions the self-restraint of his soldiers in not laying hands on the numerous bronze utensils (χαλκώματα) with which the houses of the Cardūchi (the Kurds of Armenia) were furnished. But even clay utensils were painted with extraordinary care and beauty of design, as the Greek vases in all large museums show. Such, we may be sure, were not committed to slaves for daily use, who had to eat and drink out of meaner vessels. At Priēne, in the recent excavations there, pottery was found marked " for the grooms," or " for the cooks " (ἱπποκόμοι, μάγειροι).

Vessels.

We may distinguish several main classes of such utensils:

1. Vessels for storing food, such as wine, olive-oil, honey, water, figs, salt meat, grain, etc. These include the huge *pithos* (πίθος), sometimes six feet high and three feet in diameter, so capacious that when Pericles compelled the country people to live in

Vessels used as receptacles.

FIG. 107.—Casks found at Troy.

crowded Athens during the first year of the Peloponnesian War many camped in these *pithoi* (popularly called φιδάκναι) for shelter. Everybody has heard of Diogenes and his "tub."

These casks, when used for oil or wine, were regularly sunk into the ground to most of their depth.   Athenian houses

FIG. 108.—Amphora.

were also provided with cisterns, round or square, which were dug in the ground and then plastered.   In these also oil and wine could be stored.   Xenophon tells us that even in the mountains, among the wild Cardūchi, wine was so plentiful that it had to be kept in this way (ἐν λάκκοις κονιατοῖς).   Special bins (σιπύαι) for storing grain also belong in this class.

The *amphora* (ἀμφορεύς, originally ἀμφιφορεύς), so called from its two handles, was smaller than the pithos.   This might have a foot or base, or else it ended in a point at the bottom ; in this case it lay horizontally, or was leaned against the wall.   The normal amphora had a capacity of about ten gallons (page 244). Among the provident Mossynoeci large numbers of amphoras were found by Xenophon's troops containing pickled dolphin.   A variety of the amphora, used especially for storing wine, was the *stamnos* (Fig. 109).

The general term applied to jars used in storing liquids to be transported was *kera-*

FIG. 109.—Stamnos.

mia (κεράμια; cf. κέραμος, *pottery*, whence "ceramic").   In the *Anabasis* the people of Sinōpe and Heracleia hospitably

send abundant wine to the Greeks in these keramia.   There
were other large jars called *bīkoi* (βίκοι), in which Cyrus was
in the habit of sending pres-
ents of wine to his friends.

The *hydria* (ὑδρία), originally a water-jar, was in extensive use for all purposes.
It resembled the older *kalpis*
(κάλπις) mentioned in Homer,
and had one or more handles.
Girls who carried water from
some spring to the house bore
these hydrias on their heads,
supporting them by means of
a pad (τύλη).   The process is
clearly seen in the vase pic-

Fig. 110.—Hydria.

ture given in Fig. 13; see also Fig. 11.   Money was often
buried in such vessels, which have preserved it faithfully
for modern excavators to find.

Fig. 111.
Lekythos.

The *lekythos* (λήκυθος) was indispensable to
the Greek whenever a small pitcher or jug
was required, and many beautiful specimens
are extant (Figs. 111 and 136).   With it full of
oil he went to the gymnasium, the palaestra,
or the bath.   In the house it was as useful
as the hydria.   We hear sometimes of *lekythoi*
made of leather.   From it the oil was often
poured into a little round flask, whence it
could be slowly " dropped " into the hand.
These flasks varied greatly in shape.   One
familiar type, called the *alabastos* (ἀλάβαστος,
the "alabaster" of the New Testament), is
shown in Figs. 112 and 160.   Another type,
the *aryballos* (ἀρύβαλλος), appears in a late,
but beautiful, example in Fig. 159.   Compare also Fig. 72,
where it hangs on the wall of the palaestra.

2. Vessels in which liquids were mixed or food was boiled. The mixing bowl was the *krāter* (κρατήρ, in Homer

Cooking vessels and mixing bowls. κρητήρ), broad and deep. It had, as a rule, two handles, since it was heavy, and must frequently be carried from one room to another. Its base was broad and firm, and it was often set in a kind of huge saucer or stand (ὑποκρατήριον), which caught whatever overflowed from the krāter in the process of filling and mixing. Here we may notice the strainer or colander (ἠθμός) through which the wine had to be filtered, since modern methods of clarifying were unknown to the Greeks. The strainer was a bronze or silver utensil, shaped somewhat like a cup, and perforated in beautiful patterns, like that shown in Fig. 113. The krāter was filled only for immediate

Fig. 112.
Alabastos.

needs, when the wine was drawn into it from a keramion, and from the krāter in turn dipped into the cups. The

Fig. 113.
Wine strainer.

Armenians, however, seem to have stored their beer in it. Xenophon mentions also their outlandish custom of stooping over and drinking directly from it "like an ox."

The most important vessel in the kitchen was the *chytra* (χύτρα), a kettle or pot having a variety of shapes, with either one or two handles, and commonly set on a tripod (Fig. 129). Another kitchen utensil was the

Fig. 114.—Krāter.

lebes (λέβης), also kettle-like in shape, made usually of bronze, and either resting on three legs or set on a tripod.

3. Vessels for drawing liquids. Chief among these is the wine pitcher (οἰνοχόη), which had a single handle (Fig. 115). With this pitcher

Vessels for drawing. the wine could be dipped from the krāter into the cups. Another pitcher (the πρόχους), was that from which water was poured over the hands of the guests after the dinner, and just before the symposium began. The *kyathos* (κύαθος) had a bowl shaped like the modern cup. It was, however, not used for drinking so much as for drawing, since the handle rose high above the brim, giving the effect of a ladle.

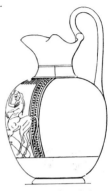

FIG. 115.—Wine pitcher.

4. Vessels for drinking (ποτήρια, ἐκπώματα). The *phialé* (φιάλη), which belongs to this class, was a shallow, saucer-like dish without handles

Drinking-cups. or base. Silver cups of this kind were highly esteemed as presents and prizes. This and the *cylix* (κύλιξ, Fig. 116) were the cups in commonest use at symposia. The cylix had a rather shallow bowl, like the phialé, but differed from it in having two handles and a base. Another cup-like bowl, seen oftenest in the country, was the

FIG. 116.—Cylix with tall base.

skyphos (σκύφος), with two small handles close to the rim. Similar to this was the *kotylos* or *kotylé* (Figs. 117 and 218). There were also goblets of various shapes, among which the *kan-tharos* (κάνθαρος) and the *karchesion* (καρχήσιον) are perhaps the most commonly mentioned. The kantharos appears in Fig. 145, where it is carried by Dionȳsus and by the Spirit of Comedy preceding

him.   The drinking-horn (κέρας), which had descended from
the earliest days of primitive man, survived in shape, at
least.   Such was the *rhyton* (ῥυ-
τόν), made of earthenware or metal.   Some drinking-horns had a
small hole in the bottom, which,
when not closed up by the thumb,
allowed the wine to pass in a
steady stream into the mouth.
Actual horns were still used by
the Thracians in Xenophon's
time.

Fig. 117.—Kotylos.

The Armenians knew the practice of drinking
through straws.   The *kōthon* (κώθων) was a bottle or flask

Fig. 118.—Drinking-horns.

with narrow mouth,
frequently carried
by soldiers, sailors,
and travellers gener-
ally, and answered
to the modern can-
teen.   Another bot-
tle-like vessel was the *lagynos* (λάγυνος), which was often
encased in wickerwork, as in Italy to-day.

5. Vessels for washing and bathing.   The *chernibeion*
(χερνιβεῖον) was the basin
in commonest
use for wash-
ing the hands.

**Bathing
utensils.**

It was employed not only
for the *chernips* (page 267),
the ceremonial handwash-
ing preliminary to a sacrifice or other religious function (χείρ and the stem νιβ-,
wash), but also in domestic life.   Then there were
larger bowls (λουτῆρες, λου-

Fig. 119.—Bathing bowl (λουτήρ).

τήρια) for bathing when the whole body was not to be im-
mersed ; and regular tubs or troughs (πύελοι) large enough
for the whole body. These answered to the royal bath-tubs
(ἀσάμινθοι or δροῖται) of earlier times, which are mentioned
in Homer. In the public baths, of course, there were much
larger troughs or tanks, made of slabs of stone or marble,
and capable of holding many persons (page 174). They
were deep enough for diving, whence their name *kolym-
bēthrai* (κολυμβῆθραι, from κολυμβῶ, *dive*).

FIG. 120.—Bronze lamp shaped like a boat.

6. Vessels used for illumination. In Homer, the only
device known to light a room, besides the fire on the
hearth, was the torch (λαμπτήρ). Those used

Lamps.

in lighting one's way from room to room were
called *daïdes* (δαΐδες). They were sometimes placed in earthenware holders, making thus a stationary lamp. The dis-
covery that olive-oil—as yet unknown in Homer—could
be used for lighting made
a most important advance
in the history of illumination, and led further to
the manufacture of bronze
and terra-cotta lamps (λύ-
χνοι) in great variety.
These were often boat-
shaped, with two openings.
The one, usually in the

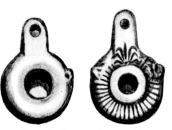

FIG. 121.—Lamps of terra-cotta.

middle, was used in filling the lamp; the other, at one end,
was for the wick (θρυαλλίς), which was made of flax. Some

larger lamps had two and three openings for wicks. Frequently they were supported on high stands, so that the
light might be thrown farther. Niches for lamps were sometimes built in the wall of a house, six or seven feet from
the ground (page 34). In later times lamps with numerous wicks came into use, but on the whole the lighting of
a house in the classical period was imperfect and unsatisfactory, and the smell of the wick, unprotected from sudden
drafts of air, must have been nauseating. This was doubtless counteracted to some extent by the burning of incense

FIG. 122.—Brazier.   FIG. 123.—Brazier of terra-cotta.

(θυμίαμα) in braziers or censers (θυμιατήρια), the beauty of
which, to judge from existing specimens, must have added
much to the adornment of the home (Figs. 122 and 123).

Since street-lighting is a comparatively modern invention, torches were needed by all who went abroad at night.
Torches. The rigorous discipline of the early Spartans
required them to dispense even with a torch.
An Athenian, however, on a moonless night sent his slave
to buy a small torch, which the slave then carried in front
of his master. Torches were made of pine-knots, or dry
sticks fastened together and smeared with pitch. In Athens
they were somewhat expensive, and seem to have been less
commonly used than among the Romans. Aristophanes
represents the moon as saying that she saves the Athenians no less than a drachma a month (eighteen cents) by

her light.   Torches were, however, necessary at weddings
(page 123) and funerals (page 295).

Torches were inconvenient when carried in the hand,
on account of the hot pitch which dropped on the fingers.
It was this, one of the comic poets tells us, that led to the
invention of lanterns (λυχνοῦχοι).   These were cases made
of transparent horn or bladders, into which a house lamp
could be put.   Sometimes a mere basket or small pot was
used instead, like the pitchers of
Gideon's men, with "lamps within
the pitchers" (*Judges* vii, 16).

7. Vessels used as dishes.   Dishes and platters, in which solid foods
could be kept and served, were of
Dishes.   many kinds and shapes,
            according to the nature
of the food they were designed to
hold.   Some names of them are
tryblia (τρύβλια), deep dishes, and
diskoi or *pinakes* (δίσκοι, πίνακες),

Fig. 124.—Platter, lekythos,
and toilet-box.

flat plates or platters.   Here we may notice also toilet-
boxes (πυξίδες) for holding ointments, rouge, pins, and the
like.   Many fine specimens have been
preserved (cf. Figs. 124 and 125).

8. Basket-ware.   This embraces a
large number of utensils in wickerwork, used for holding bread, cake,
Baskets.   flowers, wool, and women's
            handiwork generally.   The
kalathos (κάλαθος), not unlike a modern
waste-basket in shape and height, was

Fig. 125.
Toilet-box (πυξίς).

intended especially for wool (Figs. 97, 98).   The *kanoun* (κανοῦν) was a shallow sacrificial basket, in which were carried
the knife, the barleycorns, and the wreath of flowers for
the victim's head.   The *spyris* (σπυρίς, in familiar language
σπυρίδιον) was a round market-basket.

Wine was frequently carried in goatskins (ἀσκοί, from αἴξ, *goat*). Indeed, no picture of an ancient street scene would be complete without the hucksters carrying skins

Goatskin bags.

(translated "bottles" in the New Testament, e. g., *S. Matt.* ix, 17) containing wine, water, oil, milk, and olives. The skin of the animal was sewn together tightly and covered with pitch, one foot being left open to serve as an outlet. The shape of the goatskin survived in many vessels of pottery.

Grain and other dry edibles were transported in sacks (θύλακοι). Washerwomen carried their clothes to the river in bags (μάρσιποι).

CHAPTER XI

ARTICLES OF FOOD

ANCIENT and modern life offer a striking contrast in the kind and quality of food known to each. As regards the Greeks, the fare was characterized in general by frugality and lack of variety, due, of course, to the limited territory from which food supplies could be drawn. In later times, when the victories of Alexander and the further conquests of the Romans had introduced to Greece and Italy the products of strange lands, the nature of the food underwent a corresponding change.

In Homer, bread and meat are the staples which suffice to satisfy the appetites of the warriors in the *Iliad* or the **Homeric** suitors in the *Odyssey*. The flesh of cattle, **viands and** sheep, goats, and pigs was roasted whole on **meals.** spits hung over huge fires. Steaks, marrow sucked from the bones, and especially fat, were eagerly devoured. Meat was never boiled, but always roasted or broiled. Fish was substituted for it only when the eater could get nothing else, though the poet mentions the practice of fishing by hooks, harpoons, and nets. Barley-meal and wheat-flour were baked without leaven into large loaves or cakes (ἄρτοι). Wine (οἶνος, μέθυ) was the only drink, and two kinds of it are mentioned—the Pramnian, used especially in making a compound called *kykeon* (κυκεών), consisting of barley-meal, grated cheese, and sometimes honey; the Ismarian, accounted the best, and brought from the sunny, fertile slopes on the coast of Thrace. It was from this region, probably, that the cultivation of the vine extended

into Attica and the rest of Greece. Milk (γάλα), derived
from sheep and goats, was drunk only by such characters
as Polyphēmus.

The meals in the Homeric age were the early morning
breakfast, ἄριστον; the dinner, δεῖπνον, when hot meat was
eaten; and the evening meal, or supper, δόρπον.

In the period following Homer, the wealthy Ionians indulged in a greater luxury of viands. It was at this time
that figs (σῦκα), quinces (μῆλα κυδώνια), pomegranates (ῥόαι), and the olive (ἐλάα) came into
use. The art of cookery developed in all
wealthy communities; and not only in eastern Hellas, but
also in Sicily and Lower Italy. In the last-named region,
the people of Sybaris, who have become proverbial for their
luxurious tastes, granted a patent for one year to the cook
who invented a new dainty. In some places the indulgence
of the appetite went so far that crude sumptuary laws were
passed to check it. In Locris there was a legal prohibi-
tion against the drinking of unmixed wine; for wine was
regularly drunk with double its quantity of water.

In the classical period we find Athens and Sparta pre-
eminent for frugality. Food and drink (σῖτα καὶ ποτά)
were limited in variety and
generally poor in quality.
Sparta's ill-savoured black
broth (μέλας ζωμός) was notorious. While
the Thessalians were noted, and even
denounced, for their good tables and
extravagant appetites; while the profitable commerce of Corinth and the fertile fields of Sicily brought wealth to
their inhabitants, which was spent in
gratifying the senses; while all Boeotians were accounted stupid gluttons,

Fig. 126.—Movable oven.

Athens, on the contrary, maintained the golden mean of
simpler tastes in this as in other matters. Even among

Increase of luxury.

Frugality of Athens and Sparta.

wealthy families an allowance of three drachmas a day (scarcely fifty cents) was deemed extravagant beyond all conception for the maintenance of three children and two servants. A poor man was satisfied with the simple barley-cake (μᾶζα) or porridge (ἔτνος) of flour or meal, a dish which had descended from remote times. A few dried figs or a leaf of lettuce or thyme growing wild on the hills would suffice him for a long time.

Meat (κρέας) was eaten on special occasions, at a banquet or public festival, when it was offered to the gods. Hence, meat is often called *hiereia* (ἱερεῖα), with **Meat.** reference to its having first been consecrated (ἱερά). Sheep, pigs, and goats were perhaps the commonest offerings, and therefore most often eaten at domestic sacrifices. A whole lamb could be bought for eight drachmas, or less than one dollar and a half; but that sum was beyond the means of many in those days of cheap labour, low wages, and scarcity of money (cf. page 248). Beef, as a rule, was obtained by the poor only at the greater public sacrifices (ἑκατόμβαι, ἑστιάσεις, page 62). The army in the field, of course, ate what rations (σιτία) it could get; and not infrequently soldiers serving in foreign countries the products of which were more abundant than those of

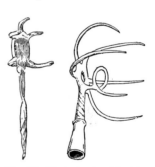

FIG. 127.—Hooks (κρεάγραι) for taking boiled meat out of the pot.

Greece fared better than they would have done at home. Thus, the people of Heracleia, on the Euxine, provided the retreating Greeks with 3,000 medimnoi (see page 244) of grain, 2,000 casks of wine, 20 oxen, and 100 sheep. To have nothing to eat but meat was regarded as extraordinary, if not almost as a hardship. Among the hospitable Armenians the Greeks retreating with Xenophon were

10

feasted with lamb, pork, veal, kid, and poultry, with abundance of wheat and barley bread. In the camp oxen were roasted whole. A spit large enough to hold an ox over the fire is mentioned in the *Anabasis* (βουπόρος ὀβελίσκος). Meat was also boiled at this later period. At a dinner the meat was brought in already carved in proper portions (κρέα νενεμημένα), and the guests ate it with their fingers.

Hot sausages (ἀλλᾶντες) were highly esteemed, and venders of them (ἀλλαντοπῶλαι) did a profitable business in the streets. But the choicest of all food, in the estimation of an Athenian, was fish, both fresh-water and salt, eaten either fresh or salted down (τάριχη). In fact, the word *opson* (ὄψον), which properly signified any relish eaten with bread, and sometimes anything at all that was edible, came to be applied to fish as the food of foods. Xenophon mentions with pride the

Fish and game.

Fig. 128.—Preparing a fish.

fact that in the little stream flowing through his estate in Elis there were fish in plenty. But fish from the sea was more in evidence on the Greek table than fresh-water fish. We hear especially of herrings, sardines, anchovies, and tunny; fishermen, not sailors, were the "old salts" (ἁλιεῖς) of the Greeks. Their boats (πλοῖα ἁλιευτικά) were equipped for sailing in deep water. Eels were the favourite dainty from the inland lakes, especially Lake Copāis in Boeotia. Mussels, turtles, and oysters were also eaten; but the oyster of the Mediterranean would have seemed small and poor to an American. Game was plentiful and often eaten; there were hare (λαγώς), wild boars (σύες), venison (κρέα ἐλάφεια), wild ducks (νῆτται), and geese (χῆνες); partridges (πέρδικες); pigeons (περιστεραί); also quail, thrushes, and blackbirds. Bears (ἄρκτοι) and chamois (δορκάδες) were hunted and doubtless occasionally eaten.

Many vegetables which are to-day practically essential to life were unknown or undeveloped. It was a world where

Vegetables. there were no potatoes, no green corn, no tomatoes, no squash, no melons, though pumpkins from India were known, if not commonly eaten. A few kinds of green vegetables (λάχανα), such as spinach, lettuce, and cabbage, were sold in the market by women (λαχανοπώλιδες); also peas and beans (grouped together under the term ὄσπρια), eaten either raw or cooked with oil and vinegar or with honey; radishes, onions (κρόμμυα), garlic (σκόροδα), leeks, and other roots, including perhaps turnips (γογγυλίδες). Pease porridge (ἔτνος, λέκιθος) was a regular part of the Greek diet. It could be bought from hucksters in the street.

FIG. 129.—Movable oven with pot (χύτρα).

Fruits. The chief products of Attica, in addition to those just mentioned, which were grown in small gardens, were figs (σῦκα) and olives (ἐλᾶαι). There were some vineyards also, the grapes from

which, when not used for making wine, were dried into
raisins (ἀσταφίδες). Figs, too, were eaten dried; fresh fruit,
in general, was not so highly esteemed as it is to-day, because the more wholesome varieties of apples and pears
were as yet undeveloped. How far the art of grafting was
practised in the fifth century is unknown; but Xenophon
possessed an orchard of cultivated trees (ἡμέρων δένδρων)
which produced all kinds of edible fruits. Apples, pears,
and pomegranates good enough to eat were known in the
time of the *Odyssey*. Plums, peaches, apricots, and cher-
ries were not introduced until later, some of them in
Roman times. Oranges were entirely unknown. While
figs were a staple product of Attica, dates (αἱ βάλανοι τῶν
φοινίκων) were imported from Asia Minor. Xenophon records that the dates eaten by Greeks were small, and in
their native country were thought fit only for the slaves.

Nuts (κάρυα), eaten raw, were highly esteemed as dessert
(τραγήματα) just before the symposium, since they provoked
thirst. They often came from the interior of
Asia Minor, especially the region just south of
the Euxine. The commonest were walnuts and almonds.
Chestnuts were little known in the fifth century; Xenophon
thinks it necessary to describe them as having no inside
division, like the walnut, and he has no special name for
them. They grew in Paphlagonia, where the natives ate
them boiled. Almonds (ἀμυγδάλαι) were highly relished.
An oil or salve of bitter almonds (χρῖμα ἀμυγδάλινον) is mentioned as a useful substitute for olive-oil.

Nuts.

Grain (σῖτος) was known in a considerable variety of
forms. We hear of wheat (πυροί), barley (κριθαί), millet
(μελίνη, κέγχρος), and spelt (ζειαί). But oats and
rye were lacking; the former was considered a
mere weed, since it did not grow well in the
warm climate of Greece. The Athenians prided themselves
on their bread, and fancy baking, the business of the *artokopoi*
(ἀρτοκόποι), flourished even in frugal Athens. These men

**Grain and
its products.**

made elaborate cooking at home unnecessary. They baked and sold many kinds of bread and rolls from wheat and barley, sometimes sprinkling them with poppy seeds, as in Germany to-day, or with the seeds of flax or sesame, which answered to caraway-seed. Sesame came from Asia Minor; the Ten Thousand found it growing, for example, in Cilicia and Bithynia. In Athens, too, lentils were sometimes mixed with the dough, making a peculiar kind of roll called *gouros* (γοῦρος). Leaven or yeast was sometimes employed; Xenophon mentions raised bread (ἄρτοι ζυμῖται) as forming part of the feast provided by Seuthes. The

Fig. 130.—Dessert.

bread in the market was regularly inspected by the market commissioners (ἀγορανόμοι), who saw to it that the loaves conformed to a standard of weight fixed by them. A very large loaf, measuring three choenixes (page 244) was appropriated by a greedy

Bread and cake.

Arcadian at Seuthes's feast. The only sweets that were known consisted of different kinds of cakes (πέμματα, πόπανα) made with honey. Candy and puddings in the English and American sense were not yet devised. Eggs, however, soon came into use in cooking, and sauces of many kinds, chiefly for meat, fish, and game, were elaborated. (These were called καταχύσματα; also ἡδύσματα, since ἡδύς may be used of anything that is pleasant to the taste, and ἡδονή is the regular word for "flavour.")

Seasoning was done by salt, mustard, garlic, onions, and

a few herbs (ἀρώματα), like pennyroyal, marjoram, and silphium. Of these, silphium was the favourite, and the people of Cyrēne, on the north coast of Africa, ac-
Silphium.   quired wealth through its export in enormous
quantities. But there was no pepper; there were no other
spices, extracts, sugar, or butter. For sugar, honey was
used; bees were kept in hives, but wild honey from the
woods and mountains, especially Hymettus, was still gathered as it had been in more primitive times. Olive-oil was
the regular substitute for butter, which did not find favour
among the Greeks until very late times. In the fourth century B. C. it was known only as a Scythian prod-
Cheese.   uct. Cheese (τυρός) was a favourite article of
food, in large measure taking the place of butter at meals.
In cooking, oil was used for fish, flesh, and greens alike.
Lard or fat seems not to have been used for
Oil.   this purpose. In the Homeric age pieces of fat
(στέαρ) were eaten like any other part of the animal, and
the blubber of dolphins was preserved for kitchen needs
in Thrace. In Armenia a salve made from lard served in
place of olive-oil.

Wine (οἶνος) always remained the chief drink, in classical as in Homeric times. These were the days before tea,
coffee, cocoa, cordials, spirituous liquors, and
Drinks.   mineral waters were known or heard of. Milk
(γάλα) was not often drunk except in the country. It was
taken from sheep and goats, seldom, if ever, from cows.
But though wine was virtually the only drink, the Greeks
on the whole were temperate; the Thessalians were the
most conspicuous offenders in overindulgence. Among all
Greeks, however, a mere water-drinker was a rare exception,
and Demosthenes was scornfully ridiculed for his total ab-
stinence. The water-drinking of Persians and Iberians was
a subject of remark.

Of wine there were many sorts. Those most highly
prized came from Chios, Lesbos, Thasos, and Secyon. It

was put up for export in large goatskins (ἀσκοί, page 142) or earthenware jars (κεράμια, page 134), and sometimes pitch, **Wine.** sea-water, lime, or herbs were put in to preserve or heighten its flavour. This use of pitch survives in modern Greece. A wine made of dates is mentioned in the *Anabasis*.

Wine was scarcely ever drunk pure (ἄκρατος); it was mixed with water, which in most cases predominated. **Mixing.** Half and half (ἴσον ἴσῳ) was the maximum of wine ever allowed, and this mixture was not so common as that of three parts of water to two of wine. The practical reason for this lay in the greater sweetness and more fiery character of Greek wine, as compared with most wines drunk to-day. Even milder dilutions, such as three to one or five to two, were common. This accounts for the prominence of the mixing bowl (κρατήρ) on all occasions where drinking was in progress. If chilled wine was desired, it was put into coolers (ψυκτῆρες) with snow or ice. As we saw on page 136, it was cleared with a strainer before drinking.

The first meal of the day, taken immediately on rising, at dawn, was as simple as the modern European " rolls and coffee." **The three meals.** Breakfast consisted of a barley-cake (μᾶζα) or roll dipped in a little pure wine, or *akratos*; hence this meal (the ἄριστον πρωινόν) was also called the *akratisma* (ἀκράτισμα). A little before noon, when the morning's work in the agora or the courts was over, the Athenian took his luncheon, or *ariston* (ἄριστον); it was usually of a simple character, with perhaps some salt fish, or sausages, or ham. The time of day at which this meal was taken is made clear from many passages in the *Anabasis*, where the context shows that the troops had been up and busy about their duties some time before they partook of the ariston—for them, at least, a combination of breakfast and luncheon. About sunset came the chief and most elaborate meal, the dinner, or

deipnon (δεῖπνον). The man of the house, if he had no
guests, ate with his wife, who, with the children, sat beside
the couch on which he reclined (Fig. 131).   As to the hour
of meals, we observe among the Athenians the same tend-

Fɪɢ. 131.—A family meal.

ency to set the dinner later and later in the day that is
noticeable in civilized countries to-day, thus crowding out
the old-fashioned "supper."   So in Athenian town life the
supper (δόρπον) disappeared with the custom of lunching at
noon and dining at night; but the phrase "supper time"
or "tea time" (ἀμφὶ δορπηστόν) survived to denote the early
evening.

CHAPTER XII

CLOTHING

THE nature and the fashion of clothes which people wear are mostly determined by the climate in which they live and the degree of civilization which they have reached. Fashion and the love of ornament also play their part, but fashion in ancient times, though its influence was distinctly and consciously felt by the Greeks, never prescribed such varieties of costume and rapid changes of style and cut as it does to-day. As to climate, the Athenians enjoyed nearly one hundred and eighty days of entire sunshine and about one hundred and fifty days more of partly sunny weather. The business of living was comparatively simple, and even the poorest had little difficulty in procuring clothing enough to satisfy ancient notions of comfort and decency, however these might be lacking according to modern ideas. On the other hand, the climate was bracing enough to require more than the scanty clothing of the tropics. Journeys into the mountains brought the hunter, the shepherd, the wood-cutter, or the military patrol into a sharper air, and in midwinter, when the north wind blew on the city from the snow-covered heights of Mount Parnes, the Athenian felt that Boreas was shooting darts at him (cf. page 2).

The Athenian climate.

Greek fashions uniform. Throughout Greece the general principles of dress were the same; only the amount of covering varied with the altitude and the latitude. In this, as in other things, the Athenian was guided by a sure and simple taste which demanded moderation

153

(μετρία ἐσθής). The contrast between the Greek clothing
and the elegant finery of the Persians strongly impressed
Xenophon. To the freebooter from Greece, therefore, garments were often acceptable prizes taken in war, and were
sometimes given as presents. The art of this period is
matchless in its treatment of the details of dress, and we
may be sure that it not only reproduced with some fidelity
the dress actually worn, but also exercised considerable influence on popular taste.

Dress is denoted by the words ἐσθής, ἱμάτια, and στολή.
But in the *Anabasis* στολή is the vaguer term applied to
the garments of the natives, not the Greeks.

The garment worn almost universally was the tunic or
chiton (χιτών), which belonged to the class of clothing that
was "put on," or "got into" (ἐνδύματα, from
ἐνδύω), like the soldier's cuirass, or the modern
shirt. For it we also have the word χιτωνίσκος.
To make it, in the case of the man's chiton, was a simple
matter. A piece of the material to be used was made on
the loom, or afterward cut, in the desired length (*a b*, Fig.
132). It was then folded so that *c d* met *a b*, making one
side closed (*e f*), the other open (*a c–b d*). The top (*a c–e*)
rested on the shoulders of the wearer, who kept it in place

The man's chiton.

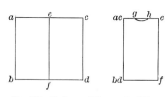

FIG. 132.—Pattern of the man's chiton.

by fastenings—pins, clasps,
or buttons—or by means of
permanent sewing. In the
latter case, of course, a space
(*g h*) had to be left open for
the neck. The arms projected just below *ac* and *e*; on
the closed side (*e*) a slit was
cut for this purpose. The fact that one side was open
(*ac–bd*) was disguised by the belt (ζώνη), which gathered
the chiton snugly to the body at the waist. The length
could be varied to suit the taste and the need of the wearer
by simply pulling up the skirt of the chiton and letting

the superfluous portion hang in a fold outside the girdle, giving the effect of a blouse (Fig. 133). This was always done by travellers or soldiers, and the term " well-girded " (εὔζωνοι) was used of troops especially adapted to active, alert

FIG. 133.—Man's chiton. FIG. 134.—Woman's chiton, with apoptygma.

movements, whether they were light-armed or heavy-armed. The term survives to-day in the Greek army. The soldier's dagger was attached to the girdle or to a shoulder-strap.

In Homeric times the material was linen. When the wearer was not engaged in hunting or fighting, the chiton was long, reaching to the ground. Even late **Material and length.** in the fifth and fourth centuries, at the religious feasts, in which ancient customs and modes of dress survive the longest, the chiton was linen, and extended to the feet (χιτὼν ποδήρης, Fig. 65). On the other hand, as early as Homer the short chiton was worn by hunters, farmers, and artisans; also by the warrior. So, in the busy fifth century, when the majority of people found it im-

156   THE LIFE OF THE ANCIENT GREEKS

possible to retain the long clothes of the aristocratic Ionians,
they introduced the shorter Doric chiton as the regular
mode. The material, too, was more often wool than linen,
because little, if any, flax grew in Greece, whereas sheep
were raised on every hillside. Xenophon, however, leads us
to believe that even this woollen chiton, being short and
open, was a poor protection against the cold of the north. He
describes the Thracian chiton as encircling the thighs, by
which he must mean a kind of shirt and trousers combined.
The poor man's tunic was of rough wool; the rich had tunics
of fine wool raised in Attica, Megara, and especially Milētus, the sheep of which were the
"merinos" of antiquity.

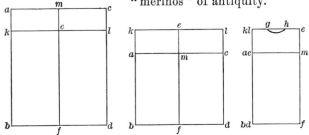

Fig. 135.—Pattern of the woman's chiton with fold.

Sleeves were rarely added to a man's chiton. The over-
hang at the shoulders (*ac*, *e*), which naturally resulted when
the arms hung at the side, formed a kind of sleeve

Sleeves. extending about half-way to the elbow. The
wearing of chitons with long sleeves (χιτῶνες χειριδωτοί) which
reached to the wrists was confined to Persians, to the rather
effeminate Greeks of lower Italy, and to the actor's costume.
The chiton was the sole garment required and worn in the
house. One who was attired in it, without any other cover-

The woman's ing, was said to be "in undress," γυμνός.
chiton. The chiton worn by women, though its general nature was the same, differed in some details from
the man's chiton. A piece of cloth (*a b c d*, Fig. 135)

was folded at *k l*, so that *k a-l c* measured the distance from neck to waist, or a little less, and *k b* (also *l d*) was

Fig. 136.—Woman arranging her chiton with girdle.

the length of the whole garment from the shoulder to the feet. The cloth was then folded, as in the man's chiton, at *e f*, so that *kl–bd* formed one side of the garment, *ef* the other. The upper part of the body (*kl-ac, e-m*) was in this manner covered by two layers of the material; the outer layer, which hung in a flap loosely, was called the *apoptygma* (ἀπόπτυγμα). The two parts, front and back, were fast-

The upper fold.

ened together on the shoulders by pins or clasps. Sometimes the open side (*kl-bd*) was sewed up from the armpit to the lower hem of the chiton. Women wore sleeves more often than men, but chitons with half-sleeves were perhaps the rule. The girdle might confine the chiton only, or both chiton and outer garment. In addition, bands (στρό-

Fig. 137.
Chiton with sleeves.

φια) answering to modern stays were sometimes worn under
the breast. The sleeved chiton, without girdle, appears in
Fig. 137.

Over the chiton was thrown a piece of cloth, usually
single, less often doubled, called *himation* (ἱμάτιον). The hi-

**The
himation.**

mation—ἱμάτια is also the word for clothes in general—was the descendant of the Homeric *chlaina*
(χλαῖνα, Fig. 11), a long woollen mantle, sometimes smooth, sometimes with a thick nap. It hung down
the back as far as the calf of the leg, being fastened together at the shoulders with a brooch or clasp. Sometimes
it was folded so as to give two thicknesses; it was then
called a " double chlaina " or *diplax* (χλαῖνα διπλῆ, δίπλαξ, or
διπλοΐς). In classical times the himation was an oblong piece
of woollen cloth, the length being to the width in the
proportion of about 7 to 5. To be correctly adjusted—
and fine gentlemen in Athens were very scrupulous about

FIG. 138.—The himation : assassination of Hipparchus.

its orderly arrangement (κοσμίως ἀμπισχνεῖσθαι)—the cloth
must be as wide as the distance from the neck to the
calf of the leg. In putting it on, one of the long sides

was grasped by both hands and swung freely round at the
left, so as to cover the left arm and shoulder; it was then
brought round the back and under the right arm, the
remaining portion being carried up to and over the left
shoulder again, where it hung over the back and rested. If
it was not desired to keep the right arm free, the wearer

FIG. 139.—Pins.   FIG. 140.—Pin made in prehistoric times.

brought the himation over, instead of under, the right arm,
adjusting it over the left as described before (Fig. 138).

    In Sparta the himation was the ordinary garment worn
by all persons over twelve years old; it could be folded
double, like the Homeric diplax, whence it received the name of "double tribon" (τρίβων
διπλοῦς), *tribon* being another term often employed for an ordinary outer coat. The Spartans wore no
chiton under it. This custom, which in Athens generally
was not deemed quite respectable, was, however, imitated
even there by persons who, through necessity or affectation,
practised austerity or asceticism in clothing or food, especially the later philosophers, such as the Cynics. The frugality of Socrates led him to wear nothing but a poor himation,
which he never changed, winter or summer. No wealthy
gentleman, however, would ordinarily have thought of ap-

Chiton and himation.

pearing outdoors ἀχίτων ἐν ἱματίῳ—that is, shirtless with his
mantle on—any more than he would have appeared γυμνός, or cloakless, in his tunic merely. Of course the himation, having no fastening at the shoulder, had to be laid
aside during any special exertion, as in dancing, or in
chopping wood, or in assaulting a height.

Young men, even of aristocratic and dignified families,
often affected a careless and jaunty adjustment of the
outer cloak, and the monuments show that
there were many individual ways of putting it
on, which varied in small details from the normal manner
described above. This was particularly the case with the
chlamys (χλαμύς), the distinguishing garment of the ephēbi
(see page 90 and Fig. 50) on military duty and parade,
and of the members of the Attic cavalry. This garment,
which was a circular mantle or cape, hung over the back
and left shoulder, generally reaching to the waist or sometimes even lower. It was gathered round the neck and
fastened either in front or on the shoulder by a clasp. The
right arm was left free for driving or for holding the lance.
To prevent the loose ends from flying awkwardly about in
the wind and impeding the rider, the chlamys was weighted
with bits of lead or clay (Fig. 261). The Thracians, on
account of the greater severity of the winters in their
country, wore long cloaks (ζειραί) which extended to the
riders' feet.

The chlamys.

Women's outer garments exhibited great variety and inventiveness in shape, draping, colour, and ornamentation.
But though the finer sorts had special names,
such as *chlanis* (χλανίς) and *xystis* (ξυστίς), the
generic term was still himatia, as in the case of
men (distinguished as ἱμάτια γυναικεῖα and ἱμάτια ἀνδρεῖα).
Sometimes they hung like a shawl, sometimes again they
cloaked the whole body and even the head. Separate veils
were not so commonly worn by Athenian women as they
were in Homer's time, when the *kredemnon* (κρήδεμνον) was

The himation
as worn by
women.

an essential article of the woman's wardrobe. The women
of the masses, at least, more often drew up their himation
over the head, or even the fold or flap (ἀπό-
Veils and   πτυγμα) of the chiton (page 157). Still the veil
hoods.   (καλύπτρα, κάλυμμα) was not wholly discarded,
and was always worn in public by young girls and brides.

We have seen that the himation,
even when draped so as to leave the
right arm free, was still wholly un-
adapted for strenuous work. In Fig.
74 we see how the athlete has wrapped
it round his waist in order not to be
impeded in his exercise; and in Figs.
64 and 96 it is clear that it had a
tendency to fall from the shoulders
when the wearer was intent on his
work, even though he might be quiet-
Working   ly seated. Working men,
men's   therefore, usually discard-
garment.   ed the himation altogether, and wore a garment which was
girded at the waist, like the chiton, but
the upper part of which was wrapped,
in the fashion of a himation, round the
back and chest, with the end passing
under the right arm and fastened by

Fig. 141.—Pendant for the breast.

a clasp on the left shoulder only. In this way the right
arm and shoulder (ὦμος) were left bare and unimpeded;
the garment was therefore called *exōmis* (ἐξωμίς). It is,
in fact, a chiton in all respects; were the chiton worn by
Hephaestus in Fig. 145 joined together under, instead of
over the right shoulder, it would be an exōmis. The rough
mountaineers of central Greece wore skins of wild animals,
with the hair side turned out; shepherds usually wore goatskins. Leather jerkins (σπολάδες) were worn by slaves over
the regular linen chiton, and sometimes even by soldiers, in

11

lieu of a metal cuirass. The Macrōnes, we learn from Xenophon, wore tunics of woven hair. Fishermen and sailors sometimes donned primitive garments made of plaited
rushes; and the huge goatskin or sheepskin blanket called
the *sisyra* (σισύρα) was not only used as a bed-covering at
night, but also wrapped round the body in cold weather by
the person lucky enough to possess one.

In all cases we note the absence of trousers among the
Greeks, although the peasants of Ionia wore a kind of

FIG. 142.—Scythians clad in trousers.

leathern greaves (κνημῖδες) when at work in the fields. But
the "many-coloured trousers" (ποικίλαι ἀναξυρίδες, Fig. 142)
of the Persians and the breeches (βράκαι) of the Gauls were
by Greeks commonly held in derision.

The colour of the chiton and the himation varied with
the taste of the wearer; but white predominated in the case
of the chiton. Dark colours, either natural or
Colours.   artificial, were worn by the labouring classes
in town and country; black was the colour of mourning.
Purple himatia, common enough among the rich and
effeminate Aeolians, Ionians, and Lydians, and frequently
seen in Athens in the days of the tyrants, were, in the
democratic fifth century, reserved for festal occasions,
though occasionally some person, bent on creating a sensa-
tion, would impress the populace by appearing in purple,

like the orator Gorgias or the madcap Alcibiades. Greek soldiers in foreign pay, like Cyrus's men, were apt to spend their money on the finery of the country where they served, and so, in the review held by Cyrus, we see the men march-

FIG. 143.—Folding garments after the wash.

ing by in red tunics. The Persian nobles, of course, wore tunics of which the material, colour, and ornamentation made them expensive.

Among women the use of garments dyed in various colours was more common. We hear of red, yellow, blue, **Ornamenta-** and green; also of shades like saffron (κροκω-**tion.** τός), frog-green, and apple-green (or yellow). Women, too, varied the tone by borders (κράσπεδα) of a different hue, which were either woven on the original web or sewed on as a separate piece. Sometimes the solid colour was relieved by horizontal or vertical stripes in another colour, the favourite combination being purple stripes on a white or yellow ground. On religious and festive occasions—as, e. g., at weddings—women appeared in clothes which had flowers, stars, and other similar patterns woven or embroidered on them.

To cover the feet was not regarded as such a necessity as it is in civilized countries to-day. Not only in the case

Foot-wear.

of the poor labourer and the ascetic philosopher, not only in Sparta, where we little expect the amenities of living, but even among the fastidious Ionians, it was no crime to be seen in the street without shoes (ὑποδήματα). The guest invited to a banquet and symposium always took off his sandals before taking his place on the couch. Out of

FIG. 144.—The sandal.

The sandal.

the sandals (πέδιλα, σάνδα-λα, Fig. 144), which were merely flat soles of wood or leather fastened by thongs at the instep and big toe, was developed the shoe with uppers; and this, in turn, was combined with a covering for the ankle, suggested, perhaps, by the greaves of the warrior,

The boot.

making a boot. The material was commonly leather, the preparation and colouring of which were well understood; but often a rough felt was employed instead. In cases of hardship, as when the soldiers' shoes gave out on the march, rough shoes or brogues were improvised of rawhide; these were made of a single piece of leather tied round the foot and ankle, and were called *kar-batinai* (καρβάτιναι). Some sandals had a bit of leather in front or on the sides, covering a portion of the foot, somewhat like a slipper. These appear to have been called *krepīdes* (κρηπῖδες). This soon led to the genuine shoe (κοῖλα ὑποδήματα), laced or buttoned, reaching to the ankle. Different kinds were named from the "country of origin." Colophon, in Asia Minor, manufactured a favourite kind called *Colophonia* (Κολοφώνια); and Sparta produced the *Lakonikai* (Λακωνικαί), worn by men. Women wore also the "Persian" (Περσικαί) and the "Secyonian" (Σεκυώνια) shoe, the distinguishing peculiarities of which it is no

longer possible for us to determine. Prominent men sometimes set a fashion in shoes, which accordingly took their
names from them, so that we hear of shoes bearing the
name of Alcibiades or Iphicrates, corresponding to the
modern "Bluchers" named from the celebrated Prussian
general. The boot (ἐνδρομίς or κόθορνος) was useful in the
field, in hunting, or in agriculture, since the covering
reached to the calf of the leg. The *kothornos* (κόθορνος),
like peasants' shoes in Europe to-day, could fit either foot.

Fig. 145.—Dionysus wearing the kothornos.

Hence the nickname Kothornos was applied to Theramenes,
on account of his wavering political convictions. (Since
all these were attached with straps, ἱμάντες, the general
term for foot-wear was ὑποδήματα; "unloose," ὑπολύεσθαι, is
used of taking off one's shoe.)

Coverings for the head. The use of head-coverings, both among men
and women, was also much more restricted than
with us to-day. Most Greeks had thick hair.
Premature baldness seems to have been rather uncommon;
at any rate, it was a subject for remark on the part of ancient wits. The people of Myconos, one of the Cyclades,

were all said to be bald, though how the notion arose it is
hard to see. Certain trades, however, like blacksmithing,
demanded a hat of some sort, as did also lengthy journeys
in the summer sun. Felt (πῖλος) or the skin of some animal, especially the dog, was early used in making caps,
whence they were called simply "felt" or "dog-skin"
(πῖλος, κυνῆ). The "felt" (πῖλος), which had no rim, was

FIG. 146.—" Dressing" garments with oil.

worn by sailors, artisans, and sometimes invalids, like the
obsolete nightcap. Hephaestus wears it in the vase picture
reproduced in Fig. 145; see also Fig. 198.

Fox-skins, also, were utilized in the making of caps
(ἀλωπεκαῖ), such as the Thracians wore, which covered both
head and ears (cf. Fig. 142). Occasionally dried rushes
were plaited together to form what would correspond to
our straw hats. The hat most characteristic of the traveller, the hunter, the envoy, the herald, and the messenger (including the god Hermes), was the *petasos* (πέτασος,
Fig. 50). This was also worn by the cavalry, being in fact
almost inseparable from the chlamys, the regular riding
and travelling cape (page 160). The older form of the
petasos—it varied naturally with time and place—showed
a sharp point or peak, with a rim turned up in front and
back. The later forms had a round crown, either high or

low, with rims both broad and narrow. The rim was frequently wider in front and back than at the sides, and
when turned up gave the effect of a sombrero. The sides,
too, might be turned down and held close to the ears by
means of the strap with which the hat was provided. The
strap was firmly tied under the chin, so that when the heat
or the weight of the covering became too great, the hat
could be thrown back and hung between the shoulders
without coming off.

Women wore no hats or bonnets in the ordinary sense,
though coverings for the head were numerous, and a kind
of petasos was put on in travelling. The himation and the
flap of the tunic, as we saw, could be pulled up so as to
cover both head and face. Kerchiefs were a favourite covering, often arranged like a modern lady's lace cap.

The comparative simplicity and tasteful beauty which
mark the dress and the whole bearing of the Athenian of
the fifth century are to be found also in the
ornaments (σκευή) which he wore. Among
savages decoration is more important than
dress. This is illustrated by the practice of tattooing,
which Xenophon notices among the Mossynoeci, a people
whom he describes as being more remote from the Greeks
in manners and customs than any other through whose
country he had passed. All the children of the chieftains
there had their backs and chests tattooed with flower patterns. The degree and kind of ornamentation adopted by
the Greeks at different periods marks with absolute sure-
ness their progress or decay in civilization. The semi-Ori-
ental fashions of Homeric times prescribed the use of gold
and bronze earrings; of necklaces or collars made either
of solid bands of gold, such as the *streptoi*
(στρεπτοί) belonging to Cyrus's Persian nobles,
or of strings (ὅρμοι) of gold, agate, or amber
beads; brooches of many kinds (περόναι, πόρπαι, Fig. 140);
bracelets or armlets of gold or bronze; gold rings set with

Personal ornaments.

The early period.

onyx; and fancy girdles, sometimes adorned with thick tassels.   Even circles, stars, or roses in gold were fastened to the

Fig. 147.—Necklace.

cloak.   All these belonged to the Homeric age; and many were retained in after years by the Ionians and Aeolians or

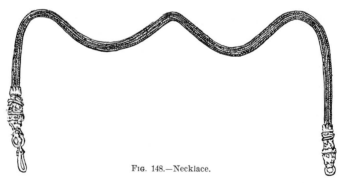

Fig. 148.—Necklace.

the luxurious inhabitants of Magna Graecia.   But in Athens, in the classical period, the men gave up many modes of dec-

oration which their forefathers had prized. The golden
cicada (τέττιξ), with which old-fashioned Athenians had
bound up their hair in queues, was discarded when the

Fig. 149.—Bracelet.

Fig. 150.—Bracelet.

mode of wearing the hair which required that fastening (see
page 177) went out of fashion. They gave up, too, the wearing of bracelets; while the wearing of earrings was a sure
sign that the person was a for-
eigner, not a Greek.

The chief decoration which
the Athenian allowed himself
Rings. was the ring, *dak-*
tylios (δακτύλιος),
usually provided with a seal, and therefore also called
sphragis (σφραγίς). Many of the soldiers, Xenophon tells

Fig. 151.—Ring.

Fig. 152.—Signet.

us, wore these, and they especially attracted the eye of
the guide who had led them through the
Chalybian territory. The soldier, however, has in every age striven to outdo the
ordinary citizen in finery, and the Greek
military indulged in rich ornament for
their armour, wearing helmets with imposing plumes, richly chased
Walking- cuirasses with tassels, shields
sticks.
with pictures and other devices, and the like.

Fig. 153.—Earrings.

The carrying of canes (βακτηρίαι) was almost universal,
among old and young (Figs. 35, 72, 74, 83, 136). They were

seen even in the hands of soldiers and actors in the theatre. In Sparta, and among the Laconomaniacs at Athens,
canes with crook handles were the fashion (σκυτάλια).

The women retained a profusion of ornaments. Among
them was the diadem or fillet for confining the hair in
Earrings. place. They also wore earrings (ἐνώτια, ἐλι-
κτῆρες) of many patterns; and necklaces and
bracelets, especially in the form of a spiral snake (ὄφις),
and anklets. They carried fans (ῥιπίδες), made of some thin
Fans. light wood or con-
sisting of a bunch
of peacock-feathers. On journeys in the hot sun their maids
attended them with parasols
(σκιάδεια), which were much

Fig. 154.—Fan.   Fig. 155.—Parasol.

like modern sunshades, and could open and shut. Similarly the Athenian girls (κανηφόροι) who were chosen to
Sunshades. carry the baskets (κανᾶ, page 141) used in sacrifice at the state festivals were attended by
the daughters of prominent metics, who carried their parasols for them. These girls were called officially *skiadepho-
roi* (σκιαδηφόροι); their position was by no means thought
to be one of dishonour.

CHAPTER XIII

CARE OF THE BODY

GREEK education, with the emphasis it laid on physical training, inculcated a respect for the body, and prescribed **Physical qualities and appearance of the Greeks.** rules for its care which were heeded by most Greeks throughout their whole lives. As a result, they produced, as it is fair to infer from their works of art, a larger proportion of handsome men and beautiful women than any other people that have ever lived; and many, even those engaged in mental labour, such as the philosophers and the dramatists, lived to a good old age. As a rule the Greeks were tall, with well-proportioned limbs, feet, and hands. Their skin was firm, their muscles supple. They had heads of moderate size, round or oval in shape; straight noses, thin lips, and dark or light brown hair, inclined to be curly. Above all, they were noted for their beautiful eyes, with a gaze keen and steady. They themselves admired tallness in both men and women. Their complexion was by nature fair, but was browned by outdoor life and the habit of exercising naked. The sight of some Persian captives, with their white skins, filled them with amusement and derision. Of course, not all Greeks conformed to the type

FIG. 156.—Portrait bust of a Greek (the historian Thucydides).

just described. Thersītes in the *Iliad*, and Socrates in later times, are notable exceptions. The ugliness of Soc-

Socrates. rates caused even his friends to compare him to a satyr, one of the grotesque attendants of Dionȳsus. He had a broad nose with spreading nostrils; his mouth was large, the lips thick, and his eyes protruded like those of a crab. He was disproportionately stout, and walked with a waddling gait. Altogether his appearance entirely belied the strength and beauty of his mind and the kindliness of heart which he showed to all. The poet Sophocles,

Sophocles. to judge from the well-known statue in the Lateran, represented the personal charm of the ideal Greek, as his dramas stand for the perfection of Greek poetry.

Fig. 157.—Painted portrait of a woman.

Regular bathing was early recognized as necessary for health and comfort. In the ruins of the

Bathing in Homer. palace at Tiryns, which belong to the Mycenaean age, we may yet see complete arrangements for baths in the house, including a channel for drawing off the water and vessels for holding olive-oil, the use of which, at least in later times, was inseparable from bathing. Baths are frequently mentioned in Homer; we hear of a kind of tub made of wood or marble (ἀσάμινθος, cf. page 139), and a tripod used when the water for bathing was to be heated (called τρίπους λοετροχόος) ; also a foot-bath.

Hot baths. Warm water (θερμὰ λοετρά) was used in the house, but baths in rivers or in the sea are also mentioned. The proper performance of religious rites demanded purity; hence the hands, if not the whole body, were always washed before a sacrifice or a libation.

The Spartans maintained the practice of bathing in cold water, avoiding hot, except after extraordinary exertion. Even then, the warm bath was followed by another in cold water, with a vigorous rubbing afterward. In the more luxurious parts of Greece the use of warm baths, and even steam baths, became general; but the custom was condemned by the more conservative among the Athenians. The hot springs of Sicily were famous, and their first use was ascribed to Heracles, who, according to the myth, refreshed himself with them after his Labours, and thereby gave a certain sanction to their use by his followers.

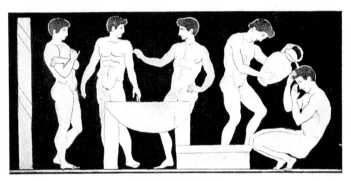

Fig. 158.—At the bath.

At home bathing was performed with a wash-basin or at a fountain in the court, if the house was thus supplied. There was no special bath-room. The bather **Bathing at home.** washed himself with water held in a round or oval basin (λουτήρ, Figs. 119, 158), or else sat in a tub or trough (πύελος, page 139), while another stood by and poured the water over him. Public baths (βαλανεῖα), **Public baths.** with elaborate systems for supplying hot water, and with separate dressing-rooms, were not erected until a somewhat late period. In the fifth century they were not viewed with great favour, on account of the

use of hot water, and because the gossip and idling therein
tended to undermine the morality of young men who resorted to them.   Probably the baths of this period were
simply attachments of the gymnasia and the palaestrae,
outside the city walls.   Later, state institutions (βαλανεῖα δημόσια) were built
and placed in charge of city officials (the
ἀττυνόμοι, page 16).   At first, as we have
noticed, there was no dressing-room (ἀπο-
δυτήριον), so that bathers' clothes were at
the mercy of sneak-thieves.   The bather
might use a separate tub or bathe with
others in the tank (μάκτρα, κολυμβήθρα,
page 139).   After the plunge the bath-
tender (βαλανεύς) or one of his assistants
stood ready to pour cold water over the
head and shoulders, or to supply various cleansing substances with which the

Fig. 159.—Aryballos
(late form).

Soap. bather rubbed himself.   Soap, a Saxon invention, was not known until the time of the Roman
Empire.   Its place was supplied by *konia* (κονία),
a kind of lye made from ashes, or by nitre (νίτρον),
or by a refined earth brought from the island of
Use of oil. Cimōlus.   But more important than
these, in popular regard, was the rubbing with oil, to keep the skin smooth and soft.
The oil was brought from home in a flask (λήκυθος,
ἀρύβαλλος, or ἀλάβαστος; page 135).   The bather
also took care to provide himself with a towel
(ὠμόλινον) and a strigil (στλεγγίς, page 81), by
which the superfluous liquid was scraped from the body
before dressing.

Fig. 160.
Alabastos.

Cost of a public bath. The price of a bath with all these extras
—the douche, rubbing, lye, and scraping—was
extremely low: two chalci, less than a cent, was charged.
Baths were regularly taken at home or in public places by

the scrupulous just before going to a banquet, and Plato in his *Symposium* likes to dwell on Socrates's conformity to this requirement of polite society.

The fondness for using oil was akin to the liking for salves and perfumes. The perfumery shops (μυροπώλια) were favourite resorts in Athens, and they dispensed all kinds of ointments and scents. Even in far-away Armenia we hear of ointments made of lard, sesame-seeds, bitter almonds, and turpentine. But myrrh (μύρον) was the most popular in Athens.

Use of unguents.

Closely allied in function to the bath-tender was the barber (κουρεύς); and no resort was more often visited by the Athenian than the barber-shop (κουρεῖον). Both bath-tender and barber were proverbial for bustling officiousness and garrulity. All the news of the day was gathered at the barber's and dispensed by him. The great disaster at Syracuse was first heard of in a barber-shop in the Piraeus, and the barber ran all the way to the city, five miles away, to tell the news. The old joke of

Barbers.

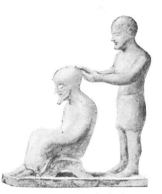

Fig. 161.—At the barber's.

King Archelāus of Macedon often reappears to-day. "How shall I cut your hair, sire?" asked the barber. "In silence," he answered.

The mode of wearing the hair differed widely in the several Greek states. In the Homeric period, and for some time after, the hair was worn long. This fashion was expressed by the verb κομᾶν, and we have "long-haired" (κάρη κομάοντας), therefore, as the standing designation of the Achaeans in the *Iliad.* One notable exception in the early age of Greece was the

Mode of wearing the hair.

practice of the Abantes in cutting off the front of their
hair. They were a warlike people in Euboea, accustomed to

FIG. 162.—Women's head-dress.

hand-to-hand fighting, and cut off their hair, so Plutarch
says, in order to prevent their enemies from getting a hold.

At Athens the athletes kept their hair close-cropped.
But the Spartans retained the Homeric custom. Before
the Spartan boy reached his majority his hair was cut regularly; after that time he wore it long, and it was the object of special care, as we read in the story of the Spartans
at Thermopylae. In Athens, to be sure, there were not
wanting persons who
copied Spartan man-
ners in all
Athenian fashions. respects;
but when
the Athenian lad be-
came a citizen, and had
dedicated to some di-
vinity the locks which
had grown long in child-

FIG. 163.—Children's hair.

hood (see page 89), he thereafter kept his hair moderately
trimmed, being of course guided by his own taste. Doubtless we see the customary treatment of the hair in the ideal
statues of Zeus or of Asclepius (Fig. 250) or in the portrait
of Thucydides (Fig. 156) which belong to this period. As
in other things, so in this also the later Athenian adopted
the golden mean. Before the Persian Wars the men of

Athens wore their hair long, either gathered in a kind of knot (κρωβύλος) on the top of the head, where it was held

in place by a gold brooch, or hanging at the back like a queue. This the Athenian of the time of the Peloponnesian War discarded

Fig. 164.—Shears.

(cf. page 169). On the other hand, he avoided an extremely close crop, which was adopted by most slaves; but these also braided and coiled the hair at the back, possibly according to the custom of the country whence they had come.

The cut of the beard was also a matter of attention. In the older period, as is shown in an old-style vase from which Fig. 75 is taken, the beard had an artificial, wedge shape, which was sometimes retained in later times by slaves and in the caricatures of the comic stage. The citizen of Athens allowed it to take its natural shape, with occasional trimming. The Spartans, like most military folk, liked to grow a ferocious mustache (μύσταξ), until the Ephors felt they must make a law restraining the custom; but no Greek ever wore a mustache without a beard. Other parts of the beard were the side-whiskers (γένειον) and the long beard (πώγων). To keep the face closely shaved, as was the custom among the free-born after Alexander's time, must have required some courage, for razors (ξυρά) were rough and clumsy; shaving at home was practically impossible.

The beard.

To the barber's the Athenian repaired to have his nails trimmed and his corns cut. The barber also performed certain minor surgical operations, such as removing warts and superfluous hair. On his way from the barber-

Duties of the barber.

Fig. 165.—Razor.

shop or the bath to attend a banquet, the Athenian would stop at a perfumer's and have his hair and beard scented with myrrh; but this was often supplied by the host.

12

The men of Athens, as we saw, gave up the knot or queue

Women's head ornaments. worn by their elders, and the care of the hair, except the every-day combing after the bath, was left to the barber. Brushes had not been invented. Women, on the other hand, could not resort to a hair-dresser's, and had to depend on their own taste and the help of their slaves for the arrangement of the hair. Sometimes it was left to flow unrestrained down the back; but more

Fig. 166.—Woman's coiffure.

often it was combed back and gathered in a knot, more or less high, or in a twist which extended backward—the " Psyche

Fig. 167.—Pendant to be hung at the ear or the temple.

twist " (Fig. 162). Bands or fillets (ταινίαι) for the hair and brow formed a conspicuous ornament among women. Besides the simple ribbon, there was the wider band of cloth or leather, studded with gold, which served to keep the coil of hair in place; an arrangement of this kind is seen on the head of Hēra, Fig. 245. Nets, too, frequently served this end. For this purpose were also used combs, hairpins of bronze, ivory, bone, gold, or silver, and especially gold diadems (στεφάναι). Besides wearing ear-rings, women also hung elaborate ornaments of gold or silver from the side of the head or from the temples (Fig. 167; cf. Fig. 141).

CHAPTER XIV

SOCIAL LIFE AND ENTERTAINMENTS

In the outdoor life of the men, in their gatherings in the market, the palaestra, the bath, and the gymnasium,

Opportunities for social intercourse. and in frequent meetings of tribe and deme, and especially phratry, we see numberless opportunities for intercourse and social contact. The attractiveness of barber-shops in the eyes of the male members of the society caused them to be named "wineless symposia"; and the whole tendency of Greek life was to find amusement in concourse. The quiet attractions of study and reading, while not seldom appreciated, were nevertheless diminished by physical drawbacks (cf. page 108); the poorness of the writing materials, the closely written pages, with words undivided one from the other, the inadequacy of the light indoors, except in the court, and everywhere at night, made reading a source of entertainment limited to the few. Serious persons took delight in conversation of an improving nature with a few chosen companions, walking about the suburbs or on the banks of the Ilissus, or sitting on the stone benches at the gymnasium. This would happen in the long afternoons, when

Occupations of the day. the luncheon ($\mathring{a}\rho\iota\sigma\tau\sigma\nu$) had been followed by a brief rest at home while the sun was hottest.

All the games begun and practised in childhood (page 76) furnished amusement for the adult. Many an hour was whiled away in playing draughts ($\pi\epsilon\tau\tau\epsilon\acute{\iota}a$, Fig. 227), or in the game called by the Italians *morra*, in which the two players suddenly extend one or more of the fingers of the right hand and guess at the total number extended by both; whoever guessed nearest was the winner. In the accompanying picture (Fig. 168) each player grasps with his left hand a short pole to prevent the unfair use of the left hand in the excitement of the game.

In general, the Greeks went to bed early, and often rose before dawn. All sports, theatrical performances, and social calls occurred during the earlier part of the day; the

FIG. 168.—"How many fingers?"

sports extended into the afternoon, which generally closed with the bath and the preparations for dinner. The banquet (δεῖπνον, εὐωχία) was the only kind of entertainment

The banquet. to which one might resort at night. It took place almost always after sunset. One or two exceptions are mentioned by Xenophon, but these were due to the varying custom of other localities or to the exigencies of camp life, as when the soldiers were feasted by the Armenians and by Seuthes. Also at the state festivals the public entertainment of each tribe (ἑστίασις) took place in the daytime.

To the banquet all were glad to resort when occasion
offered—the old and the young, the grave and the frivo-
lous, Socrates and Alcibiades. The recluse or the miser
who drank only water, and the churl who never entertained,
but ate by himself in the dark, were rare. The host presented his invitation orally, sometimes through a friend or
slave, often in person; never by formally writ-

The
invitation.   ten notes. Often, too, the invitation (κλῆσις)

was issued only a day or two previous to the
feast, or even on the morning of the day when it was to
occur. There was no conventional phrase dictated by society Sometimes the host announced that he was to en-
tertain some distinguished person or celebrate a wedding,
and in graceful, complimentary words would entreat the
presence of his friend to help him; or he would call out
more familiarly, " Be sure to come to my house " (ὅπως
παρέσει μοι), at the same time stating the reason. Perhaps
the most formal phrase, employed when the guests were not
intimate friends, was " I invite the gentlemen to dinner "
(τοὺς ἄνδρας ἐπὶ δεῖπνον καλῶ). The guests were at liberty to
invite any friends of theirs, and old acquaintances always
felt free to drop in unbidden at these hospitable gatherings. Women were invited only to wedding feasts.

With the increasing art exhibited in cookery during the
last years of the fifth century arose a number of professional
male cooks (μάγειροι), who were almost always

Professional
caterers.   hired for private banquets. Even here the

wife of the host came into no relation with
her husband's social set, and had nothing to do with the
ordering of the dinner or the direction of the slaves who
attended the guests. The *chef* brought his own assistants,
as well as the utensils required for special dishes, either
owned by himself or hired in the agora.

On arriving, the guests (σύνδειπνοι) were greeted with the
simple " Hail ! " (χαῖρε), or " You have come just in time "
(εἰς καλὸν ἥκεις), or the more affected " I salute you " (ἀσπά-

ζομαι). Handshaking was not so common as with us, since
it had a deeper meaning, and was ordinarily reserved for
the formal, ceremonious conclusion of a com-
**The
reception.**   pact or treaty. Bowing was regarded with disfavour, as being akin to the slavish salaam of
the Persians and other Orientals (προσκύνησις). By the
Greeks this mode of salutation was offered only to the gods,
on the appearance of an omen or the like. Of course,
among members of the family or very intimate friends
the embrace (χερσὶ περιβαλεῖν) and the kiss (φίλημα) were as common as they are in Europe to-day.

On reaching the court of the house, each newcomer removed his sandals and allowed his feet to be washed by
the slaves before he took his place on a couch.
The dinner.   For the men in Athens, unlike the Homeric
heroes, reclined at table, usually two on a couch. After all
were comfortably settled in the order appointed by the
host, and water had been poured over their hands, the
small portable tables (page 130) were brought in laden

with the food, and
disposed near the
couches. The
Thracians hospi-
tably placed them

FIG. 169.—Cylix with low base.

nearest their
guests. Thin
soups, or *consommés*, were unknown, and broths cooked
very thick were rarely served at these special dinners.
The obvious reason for this was the lack of spoons, which
were not employed for table use until later; when broth
was eaten, it was scooped from the plate with
The menu.   pieces of bread (μυστῖλαι). Solid food, with
which the dinner commonly began, was brought in already cut up. The guests helped themselves and ate with
their fingers, forks being unknown. Instead of napkins,
they wiped their hands with bits of bread (ἀπομαγδαλιαί),

which were then thrown on the floor to be eaten by the
dogs. Vinegar, mustard, and other condiments stood ready
in cruets (ὀξύβαφα) on each table. Wine was the only
drink, and it was taken sparingly during this portion of the
entertainment. At the end of the meal each guest took a
swallow of unmixed wine in honour of the "Good Divinity" (ἀγαθὸς δαίμων), a ceremony which, in its pious recog-
nition of man's dependence on the gods, corresponded
somewhat to the saying of grace. After this the tables
were removed, the floor swept clean of all crumbs, bones,
and the like, once more water was poured over the hands,
and then the company sang in unison a paean accompanied by the flute-player (αὐλητρίς), who was always present
on these occasions (Fig. 172).

And now the symposium began; besides *symposion*
(συμπόσιον), a common name for it was *potos*, the "drink-

The sym-
posium.

ing" (πότος). Smaller tables were set before
the guests, on which were dried fruits, nuts,
and other light viands of a thirst-provoking

nature (see page 148). These
constituted the "second tables"
(δεύτεραι τράπεζαι, or τραγήματα),
corresponding to dessert. The
feasters anointed the hair and
beard with myrrh ; they put garlands on their heads, round their
necks, and on the breast; and
then the slaves (οἰνοχόοι) mixed
the wine in the great bowl (κρατήρ). Water predominated in this
mixture, as we have seen before
(page 151). Three bowls were

FIG. 170.—Krater.

filled and emptied in the course of an ordinary symposium.
The first cupful out of the first bowl was consecrated to
the Olympians, especially Zeus; the first out of the second
mixture, to the Heroes ; and from the third, to Zeus the

Saviour. The host then drank to (προπίνειν) the health of his guests, after which they all drank singly to each oth-

Toasts.

er, going round the circle from left to right. When one was challenged to drink with an-other, it was considered proper form to empty the cup at a single draught (ἀμυστί). At the beginning, the saucer-shaped cups, or *phialai*, described on page 137, were used; as the drinking proceeded, the guests called for larger goblets or for drinking-horns.

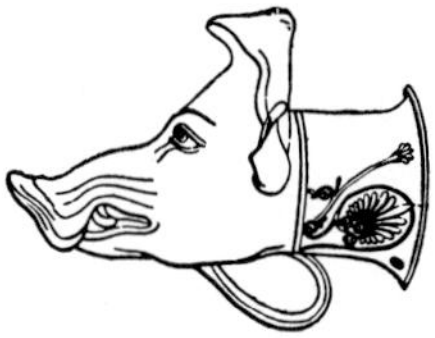

FIG. 171.—Drinking-horn.

As a rule, a toast-master was elect-ed when the symposium began. He

The toast-master.

was called by various names, such as "king," "leader of the drinking," or "symposiarch" (βασιλεύς, ἄρχων τῆς πόσεως, συμποσίαρχος). It was his duty to decide on the proportion of water to be mixed with the wine, to indicate when the time had come to exchange the larger for the smaller cups, to prescribe

FIG. 172.—The symposium.

forfeits for those who had violated the rules of the drink-ing, to conduct the drinking contest, and to propose toasts.

Amusements at the symposium.

Each guest tried to outdo his neighbour in wit, humour, story-telling, and practical jok-ing; and often the discussion of various topics propounded by the symposiarch, or occurring incidentally, was of a distinctly high order; every guest knew Homer and the lyric poets, and could quote them readily; every guest, too, in that age of keen wits and stirring national

experience, was quick at repartee, eager in debate, always
ready, even in support of some whimsical paradox, to cite
an illustration out of his own experience or his country's
history. For a long period singing remained
Singing. the chief source of entertainment. The early
education of every Greek rendered him competent to take
the lyre and sing, at least tolerably, some famous song
from Anacreon, or Simonides, or Euripides. Or rounds
and catches (σκόλια) were sung in more boisterous style by
all in turn. Especially popular were riddles,
Riddles. conundrums, and catch questions. Another
favourite was the game called *kottabos* (κότταβος), which
consisted in tossing off the last drops in the cup in such
manner that they hit a small figure, made of clay or metal,
the bobbing of which determined the success of the throw.

As luxury increased, these simpler amusements gave
way to elaborate programmes performed by professional
flute and lyre players (αὐλητρίδες, κιθαρισταί),
Professional entertainers. dancing-girls (ὀρχηστρίδες), and jugglers and
contortioners. Rich hosts were also beset with
a crowd of needy flatterers (κόλακες), who sought to enter-
tain the company by their wit,
and thus earn a right to enjoy
the feast. Their per-
Buffoons. sistence gave them a
professional character and a special name, γελωτοποιοί, and they
were tolerated, strangely as it
seems to us, even in the best and
most dignified society; their noisy
garrulity often usurped the con-

Fig. 173.—Jumping over swords.

versation, and their gluttony and wine-bibbing tended to
lower the morality of convivial gatherings; but, with all that,
they were not so much in evidence as the Roman parasite.

The flute-girls and the dancers gave exhibitions not only
in music and fancy dancing, but also in acrobatic feats, jump-

ing over knives, twirling hoops and balls, and enacting dramatic scenes of subjects not ordinarily produced in the classical drama at the Dionysiac festivals. Thus

Theatrical scenes. Xenophon in his *Symposium* describes a representation of the loves of Dionȳsus and Ariadne, given by a dancing boy and girl—a story that was dear to the Athenian, since it called to mind the exploits of his hero Theseus in the Labyrinth at

Fig. 174.—Coin of Crete representing the Labyrinth.

Crete. Such scenes portrayed in pantomime the romantic elements of a myth not touched on in the "legitimate" plays of the period, except now and then by Euripides; and their most marked characteristic, as distinguished from the public performances in the theatre, was the fact that women assumed parts in the representation. This practice was significant of great changes that were to come in the remote future; for not until modern times has the public appearance of women as actresses been countenanced, except at the imperial courts in the Roman epoch.

The party came to an end with a libation to Hermes; and the merrymakers, if they were young and reckless, departed with flutes and torches to serenade some favourite beauty. Such bands of revellers (κωμασταί) not infrequently infested the streets of Athens at night, and besides the noise with which their loud music troubled good citizens,

Social and political clubs. they sometimes came to blows among themselves or with another similar party. Out of associations of boon companions like these grew up clubs composed of young men of the aristocrats, who united for political as well as social ends. Later Athenian history was largely determined by the predominance of one or another faction whose origin could be traced from such bands.

There were also purely dining associations (ἔρανοι), corresponding in their purpose to a modern lunch club.   In these each member contributed a portion of the viands, as in a modern picnic, or else provided food for all, being afterward repaid by the others.   In the later centuries of Athenian history these clubs assumed great importance in social life, and were regularly organized for pleasure and the common worship of some special deity.   Under this later system members paid regular monthly dues, sometimes amounting to three drachmas.

CHAPTER XV

THE VARIOUS CALLINGS: THE WARRIOR

THE Greek, especially the Athenian, regarded himself as an integral part of the state; his whole life must,

Absorbing interest in the citizen's functions.

according to his view, be devoted to what he conceived to be the duties of a citizen. These duties might range from functions as high as generalship or archonship down to attendance at the public assembly (ἐκκλησία) and the law courts (δικαστήρια), or might resolve themselves into mere gossip about public leaders and public policy. At all events, his life must be free from any impediments to his political functions; he must be independent in his relations with other citizens; his time must be wholly free (cf. page 118).

Such ideas about the civic function, cherished by all Greeks, whether their government was democratic or oligarchical, were possible in a society where slave

Disdain of work.

labour disposed of all the drudgery of life. The old patriarchal life of Homer was different. Slaves there were, but even kings joined in the reaping, princes tended cattle, and princesses spun yarn and wove it into cloth and took part in the family washing. But in Athens, democratic as we are accustomed to regard its society, Socrates was the only notable figure who had a word in praise of the " dignity of labour."

All, therefore, who had to work for a living, being to that extent dependent and not free, were in general regarded with contempt. In so far as they were obliged to sell their time to be placed at the disposal of some one else,

they were *aneleutheroi* (ἀνελεύθεροι), deprived of liberty as
much as an actual slave (δοῦλος). Further, many artisans,

Social
distinction
between the
worker and
the independ-
ent citizen. like tailors and cobblers, led such a sedentary
life, outside the invigorating influence of sun-
light and fresh air, that physically they could
not measure themselves with the gentleman,
eleutheros (ἐλεύθερος), who was nurtured in the
free life of the market, the gymnasium, and the palaestra; and mentally, their narrow view of the world was supposed to make them mean and vulgar (βάναυσος). Hence
the industrial arts were called "slavish" (τέχναι δουλοπρε-
πεῖς), since they appeared to make men no better than
menials; or "vulgar" (τέχναι βαναυσικαί), with reference to
the sordid effect they had on those engaged in them.
Hesiod, to be sure, had said that "Labour is no reproach,
'tis idleness that is dishonour"; but the very fact that he
said it shows that as early as his day the contrary opinion
held sway.

Some exceptions in the case of certain activities in
which citizens engaged may be observed in the cities on the

Wholesale
traders
and manufac-
turers. coast (ἐμπόρια) where commerce flourished on
a large scale. In Athens there were numerous
wholesale merchants (ἔμποροι) and manufacturers belonging to the citizen class. These,
because of the grander extent of their operations, and the
fact that they did not work with their own hands, but
merely superintended large numbers of slaves or poorer
citizens, were not held in disrepute. Political reformers
like Pericles, recognizing the value of a thrifty artisan
class, sought occasionally to compensate for the social disabilities that attached to artisans by giving them political
advantages equal to those enjoyed by persons who derived
their income from landed estates. And Solon, long before
Pericles, exempted sons from the duty of supporting their
parents in old age if the latter had neglected to teach their
sons a trade. These exceptions, however, only prove the

general rule ; and as slaves and foreigners (μέτοικοι, see page 64) increased, the poorest citizen often preferred to earn a few obols a day by sitting in the ecclesia or the courts of law, rather than win double the sum as a retail dealer or handicraftsman. In later times, and even to some extent as early as the fifth century, many hired out Citizens as in the capacity of mercenaries under some for-
mercenary eign leader, in the hope of getting suddenly
soldiers. rich through loot and plunder, and so become an "object of envy to their friends at home." This was especially true of the poorer districts of Peloponnēsus; more than one half of Cyrus's Greeks came from Arcadia and Achaia. It was the glimpse of the wealth, as well as the weakness, of Persia which tempted Greeks to become mercenaries and freebooters.

Since, therefore, the soldier's life came to almost every Greek, we can not gain a complete picture of the ordinary citizen's career without a brief glance at his military and political occupations, considered with special reference to the Athenian.

The martial spirit of the Athenians in the fifth century is attested not only by their achievements from Marathon (490 B. C.) to Arginusae (406 B. C.), but also by
Military their works of art. An extraordinary number
service. of vases depict scenes relating to war, and children were given names like Scyrocles, Naxiades, and Nau-
pactus to commemorate their fathers' prowess in battle. The warlike temper of this period was more conspicuous than in the time of Demosthenes, who found it impossible to rouse his people as he desired to resist Philip. With all this, and in spite of the ready response of volunteers (ἐθελονταί) to the calls to service, the normal way to raise an army for a special enterprise was by a draft (κατάλογος), in which citizens were listed by lot to serve in the heavy infantry or in the cavalry. In the middle of the fifth century Athens maintained a standing army of twenty-five

hundred heavy-armed men, *hoplites*, and a fleet of twenty ships. The usual age for field service extended from the twentieth to the fiftieth year; but, as we saw before (page 90), young men (ἔφηβοι) between the ages of eighteen and twenty were engaged in light military duties,

The new recruits. during which they were instructed in the art of fighting in heavy armour (ὁπλομαχεῖν), in throwing the spear, and in tactics (τὰ ἀμφὶ τάξεις). They also served as patrols (περίπολοι) on the frontier. Their drill ground was the Lycēum, which also formed the rendezvous for the start (ἔξοδος). Spectators were allowed at

Fig. 175.—Preparing for the rendezvous.

the drill—a contrast to Spartan practice, which excluded all those not participating. At the end of their two years of preliminary training the ephēbi were mustered in the theatre, and each received from the state a spear and shield.

Older men might be called upon for military service, even after they were fifty years old, but, as a rule, only for garrison duty. To this they were liable

The military age. until they were sixty. Socrates served four times, with conspicuous valour, between the age of forty and fifty.

The hoplites and cavalry were, in Solon's time, recruited only from the three upper classes—Pentecosiomedimni,

Hippeis, and Zeugītae. Later, in the Peloponnesian War,
the Thētes also were drafted for hoplite service; and in
Divisions of one great emergency—namely, at Arginūsae in
the land 406 B. C.—even slaves were called out. Metics,
forces. to the number of three thousand, were kept
armed for defense. The quota from each tribe (φυλή)
formed a division by itself, called *taxis* (τάξις, or simply
φυλή). The number of men in each taxis varied according
to the urgency of the call. The first summons to arms in
the Peloponnesian War brought out more than one thousand men in each tribe. Each tribal quota had its own
commander (ταξίαρχος), and was divided into companies
(λόχοι), each under a captain (λοχαγός). Though each tribe
fought, as a rule, by itself, members of different tribes might
mess or sleep together. Men grouped as comrades in this
way were said to belong to " the same tent " (ξύσκηνοι).

At the call to arms, which usually ran, " Rations for
three days " (σιτία ἡμερῶν τριῶν), the citizen who was to serve
in the hoplites
The soldier's packed his knap-
equipment. sack or wallet
(γύλιος), and took down his
lance and shield from the
chimney, where he kept them,
the shield being enclosed in
a case (σάγμα) to protect it
from smoke and dust and
prevent tarnishing (Fig. 175).
The spiders spinning webs in
the shield are a part of the
picture of peace which the
poet Bacchy-
The lides gives us.
breastplate.

FIG. 176.—Putting on the breastplate.

The soldier then adjusted his chiton, often of
a gay hue, red or purple (hence called φοινικίς) ; over this he
buckled his cuirass (θώραξ), which was made of leather or

linen covered with metal plates or scales, and was fastened
in front by clasps running vertically. Strong as it was,
it was not seldom pierced by a javelin or an arrow. The
shoulder-pieces were drawn from behind over the shoulder and fastened in front to the main piece on the breast.
From the hips downward hung flaps (πτέρυγες), consisting
of pieces of leather or felt, either single or double, designed to protect the thighs and the groin. The cuirass
made entirely of bronze, and used in the Homeric period,
had been given up. The warrior then strapped round his

Greaves. legs below the knees the greaves (κνημῖδες), made
of metal, lined with soft padding to prevent
chafing. Another strip of padding round the ankles served
as a support for the greaves below. On his head, too, he
placed a padded band, tied with a knot at the back, which
eased the pressure of the helmet and kept it more firmly in

Helmet. place. The helmet (κράνος), usually of bronze,
but also of leather, had movable cheek-pieces,
but the parts which covered nose and forehead were solid.
The helmet was surmounted with one or more plumes
(λόφοι, Figs. 175, 176, and 180); generals and taxiarchs had
three. A short sword or knife (ξίφος, μάχαιρα) hung at the

FIG. 177.—Greave.   FIG. 178.—Helmet.   FIG. 179.—Helmets.

left side by a strap from the right shoulder. With his
shield and lance in hand, and a mantle, which was thrown
aside when he went into action, the hoplite was now ready
to join his comrades at the rendezvous. The shield was
either round or oval, and was heavy, since it often reached

13

from the eyes to the knees. Hence an officer, or any other soldier whose duties required him to be thus assisted, was **The shield.** frequently attended by a shield bearer (ὑπα-σπιστής). The shield was held by straps, through which the left arm was thrust, the last strap being grasped in the hand. Often its external surface was covered by some device, which was meant to serve as a mere ornament, or to symbolize some trait of the wearer or his family, or even to strike fear in the enemy by the frightfulness of the picture (Figs. 88 and 175). The spear (δόρυ) was long—sometimes nine feet—and consisted of a stout

Fig. 180.—Hoplite.

shaft furnished with an iron head (λόγχη). Athens had thirteen thousand hoplites ready for offensive operations at the first inroad of Sparta in 431 B. C.

Besides these hoplites (ὁπλῖται), so called from the elaborate and heavy nature of their accoutrement (ὅπλα), **The cavalry.** the next important arm of the service was the cavalry (ἱππεῖς), a small and exclusive body of about one thousand men, commanded by two hipparchs (ἵππαρχοι), each leading five tribal divisions (φυλαί). The cavalry, like the hoplites, was recruited by a draft made by the hipparchs from each of the ten tribes; but naturally the list would be filled up from the richer citizens, or those who were able to keep a horse. Each tribe was commanded by its own phylarch (φύλαρχος); and no one might enter the cavalry until he had been approved by the Council **Test required.** (βουλή), after a scrutiny (δοκιμασία) more or less strict, which determined whether he possessed the necessary property qualification and was of genuine Attic descent, whether he was rich enough to own a horse, and whether he knew how to manage one (cf. page 90). Most people entertained exaggerated notions of the superior safety enjoyed by horsemen on the battle-field, and particularly in a retreat. Many, therefore, when a war broke out, were anxious to join the cavalry, and sometimes managed to do so without the necessary qualifications. The trooper was armed sometimes with a

FIG. 181.—Greek sword.

lance, useful in a charge; sometimes with a pair of javelins (Fig. 186); sometimes with a short, dagger-like sword for close combat; but he had no sabre for a cutting stroke. His cuirass seems to have been heavier than that of the hoplite. Shields were used only when the members of the troop did sentinel duty on foot.

The Athenian cavalry seems not to have been very efficient, though it was the pride of the Athenians on the occasion of a public parade, and entrance into it was eagerly sought by the young aristocrat. But the Greeks had neither saddle nor stirrups, and often rode without even a saddle-cloth (ἐφίππιον στρῶμα), so that the rider was easily unseated. The horses were not well trained, and frequently stampeded. Xenophon's words of comfort to his troops when they were in need of cavalry, while half jocose and paradoxical, yet show the weaknesses of the Athenian cavalry—weaknesses which were not shared by the more practised riders of Boeotia, Thessaly, and Syracuse. Forty years later, at the battle of Mantineia (362 B. C.), the Athenian cavalry still felt their inferiority to the Thebans and the Thessalians. In spite of that, their desperate bravery gave them the victory.

The light-armed soldiers, employed in skirmishing (ἀκρο-βόλισις) and in guerrilla warfare generally, consisted of bowmen (τοξόται), slingers (σφενδονῆται), and javelin-hurlers (ἀκοντισται). Bowmen, to the number of sixteen hundred, were recruited from the Thētes, or that portion of the citizens not ordinarily liable to service as hoplites, and

The light-armed service. from the tributary allies (σύμμαχοι, νησιῶται) of Athens. Sometimes they were mercenaries hired by the state from places not under Athenian rule; Cretan bowmen were the most noted for their skill. The slingers were always foreign mercenaries or tributary allies, and native Greeks never served as "peltasts" (πελτασταί), so often mentioned in the *Anabasis*. These were Thracians, who used a light, flat shield called the

Fig. 182.—A slinger (σφενδονήτης).

pelté (πέλτη), which was not strengthened by the plates of bronze or layers of hide belonging to the hoplite's shield. The Athenians also employed two hundred mounted bowmen (ἱπποτοξόται), chiefly Thracians or Scythians hired or owned as slaves by the state. As con-

Athenian agility. trasted with Sparta, therefore, the Athenians were capable of more agile tactics. An engineering force was required in sieges, the chief duty of which was to build walls under cover of which the besieging party could occupy a position close to

Fig. 183.—Peltast.

the city invested. It was therefore composed of masons, who selected the stones and put them together (λιθολόγοι, τέκτονες).

There was no special commissary department. When the rations brought by each man at the start were exhausted, the generals and captains sent out foraging parties, who got what they could for their own company or division. The distribution then took place under the supervision of certain officers detailed for this work, called, like the commissioners in a city market, *agoranomoi* (ἀγορανόμοι, page 20). Baggage-carriers (σκευοφόροι) had charge of the provisions

Commissary and baggage.

Fig. 184.—Greek arrow-heads.

and other belongings of officers, cavalry, and the richer hoplites. Poorer soldiers had to carry their own supplies (ἐφόδια), which were sometimes given to them by generous comrades.

The army and the fleet were under the command of ten generals (στρατηγοί), one from each of the ten tribes. These held joint command, having superseded the archon polemarchos (πολέμαρχος) in this office early in the fifth century B. C. Their first achievement as officers in supreme authority was the victory at Marathon in 490 B. C.

Discipline.

Although regular drill was kept up both in Athens and Sparta in peace as well as in war, military discipline in Athens seems not to have been very rigid, when measured by modern standards. One reason was the limited authority of the generals. They were responsible to the Council of Five Hundred (βουλή), and on their return from a campaign might be attacked in a lawsuit by any sycophant (page 19) on some slight charge. The democratic character of a Greek army is well shown by the fact that all the generals, including Xenophon, who had conducted the Cyrean Greeks safely out of the grasp of Tissaphernes and the Persians, were

Authority of the generals.

nevertheless required to render an account to their own soldiers of their generalship. Further, breaches of discipline, desertion, and cowardice were punished not by the generals, but by the courts at home, after a regular trial in which the officer whose authority had been violated might be only a witness, or, at most, a prosecutor. For all these reasons, although the value and need of discipline were acknowledged, the spectacle of an undisciplined force was too common in Greek military history, and rigorous officers like the Spartan Clearchus were generally hated.

In early Greek history citizens were not paid for their services in war. In Athens the custom of paying for military service doubtless began with the growth of wealth that came with the widening of her empire. The pay (μισθός) in Athens was a drachma (page 246) a day for a hoplite; a cavalryman must have received more, for in time of peace he was allowed a drachma daily for his maintenance alone. Public burial was given to soldiers killed in battle, and their families were cared for until the sons

Pay.

Fig. 185.—The soldier's return.

became of age. On leaving home for service in the field, the soldier made careful provision for the future of his family, usually making a will and entrusting his money to a near relative or friend. All these preparations for the worst were the more necessary since the chances of getting a letter safely to his friends at home were few, and they might never even hear of him again.

Another way in which the private citizen, especially of the lower class (Thētes), found occupation and rendered public service, was on board the fleet. From **The navy.** the middle of the fifth century twenty triremes were annually in commission, to preserve the Athenian empire and keep the crews in efficient practice. The state had three hundred seaworthy ships at the beginning of the Peloponnesian War. It was the duty of the Council (βουλή) to keep the ships up to their full number, and to assign to wealthy citizens in turn the task of equipping them. This task was one of the public services (λῃτουργίαι) by which the state expenses were frequently met (see page 62). The citizen or

FIG. 186.—Trooper ready to start.

citizens chosen for this duty were called trierarchs (τριή-ραρχοι), and attended to the caulking, rigging, manning, and general equipment. The cost of this was great, often amounting to fifty minae (page 246); for the manning and maintenance the trierarch received money from the state, for which he gave strict account at the expiration of his service.

The earliest kind of ships had fifty rowers seated on the same level, and was undecked. These penteconters **Greek ships.** (πεντηκόντοροι) were used as war-ships first by the Phocaeans, who settled Marseilles; this use survived even after triremes had been invented. We first hear of the trireme, with rowers on three levels, or banks,

in the early part of the sixth century. The earliest had no
upper protection for the rowers. Later a wooden protection was devised, but complete decks (καταστρώματα) were
as yet unknown during the Persian Wars, so that at Salamis
there was room for only four bowmen and fourteen hoplites
in each trireme. The need of transporting soldiers in war-
ships to distant fighting grounds led to Cimon's improve-
ment, by which the ships were given broader beam, and the
decks at bow and stern were joined by bridges on which a
considerable number of marines could be brought into

Fig. 187.—Ship with one bank of oars.

action. Such ships, however, were chiefly employed as
transports for men and horses. For the men-of-war (νῆες
ταχεῖαι) such as were in use in the Peloponnesian War, a narrower beam was better in manœuvres, and they accordingly
held even fewer hoplites than the ships engaged at Salamis.
Being ten in number, the hoplites could effect little and
were regarded anyway as landlubbers (χερσαῖοι). The ship
itself was a mighty weapon in the hands of the rowers;
Size of the   with its powerful ram it was so manœuvred as
trireme.   to sink the enemy, or at least snap off his oars.
        For such manœuvres a trireme was necessari-
ly long and relatively narrow; they were therefore called
"long boats" (μακρὰ πλοῖα). The average dimensions may
be roughly guessed from the ruins of dock-yards (νεώσοικοι)
in the Piraeus. These have a width of over nineteen feet,

and a length varying from about one hundred to one hundred and twenty feet. Hence the width of a trireme is supposed to have been about fifteen feet, its greatest length about one hundred and twenty feet.

Besides being narrow, they had a low board and drew but little water, hardly three feet; hence operations could be carried on in very shoal water and far up a
The oars. stream. We actually hear of cavalry brought into action against a trireme in the water; and hoplites are known to have waded out from shore and boarded an enemy's trireme. The oars (κῶπαι), therefore, must have made a rather small angle with the water's surface; in close encounters they were sometimes snapped in pieces by a passing ship. Their exact length is unknown; neither can we tell how far apart were the oars in the same row. The rowers sat on benches arranged in three rows, each only slightly higher than the other (Fig. 188). It is a mistake to suppose that the trireme rose very high out of the water. Its light draft proves that the hold was not much more than seven feet deep, the distance from the water-line to

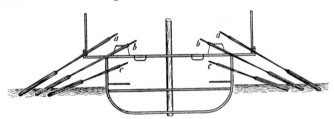

Fig. 188.—Section of a trireme.

the deck being between three and four feet. The men in the top row, called *thranītai* (θρανῖται), wielded, of course, the longest and heaviest oars, and received the highest pay.
The rowers. Those in the middle row were called *zygītai* (ζυγῖται), those in the lowest *thalamītai* (θαλαμῖται). The thalamītes (*c*) sat in the hold (*thalamos*) of the vessel, his bench being only a little above the water-line.

The thranītes (*a*) derived his name from the stool or seat (*thrānos*) that rested on the deck, or if a deck was wanting, on the platform (πάροδος) that surrounded the ship; he sat perpendicularly over the thalamītes. The zygītes (*b*) had his place on the level of the cross-beam (ζυγόν) which connected and strengthened the ship's sides. He was not directly under the thranītes, but probably a man's breadth farther in. Since the oars differed in length according to the row from which they projected—the longest from the topmost, the shortest from the lowest row—considerable practice was necessary in order to get an even stroke. The oar of the thranītes seems to have been a foot longer than that of the zygītes. The time was given by an officer called *keleustes* (κελευστής), who used a flute, a pipe, or his voice in a rhythmical call.

A trireme fully manned carried two hundred men. Of these, thirty were officers, marines, and sailors who attended to the rigging, the steering, and the raising and lowering of the mainmast. Official records which have been preserved make known the fact that there were on board one hundred and seventy oars—presumably sixty-two for the thranītai and fifty-four each for the zygītai and the thalamītai. This must include oars held in reserve against accident—perhaps a score—leaving one hundred and fifty for active service. But not all were in use at the same time, for we hear of companies or "watches" (λόχοι), into which the rowers were divided, doubtless to relieve each other on long voyages. It is said that the highest possible speed for a ship one hundred and twenty feet long can be fully attained by fifty oars, whence it is natural to assume that for long voyages there were three watches of fifty men each, especially since the officers next under the commander (ναύαρχος) were called "commanders of fifty" (πεντηκόνταρχοι). We may, therefore, conjecture that on ordinary occasions fifty rowers were at work (eighteen

Number of men in a trireme.

Watches.

θρανῖται, sixteen ζυγῖται, sixteen θαλαμῖται), while the remaining one hundred rested until their turn came.

It is impossible, from our scanty evidence, to measure the speed attained by a trireme. Modern estimates vary

Speed of a trireme.
greatly, from three and a half to fifteen miles an hour. With a fair wind the Greeks under Xenophon were able to sail from Cotyōra, on the Euxine, to Sinōpe, one hundred and fifty miles away, in a day and a night. The sails, which were square, aided somewhat the progress of the ship, for every trireme carried two masts; but when a fight was to take place near shore, as usually happened, the mainsail was often left on land. All sail was then taken in, and the

Fig. 189.—Going on board.

mainmast (ἱστὸς μέγας) was lowered and stowed in the hold along the keel (τρόπις). The foremast (ἱστὸς ἀκάτειος) carried a smaller sail, and was not lowered. In battle, therefore, the propelling of the ship devolved upon

Manœuvres in battle.
the rowers, who had to be trained by long practice to carry out the different manœuvres employed for running the enemy down. Here, too, considerable skill was required of the pilot (κυβερνήτης). In place of the modern rudder, an oar (πηδάλιον) projected at each side near the stern; the two were connected by a crosspiece held by the helmsman, and could easily be unshipped when not in use. The pilot had general command over the men in the stern, while another officer in the bow

(the πρῳρεύς) directed the men in the forward part of the ship.

The prow, with its sharp edge or "nose," readily suggests the head of an animal, and in Greek, accordingly, various terms are used of the parts of the prow which carry out this figure. Thus, on each side of the prow (πρῷρα) were huge "eyes," (ὀφθαλμοί, Fig. 190), some of which were actually hawse-holes, while others were purely decorative, as on Chinese boats. The prow also had "ears" (ἐπωτίδες) or catheads, beams extending forward obliquely, which served as a protection when another ship was rammed. Additional protection was

The prow with its ram.

FIG. 190.—Coin showing a ship.

furnished by wicker mats, hides, or cloths hanging over the sides. The ram itself (ἔμβολον) was a sharp beak or spur covered with iron, lying at the water-line or slightly below it. Both stem and stern rose high out of the water (Fig. 189), and the stern-post often ended in an ornamental figure, a swan's or a goose's head. Each ship had a name, sometimes chosen from mythology, sometimes selected with reference to the good omen a high-sounding name made for the future success of the vessel in war. Some names recently found on an inscription in the Piraeus have a very modern sound, such as the *Danaé* (Δανάη), the *Wonder* (Θέαμα), and the *Invincible* (Παγκράτεια), because this modern custom is one of many inheritances from the ancients.

At the beginning, as at Salamis, officers, marines, and rowers were Athenians. The marines and rowers were regularly taken from the class of Thētes. Later, rowers were also supplied from the metics, slaves, or mercenaries.

The two special state galleys, the *Paralos* and the *Salaminia*, were manned by citizens.

It is usual to say that the Greeks were timid sailors, and that discipline, though better than in the army, was not

Greek seamanship. perfect. On the other hand, there was some reason for the excessive caution of the Greek sailor in the fact that the trireme had such a low board, and might easily founder in a rough sea. It was sometimes necessary to strengthen the ship by passing ropes lengthwise round it on the outside. Hence, in long voyages the skipper kept as near shore as he could. The fleet bound for Sicily went first to Corcȳra, whence it could cross the stormy Adriatic at its narrowest stretch, and then it kept to the eastern coast of Italy until it reached Catana. That the Greeks, when on shipboard, had the true sailor's instincts of neatness and readiness, is attested by Xenophon, who speaks with admiration of the careful way in which ropes, yards, sails, and provisions were stowed, with a view to save space and to have them in readiness when sudden need arose. When not in use the trireme was hauled up on shore, or docks (νεώρια) and ship-houses (νεώσοικοι) were built for them in the principal seaports, as at the Piraeus.

Even in time of peace, therefore, there was abundant occupation in the military and naval service for all classes of citizens. In Athens five hundred men were necessary to guard the dockyards and arsenals, fifty kept watch at the Acropolis, which, however, was probably not otherwise fortified, and some sixteen hundred maintained order in the city and the country districts, particularly on the border; besides these, two thousand men served in garrisons throughout the various cities and islands belonging to the Athenian empire.

CHAPTER XVI

THE VARIOUS CALLINGS: CIVIC FUNCTIONS

WE must next glance briefly at the Athenian constitution, in so far as its operation affected the daily life of the

The private citizen in politics.
citizen. And here again the state, made thoroughly democratic by political leaders since Pericles came to the front, opened her offices to the poorest citizen and paid him for the services he rendered in the courts, in the popular assembly, and in the Council.

All citizens over thirty years old in good standing were eligible to the Council of Five Hundred, or *Boulé* (βουλή),

Membership in the Council.
the highest legislative body in Athens. The members were elected annually by lot, fifty from each of the ten tribes (φυλαί); the wards or demes in each tribe were represented in this body of fifty according to the number of demesmen (δημόται) each contained. Since the lot might fall on an unsuitable candidate, it was provided that every man so chosen should submit to a public examination (δοκιμασία) before the out-

going Council. If he was approved, he took the oath of office and entered upon his duties on

FIG. 191.—Obol and half-obol.

the 14th of the month Skirophorion (about the 1st of July), and held office for one year. Each member (βουλευτής) received five obols—about fifteen cents—daily, was exempt from military service, and enjoyed the right of a front seat (προεδρία, page 63) in the theatre.

206

Such a body was obviously too large for the transaction of ordinary routine business. To meet this difficulty, the contingent from each tribe served in turn as a special committee, under the name of *prytanes* (πρυτάνεις), **The prytanes.** for handling ordinary matters. The year was thus divided into ten parts, each called a *prytaneia* (πρυτανεία), and the order in which the tribes served in this capacity was determined by lot at the beginning of their year of office. The prytanes had their office in a building called the Tholos (θόλος), a round structure in the agora near the Council-chamber (βουλευτήριον; see page 42). There they took their meals, and offered sacrifice for the prosperity of the state. Besides receiving reports of officials, giving audience to embassies, and exercising a general police supervision over the city, they prepared the "order of the day," or "docket" (πρόγραμμα), for the next meeting of the Council or the popular assembly. During their prytany, their pay was increased to six obols (one drachma) a day, and from the beginning of the fourth century each prytany received a vote of thanks from the Council and the popular assembly. They chose by lot a chairman (ἐπιστάτης) to serve for one day and one night only, in order that he might not have opportunity to gain undue influence. It was his duty to preside at the meet-**The president.** ing of the whole Council or of the assembly, and to have in his keeping the state seal and the keys of the temples in which the public funds and documents were deposited. Thus the humblest citizen might, for at least one day in his life, exercise important responsibility. The courage of Socrates, when chosen to be chairman, in refusing to put to the vote an unconstitutional motion which called for the summary execution of the generals who fought at Arginūsae, has often been told.

The entire Council met daily in their chamber (βουλευτήριον), unless special circumstances called them elsewhere. These sessions were as a rule open to the public, but the

members were separated from the spectators by a railing
(δρύφακτοι), and each member had his own seat, distinguished by some letter of the alphabet. There
The Council-chamber. was a platform (βῆμα) in front, which every
speaker (ῥήτωρ) mounted when addressing the
Council. In the Council-chamber were statues of the gods
"who gave good counsel," Zeus Boulaios and Athēna Bou-
laia, with an altar, at which prayer was offered at the beginning of the session. A clerk (γραμματεύς), chosen during

Fig. 192.—A decree of the Council and the popular assembly.

each prytany, recorded the decrees (ψηφίσματα) of the Council. At the end of the official year every member gave an
account (εὔθυνα) of his office.

It was, however, in the popular assembly or *ecclesia*
(ἐκκλησία) that the will of the sovereign people found its
chief expression. Theoretically all Athenians
The popular assembly. over eighteen years of age might attend its
meetings; but as a matter of fact, young men
were prevented from doing so by military service until they
were twenty; and even for some time afterward, the fear of
seeming immodest before their elders kept them for a while

from active participation in debate (δημηγορεῖν). The attendance of six thousand, or about one fifth of the male citizens, was required to transact certain kinds of business. Most of those who came belonged to the city or its immediate environs; naturally, the country farmers had little time or inclination to travel to town, so that they, though greatly surpassing the townspeople in number, were insufficiently represented. It was therefore the artisans, tradesmen, and seamen of Athens and the Piraeus, with such rich citizens as possessed houses in town, who composed the assembly.

In the fifth century but one meeting of the assembly took place in each prytany, or ten in a year. In the fourth century there were four meetings, of which **Deliberative proceedings.** one occurred on a fixed day, and was deemed more important than the others (κυρία ἐκκλησία). At this meeting the election of officers was confirmed by popular vote, taken by a show of hands (ἐπιχειροτονία), and reports on the condition and security of the state, the supply of grain, and such matters, were received. Here, too, were heard public impeachments (εἰσαγγελίαι) of magistrates or private citizens, and the decisions of the archon respecting inheritance (cf. page 88), rendered since the last meeting. Once a year a preliminary vote was taken on the question of ostracizing some citizen. Extraordinary circumstances might require a special session (σύγκλητος ἐκκλησία).

The sessions of the ecclesia were ordinarily held on the hill outside the town called the Pnyx; sometimes in the agora or the Dionysiac theatre. Each member **Voting.** received on his arrival a ticket (σύμβολον), which he later presented to the proper officials, and then received his fee, amounting to an obol at first, but in the fourth century increased to three, later to nine obols. The business began early in the forenoon with a purificatory sacrifice, the blood of a pig being sprinkled round the place of assembly;

14

then followed prayers and imprecations against such speakers as might try to deceive the people in their harangues. The prytanes then stated the order of business previously decided on by the Council (page 207); any matter lying outside this order (προβούλευμα) was excluded. The voting on

FIG. 193.—The platform (*bema*) on the Pnyx.

these matters was by show of hands (χειροτονία), and therefore public; but secret voting, by ballots cast in urns, was resorted to in cases of ostracism, conferring citizenship, and other matters affecting a single individual. The decrees recommended by the Council and passed by the ecclesia were inscribed on stone or bronze and set up in conspicuous places (Fig. 192).

The chairman (ἐπιστάτης) adjourned the meeting, sometimes to the following day, if matters of business were left **Adjournment.** unfinished. This happened immediately whenever "signs from heaven" (διοσημίαι), such as lightning, earthquake, an eclipse, or even a drop of rain, seemed to indicate the displeasure of the gods.

Although both the Council and the assembly acted on certain occasions in a judicial capacity, their function was

chiefly legislative. The trial of cases at law was left mostly
to the courts (δικαστήρια). In these a large body of citizens,

The courts of law. particularly the older men, not only found
paid employment, but also indulged that love
of contest and rivalry of debate which so strikingly marked the Athenians. For they sat as jurors or
dicasts (δικασταί) to hear and decide cases pleaded before
them, and they followed with interest, if not with favour, the
arguments on both sides. From each tribe (φυλή) about
six hundred men, all over thirty years of age, were chosen
by lot from those who had announced their desire to serve
as dicasts. They formed a body, normally six thousand in
number, of whom one thousand acted as substitutes, ready
to be called on for judicial service. Each person on whom
the lot to act as dicast fell was assigned to one of the ten
divisions or courts (δικαστήρια) into which the whole number was divided; every tribe had an equal number of its
members in each court, or as nearly equal as it was possible
to arrange. The court-room to which a man was assigned
was designated by a letter (A to K); and every man carried
a "pass" in the shape of a small boxwood tablet (πινάκιον
πύξινον), on which was inscribed his name and the letter of
the section to which he belonged. Further, to make sure
that the dicast entered the court-room to which he belonged, he was given a painted staff (βακτηρία), the colour
of which corresponded to the colour of the paint at the
door of each dicastery.

There was no limit set to the term of service as dicast,
and a citizen often continued in this office until cut off by

The dicasts. sickness or death. Every year, however, he re-
newed the oath in which he swore to render a
verdict according to the laws, or, in cases where no existing
law seemed applicable, according to his honest judgment,
without fear or partiality, nor yet in enmity against any
party to a suit; to hear both sides with equal attention, to
refuse bribes, and to uphold the democratic constitution.

The oath was sworn in the names of Zeus, Poseidon or Apollo, and Demēter.

If, now, a man had a private grievance against another, he went to the magistrate who had jurisdiction in such a case as his, and handed in a written complaint (ἔγκλημα). If it was accepted, the magistrate appointed a day for the preliminary hearing (ἀνάκρισις). The plaintiff (ὁ διώκων), in the presence of at least two witnesses (κλητῆρες), then sought out the accused (ὁ φεύγων), and summoned him to appear at the appointed time to answer the complaint. This summons was called the *klēsis* (κλῆσις, πρόκλησις). At the hearing each party pre-

Preliminary hearings.

Fig. 194.—Crown of gold awarded for public services.

sented in person his own side of the question, citing witnesses (μάρτυρες), laws and decrees, private documents, and other testimony bearing on his case. The witnesses must be adult men, either citizens or met-ics. Slaves were allowed to appear as witnesses only in cases of murder; in all others their evidence was extorted on the rack. This kind of testimony, as in the Middle Ages, was regarded as especially trustworthy, and a man under complaint frequently offered his own slaves to be tortured (βασανίζειν) to prove his innocence. He might not, however, testify in his own case. On the conclusion of the hearing, all the documents and evidence in writing were put into an urn (ἐχῖνος) to await the trial (δίκη, ἀγών).

The trial. At the time arranged for the trial, which might take place on any day excepting holidays and "unlucky days" (ἡμέραι ἀποφράδες), both parties, with their witnesses, presented themselves before the court, in which sat usually five hundred and one dicasts, presided over by the magistrate before whom the preliminary hearing (ἀνάκρισις) had taken place. In very important cases two or more dicasteries sat in joint session, making one thousand and one or fifteen hundred and one dicasts in all. The odd number was maintained to prevent a tie vote; the number of dicasts was never less than two hundred and one. The court-rooms were near the agora; the oldest, called the Heliaia (ἡλιαία), gave its name to the whole judicial system, and the dicasts were often called *heliasts* (ἡλιασταί). They sat on wooden benches separated by a railing (δρύφακτοι) from the spectators, who always thronged to the trial when the participants were well-known citizens or the case affected public interests. Besides the platform (βῆμα) for the presiding magistrate, there was also one for the speakers and the witnesses.

The law required every man to plead his own case, whether as plaintiff or defendant. In the latter part of the fifth century, however, it became the custom for inexperienced speakers to hire a professional writer of speeches (λογογράφος) to compose his speech, which he then committed to memory and delivered as best he could. The time allowed each speech was limited by the water-clock (κλεψύδρα), the flow of which was stopped when the witnesses were cited. The proceedings began with prayer to the gods, after which the clerk (γραμματεύς) read the complaint (ἔγκλημα) and denial (ἀντωμοσία) of the contending parties, who were then allowed by the presiding magistrate to begin their speeches. The complainant presented his side first, frequently interrupting his speech by citing the witnesses whose testimony had been given at the preliminary hearing. These simply mounted the platform at the bidding of the speaker or the court-crier (κῆρυξ), listened to the reading of their evidence by the clerk, and acknowledged it as their own. There was no cross-examination of witnesses. Following the complainant came the defend-

Forensic speeches.

Witnesses.

ant, who in like manner appealed to his witnesses from time to time in the course of his speech.

Late in the fifth century, those persons who felt doubt about their ability to present the case with justice to themselves were allowed to bring in friends to their support; but the case must always be presented first, if only briefly, by the party concerned. By the middle of the fourth century such advocates (συνήγοροι) were very common, though they spoke with the special consent of the court, and were understood not to receive any pay for their aid. It is to the advocate, rather than to the speech-writer, that the modern lawyer bears most resemblance.

Advocates.

After the speeches were over the herald bade the dicasts proceed to a vote, which they cast immediately and on the spot, without discussion among themselves. Mussel-shells were used as ballots (ψῆφοι) in the fifth century. The voter cast his ballot into one of two earthenware vessels (called variously κάδοι, or κάδισκοι, or again ὑδρίαι); one urn stood for acquittal, the other for condemnation. Just how secrecy was maintained by this method we do not know; at any rate, it proved unsatisfactory, for another mode was adopted for most cases in the fourth century. The dicast received two round bronze ballots; one was solid, the other had a hole bored through the centre. The solid ballot (πλήρης ψῆφος) was for acquittal, the bored (τετρυπημένη ψῆφος) for condemnation. The voter, holding this ballot so that the curious might not see whether the centre was solid or pierced, now approached the urns, of which again there were two—one of bronze, the other of wood. Into the bronze urn he cast the ballot which he wished to have counted, and discarded the other by throwing it into the wooden urn. The bronze urn, containing as it did the votes that really affected the defendant, was called the "deciding urn" (κύριος κάδισκος); the other, into which the votes not to be counted were deposited, was called "the urn

Verdict.

The ballots.

without validity" (ἄκυρος κάδισκος). After the votes had been counted, the presiding magistrate announced the result.

When his duties for the day were over, the di-cast

Pay for service in the courts.

Fig. 195.—Dicast's ticket (σύμβολον).

presented a ticket or check (σύμβολον), which he had received when he entered the court, to the disbursing officers of the treasury, and got his pay. This amounted to two obols in Pericles's time, but was increased to three by Cleon.

CHAPTER XVII

THE VARIOUS CALLINGS: AGRICULTURE AND GRAZING

WHILE so many Athenians were engaged in war or in politics, the great majority were occupied in more produc-

The productive occupations. tive pursuits to get a livelihood; and these, however they may have been regarded by philosophers and aristocrats, were recognized by the more practical thinkers as forming the main support of the state, and representing in their mode of life and ways of thinking the better and more conservative interests of the democracy. This applied particularly to the rural classes, the men engaged in agriculture and grazing. Observers as widely different as Socrates, the sage, and Aristophanes, the comic poet, united in commendation of agricultural pursuits, since from them the sustenance and support of the community were derived, and the preservation of healthy bodies and of sound, if old-fashioned, ideas was assured. Although the army, the courts, the sailors of the Piraeus, and the artisans in the ecclesia take up so conspicuous a position in Attic history, it must not be forgotten that the bulk of the population of Attica were farmers or herdsmen, who had little time to travel to town and join with regularity in political movements, and did so only when their interests as a class were threatened.

Rural pursuits. The landed proprietors held the highest position socially among all classes who worked for a living. They formed, of course, the oldest element in the state, and to a great extent retained their original political, as well as social, preeminence.

Among them were a few rich men who took pleasure in managing their estates themselves, planning the crops, and joining their overseers and slaves in actual labour now and then. These exceptional persons excited wonder, as did Cyrus, when he showed the Spartan admiral Lysander his gardens at Sardis. After looking at the many kinds of trees and flowers, and seeing how carefully they were planted, and how regularly and artistically the paths were

Cyrus in the country. laid out, Lysander was overcome with admiration. " I congratulate you, Cyrus," he said, " on the man who devised all this for you." " Why," said Cyrus, " I made all the measurements and designs myself, and I planted some of the trees myself." At which Lysander said, as he looked at Cyrus's handsome clothes and the ornaments he wore : " What ! You really mean that you planted these with your own hands ? " And Cyrus answered : " Yes ; when I am in ordinary health, I never dine before taking active exercise, either in military drill or in farming."

In Attica the soil was thin and dry, yet favourable to the raising of some crops. Here, and elsewhere in Greece,

Agriculture. systematic irrigation (ἄρδειν) was intelligently practised in classical times to insure enough water, while drainage (ὀχετεύ- ειν) recovered swampy and sub- merged places for tilling. The Attic plain was well watered with canals and ditches (αὐλῶ- νες, ὀχετοί) dug from the main streams of the Cephīsus and

Irrigation, drainage, and terracing. the Ilissus. This was necessary for certain kinds of grain ; and the region extend-

FIG. 196.—Boy with pet deer.

ing from the Lycēum to the Academy was a garden of figs and olives. On the hillsides care was taken that the fer-

tile soil might not be washed away when the melting snow
sent down fierce torrents in February and March. This
was prevented by terraces, especially necessary in the culture of the vine.

Although many religious superstitions governed the
farmer in his work, nevertheless the experience of centuries
had brought down many practical hints and
helps in cultivating. The value of fertilizers
was understood, as was also the need of allow-
ing land to recover its fertility by lying fallow (νειός) for a
season or more.

Agricultural methods.

Ploughing was done at three seasons—spring, summer,
and autumn. The plough (ἄροτρον) was originally a crooked
or forked tree trunk; later it was made of separate parts fitting together and fastened either
by thongs or by pegs which nailed them together. There
was, first, the beam or stock (ἔλυμα), the end of which was
sharpened and covered with iron to form the ploughshare

The plough.

FIG. 197.—Ploughing and sowing.

(ὔννις); or sometimes a separate piece was attached to
the beam for this purpose.
A handle (ἐχέτλη) rose from
the beam at the back, and
a pole (ἱστοβοεύς) extended
from it in front; at the end
of this the yoke (ζυγόν) was
attached by means of a ring (κορώνη). The plough was
drawn by oxen and mules; horses were probably never used
for this work.

The autumn and the early spring were the times for
sowing grain and the more substantial crops (καρπός) for
which, as Plato says, the intelligent farmer is
content to wait seven months. In the sum-
mer were sown lentils, peas, beans, and other garden vegetables. Xenophon gives a picture of the farmer ploughing
(ζευγηλατεῖν) and sowing (σπείρειν), in a lonely spot infested

Sowing.

by robbers, in the interesting account of a pantomime which he witnessed in Paphlagonia.

Hay. It does not appear that hay was especially cultivated and harvested, though of course a certain amount of dried fodder was necessary when animals were housed for the winter. Any product suitable for use as green fodder was called *chilos* or *chortos* (χιλός or χόρτος). This, when dried, was used like hay, under the name of *karphé* (κάρφη or simply χιλός). Grass-land and meadows were scarce in Greece, and were usually given over to flocks and herds in summer-time.

Fig. 198.
Shepherd.

Harvesting. The harvest-time was the occasion for much sport and frolic in the fields among the reapers, who kept up ancient practices, designed to appease the "corn spirit," which had come down from most primitive times, and which allowed all kinds of practical jokes, especially at the expense of an unlucky passer-by. The reaper used a semicircular sickle (called δρεπάνη) and after the grain had been cut down it was bound together carefully in sheaves. One sheaf was left " for luck," dedicated to the spirit of the grain; the rest were gathered into carts or on the backs of the reap-

Threshing. ers, and carried to the threshing-floor (ἀλωή), a circular space paved with small cobble-stones. There the grain was spread out evenly a little at a time, and over it horses, mules, or oxen were driven until their hoofs had beaten out the kernels from the chaff and stalks (καλά-μαι). Whether flails were ever used is a question. After a thorough tossing and winnowing, done with the *liknon* (λίκνον), or cradle, a broad wicker basket which received the grain after threshing, and in which it was tossed in the air so that the wind carried off the chaff, the clean grain was poured into earthen jars (πίθοι, σιπύαι, page 133) for storing.

In the country grain was ground into flour only as
needed. Small quantities could be pounded in stone mor-
tars by female slaves. For larger amounts
Mills for grinding. mills (μύλαι) turned by male or female slaves
or by animals were required. The mill had a
flat, immovable lower millstone (μύλη) with a hard, rough
surface. On it the upper millstone (ὄνος ἀλέτης) revolved
on an iron pivot by means of a long handle; the upper stone
had a hole in the centre into which the grain was poured.
In the cities there were milling establishments (μυλῶνες)
which ground the grain brought from the interior or elsewhere on a large scale. Flour was called *aleura* (ἄλευρα) or
alphita (ἄλφιτα), according as it was made from wheat or
from barley.

In Attica grain formed one of the least conspicuous
products, and after the ruin wrought to the fields by the
Spartan invasions of the Peloponnesian War,
The products of Attica. the small farmers of Attica no longer tried to
compete with the rich grain-fields on the Black
Sea. The importation of grain, therefore, became essential to the welfare of the state, which encouraged it by
laws restraining Athenian citizens and metics from shipping it elsewhere, and laying severe penalties on all who
tried to " corner " the grain market. Whoever bought
more than fifty *phormoi* (φορμοί), or about seventy-five
bushels, of grain at a single time was liable to capital
punishment. When the grain supply from the East was
cut off by Lysander's fleet in 405 B. C., Athens and Attica
could no longer hold out, and the Peloponnesian War came
to a disastrous close.

The soil of Attica, however, was well adapted to the
cultivation of olives, figs, and grapes. Oil, figs, and wine
were therefore abundantly produced, the olives and figs
being celebrated the world over. In the cultivation of
vines and olives it was usual to dig circular trenches (γῦροι)
round each trunk or stalk to insure sufficient moisture.

The vines were propped by pointed stakes (χάρακες), though sometimes allowed also to climb on trees. Red wine was

Vineyards. produced from grapes grown on the hillsides, white wine was produced in the plains. The grapes were pressed or trodden (πατεῖν) with the bare feet in large vats (ληνοί), from which the wine flowed out into a smaller vessel, usually an amphora (page 134). The vintage, like the harvest, was attended with many old-fashioned customs of a religious nature, all in honour of Dionȳsus Lenaios, " god of the wine-press." The treaders chanted a song as they worked together in the open fields.

Olive-oil was used for a great variety of purposes: in the preparation of ointments; in the " dressing " of linen

Olive-oil. after it came from the loom; in lighting; and in cooking and eating (page 150). Consequently, the oil (ἔλαιον) was of more importance than the fruit (ἐλάα) itself, though this, too, was a regular article of diet. Olives were picked only when ripe, and put up in brine or dried. Dried olives were shipped and sold in skins (ἀσκοί). Figs were dried on crates or boards set out in the sun and wind, and pressed into cakes, as they are to-day. Grapes, in the same way, were made into raisins or currants, a name which still carries the remembrance of their place of origin—Corinth.

All growing things were regarded as being under the protection of the divinities of nature, Dionȳsus, Demēter,

Sacred olive-trees. and many lesser gods. But the olive in particular was the object of religious veneration, and like the owl (page 24) was inseparably connected with Athēna, the special protectress of Attica and Athens. An olive branch frequently appears beside the owl on Athenian coins (Fig. 199). A large number of trees in the Attic plain, called *moriai* (μορίαι), were specially consecrated to her, and any man who cut down, or even removed, the stump of one of these was sentenced to death by the Areopagus. The moriai were owned by the state, which appointed wardens or supervisors to attend to their preservation; they were responsible to the Areopagus. The state let out the tending and cultivation of these trees to

FIG. 199.—Attic decadrachma.

the highest bidder, who then had the disposition and sale of the product in his own hands.

Flowers, too, were universally cultivated in the country. However reticent in their literature the Greeks of the clas-
Cultivated flowers. sical period may be regarding their love of nature, their acts show plainly that they had open eyes for all she had to give. The lily, crocus, hyacinth, violet, and rose are familiar friends in Homer. The extraordinary vogue of wreaths (στέφανοι) for all festive occasions made horticulture a necessity; when nothing better could be obtained, even dry grass was plaited into chaplets. The favourite flowers raised in gardens (κῆποι) were those just mentioned; but many, like the poppy, grew wild in the fields. The garden
Gardens. beds were commonly edged with borders of parsley and rue. In crowded cities house gardens were hardly known until late in the fourth century; but plants were sometimes raised in pots (ὄστρακα, cf. Fig. 94), especially for the festival of Adōnis. Groves and enclosures where trees, flowers, and grass grew made the suburbs attractive places for an afternoon stroll (περίπατος).

The state appointed officers to take charge of the for-

ests, but these paid more attention to boundaries and highways than to forestry in a scientific sense. As early as the
fourth century, Attica was becoming a waste,
The forests. because the state and the people
failed to realize the importance of preserving
the once rich woodlands of Parnes, Pentelicus,
and Hymettus (cf. page 9). The trees were cut
down wastefully by lumbermen (ὑλοτόμοι), who
found their profit in the great demand for timber (ξύλα) for house and ship build-
Uses of wood. ing, furniture, and fuel. Charcoal-
burners were continually busy on Mount Parnes,

FIG. 200.
Ancient cow-
bell.

especially in the deme of Acharnae; from here they carried their baskets of coals into the city, where the cry of
" Buy coal " (ἄνθρακας πρίω) rose among the other noises of
the street. In the country wood (φρύγανα) was burned more
often than charcoal; and Socrates mentions, as one of the
advantages of country over town life, the greater abundance
of fuel for fires in the winter-time. On the march, too,
wood was gathered wherever it could be found, and split-
ting wood was one of the ordinary duties of soldiers in camp.

Perhaps most harm was done to the forests by shepherds and goatherds who deliberately burned down trees
in order to gain more pasture-land. No fea-
Grazing. ture of country life is more prominent in Greek
literature than the tending of herds (νομαί) of sheep, goats,
and cows. All these are embraced in the term " possessions,"
ktēnē (κτήνη), so common in the *Anabasis*, since they were the
chief property of man in the primitive, nomadic state. (The
larger animals, like oxen and mules, which could be used
for drawing loads, were called in general ζεύγη, or ὑποζύγια;
the smaller kinds, sheep and goats, were πρό-
Animals in βατα, though πρόβατα is also used of sheep only;
pasture. all, when out in pasture, were βοσκήματα.) From
March until September the herds wandered over the higher
mountain slopes, tended by a few lonely shepherds (νομεῖς,

βουκόλοι) and their dogs. In winter they were driven back
to the folds and stalls in the plains. Perhaps sheep were
the most conspicuous among these animals; their milk,
as well as their flesh and fleeces, was constantly required,
and great numbers were consumed in sacrifice. Hogs were
kept in droves in the open, not confined in a sty. They
were to be seen mostly in places like Arcadia, where the

FIG. 201.—The mountains of Peloponnēsus, seen from Nauplia.

oaks supplied abundant acorns for their food. Horses
were raised in droves only where the plains were extensive,
as in Thessaly, Argos, Aetolia, and Acarnania. As draft-
animals (ὑποζύγια), mules were preferred to horses, and the
sure-footed ass was indispensable in the mountain districts.
Bees. Another feature of hill life was the keeping of bees (μέλιτται), a creature whose activity
the Greeks viewed with almost religious awe. They were
kept in hives (σμήνη). Attica was as famous for the honey
of Hymettus and Brilessus as for her figs and oil. Xeno-

phon mentions a honey in Colchis which poisoned and in-
toxicated his men.

Other features of country life were of course the domestic animals, more abundant there than in the cities. Among

Domestic fowl.
domestic fowl, geese
were the favourites,
especially in Athens,
where, like other animals, they
were kept in the court (page 27);
so, too, were cranes, quail, and
doves kept mostly as pets (Fig.
202), though also eaten. Chickens were introduced from the
Orient into Greece in the sixth
century. The recollection of their
origin survived in the name still
given the cock (ἀλεκτρυών) in the
fifth century, which was common-

Fig. 202.—Woman with crane.

ly "the Persian bird" (ὁ Περσικὸς ὄρνις). Pheasants and
peacocks were imported as a great curiosity just before
the Peloponnesian War.

Dogs were exceedingly common, both in town and in
country. Some of their best-known traits, such as barking

Fig. 203. Woman with pet animal (cat ?).

at strangers and retreating when faced, madness, and the
like, are frequently referred to by Xenophon, but it is in

15

Homer, especially in the *Odyssey*, that we get the best picture of the dog as faithful guardian of master and house.

Dogs.   In the house, they lay at their master's feet while he ate, watching a chance to seize the crumbs that fell from the table. They were mostly of the fiercer breeds, and were indispensable in hunting (page 99). Hence they bore such names as Dromas, and Argos, "the fleet," or Harpalos, "quick at catching the scent." Cats were not a domestic animal in Greece, though known to the Greeks as an Egyptian animal. Tame weasels and martens took their place in protecting the storeroom from mice.

CHAPTER XVIII

THE VARIOUS CALLINGS: MANUFACTURES AND TRADES

IN most families, if not in all, a certain amount of manufacture formed part of the household duties. Thus, **Manufacturing.** many kinds of food were cooked at home, though they might also be procured ready to eat from regular dealers in the market. And more than this, the wife still plied her spinning (Fig. 98), or worked at the loom, as in the days of Homer, or superintended the slaves while they prepared the wool for spinning—washing, beating, pulling, and combing it.

Manufacture on a large scale, however, grew up in Athens and in other coast cities in the fifth century, increasing in the case of Athens the internal wealth which her political preeminence had founded. The various artisans (δημιουργοί) were not united in guilds or corporations until later times; but a son generally learned and followed his father's trade, and those who were

FIG. 204.—Workman (baker ?).

engaged in the same industry occupied the same quarter of the city, thus giving a semblance of organization for mutual protection. Hence a street might be designated as the "street of the sculptors," or the "street of the box-makers," and the like (cf. page 15). The hereditary sys-

tem certainly tended to increase the efficiency of the work
done.   Athenian citizens were not taxed or required to pay
any license fee for the trade in which
they were engaged ; but metics had to
pay such a tax, though not otherwise restricted.   Most metics plied their business in the Piraeus, where the number
of trades was extraordinary, the division of labour in some cases being
minute.

Among the producers of food we notice the millers (μυλωθροί).   These got

Fig. 205.—Making bread.

their grain—
wheat, barley,
spelt—from
jobbers (σιτο-
πῶλαι), who
bought it
from farmers of the interior, or
more often from the importers
(ἔμποροι), whose ships
had carried it from
Pontus.   The mill-houses (μυλῶνες) were supplied with the mills
(μύλαι) before described (page 220),
and these were turned by horses,
mules, oxen, or slaves; the last,
however, were set to their task
only as a punishment for extreme
misbehaviour.

Millers.

Fig. 206.—Baker's moulds.

The millers sold to the bakers
(ἀρτοκόποι), whose houses were furnished with large earthen
ovens (κρίβανοι) ; in these they baked loaves
(ἄρτοι) of a size and weight fixed by the market commissioners, besides barley-cakes (μᾶζαι) and different kinds of sweet cakes.   The baker did not always sell

Bakers.

directly to the consumer, but had his wares dispensed in the streets or the market by bread-sellers (ἀρτοπῶλαι).

The fullers and dyers played an important part in the making and preservation of clothing. Not only did they

Dyers and fullers.

wash and dye (πλύνειν) both the fleeces and the finished cloth (whence they were called πλυνεῖς and κναφεῖς), but they also attended to the cutting of the cloth into shapes suitable for different garments. In the large cities they had establishments with numerous hands, male and female, freemen and slaves. Such tailoring establishments rendered much of the domestic cutting, fitting, and sewing for the family wardrobe unnecessary, at least for the rich. The weaving of linen goods was their work exclusively, this being never done at home, where wool alone was the material. Some fac-

Cloth factories.

tories made only one kind of garment. Thus, one was devoted to the manufacture of the chlamys, another made women's shawls, while the Megarians were famous for the exōmis (page 161).

FIG. 207.—Loom.

Here, too, women's nets and other head coverings were made; but men's hats were

Hat makers.

the province of the felt manufacturers (πιλοποιοί), who produced travelling-hats (πέτασοι) and workmen's caps (κυναῖ, page 166).

The tanners (βύρσεις or βυρσοδέψαι) usually confined themselves solely to dressing the leather, but sometimes

Leather manufacturers.

they added shoemaking to their business. Their yards had to be placed outside the city, on account of the bad smell caused in the processes of tanning and dressing. The shoemakers (σκυτοτόμοι) were numerous in the neighbourhood of the market.

Personal ornaments, as we saw (page 167), were confined to articles of silver, gold, and bronze. The wearing
of precious stones was limited in classical
Jewellers. times, and the pearl-fisheries of the Aegēan,
for example, assumed no importance until later. However,
gems cut as intaglios or as cameos were used in signet-

Fig. 208.—A shoemaker's shop.

rings, earrings, and necklaces ; the principal stones were
agate, amethyst, chalcedony, and carnelian, and specimens
in European museums to-day still testify to the wonderful
skill and taste of the artists who carved them. More common than these were gold and silver ornaments. Gold was
brought from the East and from Thrace, and fashioned by
goldsmiths (χρυσοχόοι) into small objects for personal wear.
Silver was more plentiful than gold, though its value relative to gold was much greater than it is to-day. The silver-mines (μέταλλα) at Laurium (page 10) were productive
throughout the fifth century, and jewellers were able to use
silver not only for personal ornaments, but also for vases,
large mirrors, lamp-stands, and similar articles.

House-building, under the general supervision of a
master builder (οἰκοδόμος), called for the labour of workmen

engaged in many different occupations. There were first
the quarrymen (λιθοτόμοι), who cut stone and marble in the
quarries of Attica, Argolis, Sicily, and elsewhere.
Builders and From the quarries (λατομίαι) derricks (μηχα-
masons.   ναὶ λιθαγωγοί) lifted the blocks into the carts
in which they were transported to the city. After being
shaped and polished by stone-cutters (λιθοξόοι), the blocks
were set in place by masons (λιθολόγοι), who also used sun-
dried bricks or plinths of earth for house walls. The timber, supplied by lumbermen (ὑλοτόμοι) from the woods of
Attica and Euboea, was then treated by the carpenters (τέκτονες), who made the frames, upper floors, doors, sills, roof-
beams, and shelves. The roofers then put on the tiles
(κεραμίδες). When a public building was to be erected, an

Fig. 209.—At the forge.

architect (ἀρχιτέκτων) was engaged to draw plans and make
contracts for the building of the whole structure.
Furniture   As regards the manufacture of household
and cabinet- furniture, the division of labour was again car-
makers.   ried out to a minute degree. Thus, there were
door-makers (θυροποιοί), whose specialty was the construction
of handsome doors and gates, plated with bronze and other

metals, which were required in the temples and other large buildings. For beds there were the κλινοποιοί; for chairs, the θρονοποιοί; for chests, the κιβωτοποιοί; and the round legs of beds, chairs, and tables were the work of the turners (τορνευταί). Workers in iron and bronze (χαλκεῖs) produced the most varied articles of all, ranging from hairpins and mirrors to plates of metal covering walls, doors, or furniture. Among the most noted iron-workers in antiquity were the Chalybes, a non-Grecian people.

The needs of housekeeping were met by the extensive pottery trade for which Athens was famous. From an early time the potters (κεραμεῖs) inhabited the portion of the city to the northwest, near the Colōnos Agoraios, to which they gave its name, the Cerameicus (page 9). Attica had clay-pits, especially at Cape Colias (page 3), yielding material which was excellent for its strength and the facility with which it absorbed colour.

Potters.

FIG. 210.—Interior of a pottery furnace.

Almost every kind of vessel made by the Greek potter has fortunately come down to us in numerous specimens, ranging from the rough, hand-made crockery of the most ancient period, like that found near Troy, to the splendid urns turned on the potter's wheel and covered with elaborate paintings which preserve the fame of Attic and Corinthian artists, being stamped with their names or trade-marks. Among the potters some devoted themselves to the larger vessels, like the amphora and the chytra (page 134), while others made smaller pitchers, such as the lekythos, the aryballos, the wine pitcher (page 137), and the like. Other workers in clay produced lamps, modelled reliefs, made small images especially for household worship, and dolls (κόραι). The last were often made of wax instead of clay.

To complete the picture of wide and varied industry, we must add the makers of arms and armour: the manufacturers of shields, spears, bows, knives, helmets, and breast-plates (ἀσπιδοποιοί, λογχοποιοί,

Other manufacturers.

τοξοποιοί, μαχαιροποιοί, κρανοποιοί, θωρακοποιοί); and wagon makers (ἁρματοποιοί, διφροποιοί, ζυγοποιοί). Thus we see that the large cities were centres of active manufacturing concerns which, in the beauty and adaptability of their products, could well compete with their modern successors. The growth of factories was favoured by the large number of slaves imported into these cities, who worked under an overseer in the workshop (ἐργαστήριον),

Fɪɢ. 211.
Making a helmet
(κρανοποιός).

attached as a rule to the owner's house. The orator Lysias, who was a metic, inherited from his father an armour manufactory, which he carried on with his brother Polemarchus, employing one hundred and twenty slaves.

As regards the condition of the working classes, we see that the citizens who were day labourers (Thētes, τὸ θητικόν)

Occupations of the poorer classes.

resembled closely the slave class, at least in the estimation of others who were well-to-do. Their pay was very small—highest perhaps in the country, at the time when they were needed in the harvest-field or at the vintage. In town these people were employed as porters, packers in the manufactories—pottery was packed in straw, as with us—waiters at banquets. On the sea they served as common sailors; fishermen and herdsmen also belonged to their class.

Social position of artisans.

The class of artisans (δημιουργοί) comprised callings which among us are regarded as the most dignified professions. Wherever one of these vocations was in disrepute, the cause is found in the fact that the person concerned took money for his services, and was to that extent not independent of others. Even the great artists, painters, and sculptors fell under public contempt

Fig. 212.—A vase-painter's studio.

simply because they earned money. For the same reason, persons belonging to the more conservative element in politics characterized as greed the eagerness of the dicast for

Fig. 213.—Painting a cylix.

his daily stipend (page 215). A few artists, like Phidias, are said to have enjoyed the friendship of eminent men of aristocratic birth; but most of these stories of intimacy are later exaggerations which have not taken into account the conditions of ancient industrial life. In like manner schoolmasters, teachers of music and gymnastic, sophists, and even physicians were not highly regarded. Poets, however, enjoyed from time immemorial distinction in society, in spite of the fact that they made themselves rich by writing odes for princes or communities who paid them well for their flattery. Actors, as a class, were not disdained; they stood too close to the popular religion and its celebration in the lyric and dramatic performances. Opinion about them varied according to the talents and the personal character of the individual. Professional athletes, who came into prominence even before the Persian Wars, were petted and extolled by most people. Thinking men, however, like the poets Xenophanes and Euripides, were disposed to protest against the worship paid to a class who were often brutal, avaricious, and gluttonous, and it is said that Alexander did not regard them as good soldiers. Musical virtuosi, whose elaborate technique began to excite the people at the end of the fifth century, were nevertheless classed with jugglers, sleight-of-hand performers, and others hired for the entertainment of guests at a banquet or a public festival.

In the early days of Greek history there was small opportunity or desire for commercial intercourse. In Homer we hear of seafarers who undertook voyages for gain. These were mostly Phoenicians, often little better than pirates or kidnappers; they were hence called *peirātai* (πειρᾶται)—i. e., adventurers, buccaneers. These men brought into Greece Oriental products, consisting of rich garments and utensils, implements of war, and slaves, which they bartered for the raw products of Greece. It was not until the eighth

Commerce and trade.

Fig. 214.—Unloading a trading-ship.

century B. C. that Greek commerce began, being contemporaneous with the founding of the great colonies by enterprising cities like Chalcis, Corinth, and Milētus. These remained for a long period the chief centres (ἐμπόρια) of oversea commerce, and their harbours were always filled

with merchant vessels (ὁλκάδες, γαῦλοι). Corinth became
the first commercial city of the Greek mainland, standing,
as it did, midway between eastern and western
Hellas, and forming the point of connection between the Greeks of the Peloponnēsus and of the
north. The Phoenician pirate came to be replaced by the
Greek trader, *emporos* (ἔμπορος). In spite of the fact that the
emporos was often a man of ability and experience, widened
by foreign travel, he was yet not regarded with such high
esteem as the large manufacturer; for the latter simply invested his capital and left the actual work to overseers and
slaves. To the emporos attached some of the
stigma of personal labour (αὐτουργία), since, as
goods were never sent on an order, he was
obliged to journey to all parts of the trading world, and
was to that extent a labourer. And yet even he enjoyed
higher repute than the petty retail dealer (κάπηλος), whose
sedentary life, trivial gains, and reputation for avarice and
haggling made him an object of contempt. Especially
were the women and girls who plied a small retail trade
in the markets under popular disfavour; but they could
hold their own against the most presuming customer by
their Billingsgate.

The importer, on arriving at his destination, sought
out his customers, either personally or through agents, and
showed them samples (δείγματα) of his cargo
(called τὰ ἀγώγιμα or γαυλικὰ χρήματα). In large
cities a special place, called the *deigma* (δεῖγμα),
was set apart for this purpose. The Attic deigma was in
the Piraeus, and formed a sort of Exchange, where all kinds
of business and speculation were carried on. The retail
dealers selected their wares (τὰ ὤνια) and displayed them
for sale on tables; their booths (σκηναί) were in or near
the agora. These booths were sometimes made of wicker,
whence they were called *gerra* (γέρρα), the name which was
applied also to the railings of the same material by which

*Centres of
trade.*

*Stigma at-
tached to
trade.*

*The market in
an emporion.*

they were surrounded. Persons who were not citizens paid
to the market commissioners (ἀγορανόμοι) a market toll or
license for the privilege of a site. The wares, especially if
they happened to be articles of food, were displayed on platters (πίνακες), which covered the tables (ἐλεοί). So great
did the throng of tradespeople in the agora become by the
middle of the fifth century, that many of the administra-

Fig. 215.—Weighing goods for shipment.

tive offices were removed to other parts of the city. But, as
we have before seen (page 14), the centre of the agora was
kept free for the groups of citizens who spent their morn-
ings there. The porticoes or colonnades (στοαί) which
lined the sides served as comfortable strolling places when
the sun was high or when there came a burst of drenching
rain, such as is apt to fall in Athens in the springtime.

Portions of these colonnades were later appropriated by tradespeople, who gave to them much the appearance of an Oriental bazaar; but in classical times their booths were in the open air, protected, when their goods were perishable, by a kind of awning (σκιάδειον). The retailers (κάπηλοι),

Retail dealers.
like the manufacturers, were grouped together according to their wares. Thus, one portion of the agora would be assigned to the wine-dealers, and their district (κύκλος) would be spoken of as " the wine " (in the phrase εἰς τὸν οἶνον); another was assigned to lamp-sellers; another to cheese-sellers, and so on. The phrases

Divisions of the market.
" at the pots," " at the slaves," " at the books " (εἰς τὰς χύτρας, εἰς τὰ ἀνδράποδα, εἰς τὰ βιβλία) in-dicated respectively where one might buy pot-tery, slaves, and books. The master of the house, accompa-nied by a slave, did the marketing, sometimes calling in a porter to help carry his purchases home. Later, the mar-keting was entrusted to a special slave, called the *agorastes* (ἀγοραστής). The poorer classes, of course, did their own marketing, and had the disagreeable habit of carrying their money in their mouths. All this business was transacted early in the morning, the forenoon being called the time of full market (περὶ πλήθουσαν ἀγοράν, page 240).

Many wares were hawked about the streets. The dealer carried his table (ἐλεός) in front of him by means of straps

Street venders.
attached to his shoulders. Thus the streets on a busy morning would be full of hucksters calling out their goods—the sausage-sellers, pease-porridge-sellers, the charcoal-burner, and the farmer bringing his goat's milk from the country.

The measure-ment of time.
In comparatively late times there was erect-ed at the southern end of the market, where it still stands to-day, a building now known as the Horologium, or Tower of the Winds, a restoration of which is shown in Fig. 216. It is nearly octagonal, each of the sides bearing reliefs representing the winds coming

from eight different points of the compass. A bronze Triton once surmounted the slightly conical roof, and showed the townspeople by its revolving the direction of the wind. The edifice also had two contrivances for showing the time of day. One, inside the building, was a water-clock (κλεψύ-

Clocks.
δρα), fed by water from a spring on the Acropolis. The water trickled through small openings from one vessel into another. On the outside was a sun-dial (γνώμων, ὁρολόγιον). This building was probably the successor of less elaborate instruments used in the classical period for telling the time. In some sunny place a perpendicular staff was erected and the length of its shadow, marked off in feet into twelve parts, determined roughly the time of day. In the court-room, as we have seen, and probably in private houses, the

Fig. 216.—The "Tower of the Winds."

clepsydra was regularly employed. Here a given quantity of water represented a certain amount of time; but by none of these methods could the hour of the day be found with accuracy, and on a cloudy day, of course, the dial was useless. The twelve divisions on the dial or water-

Times of day.
clock, marking off the natural day into twelve parts, would be shorter in winter than in summer. These divisions, therefore, were comparatively unimportant to the

easy-going Greek, and it is not until late times that the word *hōra* (ὥρα) is used in the sense of "hour." Hence we meet with the vaguest expressions indicating time. In Homer the day has only three parts: ἠώς, from sunrise until the forenoon; μέσον ἦμαρ, noon; and δείλη, evening. By Xenophon's time more specific terms had been devised, but even these were general and uncertain in range. In the *Anabasis* we find these divisions: First, there is the time just before dawn (ἕως), indicated by the words ὄρθρος, or πρὸ ἡμέρας, or πρὸς ἡμέραν. Sunrise is denoted by ἅμα τῇ ἡμέρᾳ and ἅμα ἡλίῳ ἀνέχοντι or ἀνατέλλοντι. The morning is in general ἕωθεν or πρῴ, the middle of the forenoon being ἀμφὶ ἀγορὰν πλήθουσαν or περὶ πλήθουσαν ἀγοράν. Then comes noon, which is μέσον ἡμέρας. The word μεσημβρία, so common in other writers for "noon," happens always to mean "south" in the *Anabasis*. The afternoon (δείλη) was generally divided into two parts, early and late; for the latter Xenophon uses the word ὀψέ, and the context in other places shows that by δείλη he generally means the early evening. Sunset and evening are expressed in a great variety of phrases: ἡλίου δυσμαί and ἅμα ἡλίῳ δύνοντι; "supper-time," ἀμφὶ δορπηστόν; "evening," ἑσπέρα. Finally comes night, the beginning of which is denoted by ἀμφὶ κνέφας. In army life the night (νύξ) was divided into watches, φυλακαί; midnight is μέσαι νύκτες.

To the ordinary frequenter of the market, these divisions of the day and night, with the crude dial or water-clock for measuring them, were of less importance than the other divisions of time into months and years. The time of day he could gauge with satisfactory accuracy by glancing at the sun; but to know the day of the month—what day was lucky or unlucky, what required a sacrifice to some divinity, which was the last day of the month, the day for settling with creditors—all this concerned him deeply.

The days of the month.

In general, the Greeks were content to divide the year

into three seasons—spring (ἔαρ), summer (θέρος), and winter (χειμών), sometimes adding other designations, like ὀπώρα,

The Greek year. late summer, and ἄροτος, ploughing-time. Unfortunately for the Greek calendar, the year was based on the phases of the moon instead of the course of the sun. Each year consisted normally of twelve lunar months, a number which could be made to fit only approximately with one revolution of the earth round the sun. Consequently, it was necessary to devise cycles of years, with intercalary days and months, to make the revolutions of the sun and the moon correspond. The months (μῆνες) were given thirty and twenty-nine days alternately; and in every cycle of eight years—the one adopted in Athens—three months were intercalated, one in the third year, one in the fifth, and one in the last. Even this was by no means accurate, and Aristophanes makes the moon complain of her treatment at the hands of the Athenians, since the calendar had become so confused that the festivals of the gods were occurring at wrong times in the year. The civil year began with the first new moon after the summer

The Attic months. solstice, the first month usually corresponding with the last week of June and the greater part of July. The names which are given in the following table answer only roughly to our months; each Attic month embraces a varying portion of two of ours.

Hekatombaion	Ἑκατομβαιών	July.
Metageitnion	Μεταγειτνιών	August.
Boedromion	Βοηδρομιών	September.
Pyanopsion	Πυανοψιών	October.
Maimakterion	Μαιμακτηριών	November.
Poseideon	Ποσειδεών	December.
Gamelion	Γαμηλιών	January.
Anthesterion	Ἀνθεστηριών	February.
Elaphebolion	Ἐλαφηβολιών	March.
Mounichion	Μουνιχιών	April.
Thargelion	Θαργηλιών	May.
Skirophorion	Σκιροφοριών	June.

16

The meaning of some of these names is lost in obscurity, but it is certain that all are derived from some god or festival, like the modern names for the days of the week. Gamelion, the marriage month (page 121), was sacred to Hēra Gamelia, goddess of marriage. Poseideon belonged to Poseidon, and Maimakterion to an ancient cult of Zeus. The first day of the month was called "the new moon" (νουμηνία), and was often set as a date for paying debts; the last day had a double appellation, and was known as the "old and new" (ἕνη καὶ νέα), since the change in the moon's phase on that day marked the end of the old month and the beginning of the new. There was no division into weeks; instead, the month was divided into thirds, with reference to the waxing and the waning moon. The second of the month, for example, would be spoken of as the "second in the first part of the month" (δευτέρα μηνὸς ἱσταμένου); the twelfth would be the "second in the middle part" (δευτέρα μεσοῦντος), while in the last part of the month (μηνὸς φθίνοντος) the days were generally counted from the end.

Years were not dated from any fixed era, but were named from prominent officials : in Athens, the first archon (ὁ ἄρχων) gave his name to the year, and an Athenian document would be sufficiently dated, for example, by the words "in the archonship of Callias" (ἐπὶ Καλλίου ἄρχοντος). In Argos, the year was named from the priestess of Hēra; in Sparta, from the chief ephor. Once in a while a historian could recall a date by reference to the victory of some famous athlete at Olympia ; but the practice of dating events by Olympiads, beginning with the year 776 B. C., was not in vogue among Greeks of the classical period (page 105).

Dates.

Besides the *agoranomoi* (ἀγορανόμοι, see page 20), there were other market officials, the inspectors of weights and measures (μετρονόμοι), who were charged with the keeping of the standard weights and

Weights and measures.

measures preserved in the Tholos for the convenience of merchants. In case of dispute, the measure or weight in question was brought before them, and if found correct was stamped with their official mark.

The principal linear measures were the foot (πούς), the cubit (πῆ-χυς), and the fathom (ὀργυιά).

Linear measure. The foot varied slightly in length in different parts of Greece; so that there were three standards — the

FIG. 217.—An official weight.

Attic, the Olympic, and the Aeginētan. Since, however, Attic commerce was predominant in all parts of Hellas by the last quarter of the fifth century, the Athenian standard, both for weights and measures, was familiar to all Greeks, and we may use that as our standard here. The Attic foot, as determined by measurements of the cella of the Parthenon, which was called the Hekatompedon (page 51), was 295.7 millimetres, or about 11.65 inches; one and one-half feet made a cubit, four cubits made a fathom, one hundred fathoms, or six hundred feet, made a *stadion* (στάδιον). The following table gives more details:

2	δάκτυλοι (finger-breadths)		= 1 κόνδυλος (knuckle).
2	κόνδυλοι		= 1 παλαστή (palm).
4	παλασταί =	16 δάκτυλοι	= 1 πούς (foot).
1½	πόδες		= 1 πῆχυς (cubit).
4	πήχεις =	6 πόδες	= 1 ὀργυιά (fathom).
16⅔	ὀργυιαί =	100 πόδες	= 1 πλέθρον (plethrum).
6	πλέθρα =	600 πόδες	= 1 στάδιον.
30	στάδια		= 1 παρασάγγης (parasang).

The parasang was a Persian measure, equivalent to 3.31 miles. The stadion (στάδιον) was the length of one side of a race-course, and measured at Athens 582 feet 6 inches. The half-plethrum (ἡμίπλεθρον) is also mentioned by Xenophon, in addition to the πόδες, πήχεις, and στάδια given above.

In liquid measure, used in measuring oil and wine, the units are the *kyathos* (κύαθος), the *kotylé* (κοτύλη), the *chous*

Liquid measure. (χοῦς), and the *amphoreus* (ἀμφορεύς) or *metrētes* (μετρητής). It will be noticed that many of these names correspond to the names of certain earthenware vessels in common use (pages 134, 137). The kyathos held nearly one-tenth

Fig. 218.—Kotylos or kotylé.

of a pint, the chous about six pints, the amphoreus a little over ten gallons. The following table will show the relation :

6 κύαθοι	=	1 κοτύλη (.578 pint, U. S. liquid measure).
12 κοτύλαι	=	1 χοῦς (3.468 quarts).
12 χόες	=	1 ἀμφορεύς or μετρητής (10.4+ gallons).

Dry measure. In dry measure, used especially for grain, the denominations are somewhat different :

6 κύαθοι	=	1 κοτύλη (.49 pint, U. S. dry measure).
4 κοτύλαι	=	1 χοῖνιξ (.99 quart).
48 χοίνικες	=	1 μέδιμνος (1.49+ bushels).

The kyathos and the kotylé are each the same in Greek dry and liquid measure, but must be represented by unequal numerals on account of the difference between U. S. liquid and dry measure.   Bread was measured by the choenix; a loaf measuring three was appropriated by the greedy Arcadian at Seuthes's feast.   The medimnos contained nearly a bushel and a half.

Familiar objects in the market-place were the scales, or balance (called σταθμός). This consisted of a beam (ζυγόν), from **The scales.** the ends of which hung the scale-pans (τάλαντα, πλάστιγγε), suspended by chains. The beam might be held in the hand by means of a ring in the centre ; or, when heavy articles were to be weighed, it might turn on a pivot permanently fixed.   This kind was called *trytané* (τρυτάνη).

The talent (τάλαντον), of Babylonian origin, was the heaviest weight, and the one on which all the other de-
Weights. nominations were based. It varied greatly at different times and in different places. In Attica, in the fifth century, the talent used as the standard for weighing precious metals, drugs, and the like, amounted to about 57.8 pounds. It was divided into sixty minae of one hundred drachmas each. These are also the names of certain money denominations, which we will consider next.

Fig. 219.—Scales (τάλαντα).

The invention of coined money is ascribed to the Lydians, and is unknown in Homer, where purchases are made by bar-
Currency in ter. Cattle and horses were given in exchange
the Greek for other commodities, and sometimes gold, sil-
markets. ver, and bronze were offered in payment, their value being determined by weight. Hence it happens that the denominations of weight and of money coincide, and the talent and the mina always remained a weight of money, not a denomination coined in one piece. Into the Attic market came many coins of different states and systems of values—the Euboean, the Corinthian, or the Aeginētan, the copper coins of Western Hellas, the gold of the Eastern

cities and of Persia.   The money-changers were kept busy
counting out the regular Attic currency in exchange for

what was brought by foreign
merchants from other markets.
While the Athenians had a few
denominations in gold, such as
the small *hecté* (ἕκτη,

FIG. 220.—Attic drachma.

Fig. 221), the stand-
ard was based in the
main on silver.   In concluding bargains it was
necessary to specify whether the money (χρήματα)

Money.

was to be paid in gold or silver.   If
in the former, it was called *chrysion*
(χρυσίον); if in the latter, *argyrion* (ἀργύριον).
But these words are also used of money in general.   The drachma was the most common unit
of exchange.   Reckoned according to the value

FIG. 221.
Gold coin
of Athens.

of silver in the United States, it was worth about eighteen
cents.   The chief divisions are the obol (Fig. 191), two-obol,
and three-obol pieces.   In the following table the values are
throughout only approximate, and the superior purchasing
power of money in ancient times must be considered in
trying to fix modern equivalents.

Table of Attic money.	8 χαλκοῖ (bronze)	= 1 ὀβολός = 3 cents.
	6 ὀβολοί (silver or copper)	= 1 δραχμή = 18 cents.
	100 δραχμαί (silver)	= 1 μνᾶ (a weight, not a coin = 18 dollars).
	60 μναῖ	= 1 τάλαντον (= 1,080 dollars).

Beside these were the following: The half-obol (ἡμιω-
βόλιον); the shekel (σίγλος), familiar to the Asiatic Greeks,

Other coins.

and worth, according to Xenophon, seven and
one-half obols; the daric (δαρεικός), a Persian
gold coin, the name of which is wrongly connected with
Darius, worth twenty drachmas; the half-daric (ἡμιδαρεικόν);
and the Cyzicene stater (κυζικηνός, sc. στατήρ), a coin of the

mixed metal called electrum, consisting of gold and silver, which was used by the Lydians before silver and gold were coined separately. The stater of Cyzicus, a city on the Hellespont, was worth about twenty-eight Attic drachmas.

Fig. 222.—Attic tetradrachma.

There were also in Attica the didrachma and the tetradrachma, pieces of two and four drachmas respectively.

Almost every Greek city possessed and exercised the right to coin money. The public mint (ἀργυροκοπεῖον δημόσιον), like every other state building, was intimately associated with some god, and temples were often banks of deposit; in early Solonian times the Athenian mint was in the temple of a hero called the " Crown-wearer " (ὁ Στεφανηφόρος). Greek coinage was in general kept pure down to the third or second century; but there

The mints.

Fig. 223.—Silver tetradrachma of Laconia.

were not wanting individual counterfeiters, who made coins of debased metal (κίβδηλος), and coin clippers, who decreased their value by weight. " Fiat" money, or money made of material having no intrinsic value, was circulated from time to time. Thus Dionysius, tyrant of Syracuse, forced upon his subjects tin coins, which he compelled them to receive as tetradrachmas, although they were worth no more than a drachma; and in the second century

Purity of early Greek coinage.

the government of Boeotia made drachmas of copper, which it required to pass as legal tender of the value of a silver drachma, though the weight of both was the same. Byzantium, Sparta, and some other Peloponnesian cities used iron money. It is said that the Spartans and the Carthaginians used pieces of leather, the nearest approach to the modern use of paper money; both arise from a desire to lessen the weight of the circulating medium, it being understood that the valueless medium might be at any time exchanged for the real money which it represented. This was the case with the smaller copper coins in Greece, which, as with us to-day, had only a nominal worth, being admittedly of less weight than their face value demanded.

Prices. The price (τιμή) of articles in the market was rarely fixed, but had to be arrived at through much haggling and bargaining, often loud-voiced and acrimonious. The Attic law, however, endeavoured to exercise some restraint in relation to grain products and a few others, since it was apt to regard a rise in price, even when due to natural causes, as evidence of conspiracy against the people. Most Greeks looked on Athens as an expensive place to live in, but as compared with modern prices the majority of commodities were cheap, because of the greater scarcity of money and the relatively larger supply of some goods, notably wine. In Solon's time, an ox cost only five drachmas, a sheep only one; in the later fifth century, prices rose much higher, and a lamb cost eight drachmas, while sheep were worth from ten to twenty drachmas, according to age, size, and breed, and an ox might cost as high as a mina, though generally much less. Xenophon sold his favourite horse for fifty darics, or about ten minae. The average price of a medimnos of wheat was probably three drachmas; but in war-time it, of course, mounted rapidly, sometimes increasing at the rate of a drachma a day; barley usually cost less than wheat. Xenophon says that grain was so scarce at one point in the march across the Mesopotamian desert that two choenixes of either wheat or barley cost four shekels, or thirty obols. This would make the price of a medimnos of wheat one hundred and twenty drachmas, considerably over a dollar and a half a bushel. Bread was sold in loaves costing an obol, their size varying according to the price of grain. The expensive wine of Chios was worth a mina an amphoreus; but twenty drachmas an amphoreus, or forty cents a gallon, was regarded as an extravagant price to pay for ordinary wine. The cost of clothes and shoes was cheap or not according to the value of sheep and oxen; an inexpensive exōmis (page 161), the garment of working people, was sold for ten drachmas, and shoes, unless very highly ornamented, could be had for two drachmas. The average cost of living may **Wages.** be further guessed from the wages paid in certain vocations. The Greeks enlisted under Cyrus originally for a daric a month; later, their pay was increased to a daric and a half, or about a drachma a day. Captains (λοχαγοί) got double this sum, and generals (στρατηγοί) fourfold. The offer of a cyzicene (page 246) a month for a soldier's services was regarded as reasonable, and the aged dicast was glad enough to receive his two or three obols a day. Cripples pensioned by the state subsisted on an obol daily.

Bankers (τραπεζῖται) belonged, in the popular estimation, to the class of wholesale merchants (ἔμποροι), although **Banks.** they, like the small dealers, naturally had their tables (τράπεζαι) in one corner of the market-place. They were most- **Money-changers.** ly metics or freedmen.

Fig. 224.—Silver coin of Elis.

Their business had a threefold nature. First, they were money-changers, taking foreign currency in exchange

for the local; for this they charged brokerage. With their
scales they weighed the coins offered to them, in order to
detect any that lacked the legal weight; and they tested
the genuineness of the metal by its ring. They were themselves notorious for sharp practices and wilful mistakes in
reckoning. Secondly, they were money-lenders
(δανεισταί), ready, but always at a usurious rate,
to accommodate the spendthrift son of some
rich house. The rate of interest was not fixed, or even
limited, by law, and ran as high as twelve or eighteen per
cent. If the money borrowed was to be invested in what
was considered a hazardous enterprise, as in foreign car-
goes, the interest might be as high as a third of the principal. The borrower signed a receipt, subscribed to by
witnesses, and gave a pledge of two kinds. One was the
hand-shake, a more formal ceremony than among us; this
was called the *enechyron* (ἐνέχυρον). The other was the bond
(ἐγγύησις), by which security was offered, such as land or
other property, and which constituted a mortgage (ὑποθήκη)
on the property until the debt was repaid. Third, the banker
received money on deposit (παρακαταθήκη). But more often,
in classical times, the owner entrusted his money to a
friend, or placed it in the keeping of a god in a temple.
Sometimes, too, he hid it in jars (ὑδρίαι) in the earth, a
fortunate custom which has been the means of increasing
widely our knowledge of Greek coinage.

Money-lenders.

CHAPTER XIX

TRAVEL AND HOSPITALITY

With the increase in trade and the numerous military and colonial enterprises undertaken across the Aegēan in
Travel. the fifth century, there grew a desire for travel and exploration such as had never before existed in the heart of the Greek. Socrates speaks of himself as an extraordinary exception, when he tells us that he had never left Athens in all his seventy years except on military duty.

Yet, with all the increase in travel at this period, the difficulties in the way were considerable. Outside his own
Risks of travel. state the Greek could claim no rights, either political or personal, and one government seldom held another to account for the life of a citizen travelling in a private capacity. The word *xenos* (ξένος), which is related to the Latin *hostis*, discloses the ancient suspicion that attached to a foreigner. It meant originally not only "stranger," but also "enemy"; and even at a later day, when, through long-standing traditions of hospitality, it had come also to mean "guest" and "friend," race prejudice continued to subject the voyager to disdain. This explains why banishment (φυγή) seemed to the Greeks as severe a punishment as death. It made
Attitude toward strangers. him an outlaw, whose life might be taken with impunity by any one he met. Friendless as he was, he could receive no kindness from a host without bringing danger on the latter. Hence Euripides comments with feeling on the host's dislike of an exiled

guest.   And yet, even as early as Homer, we know that the
hard lot of the traveller was mitigated by religious feeling
and by an instinctive hospitality, which he shared, and still
shares, with the Oriental.   Religious feeling placed the
wanderer at least under the care of Zeus, Protector of
Strangers (Ζεὺς ξένιος), and an appeal in his name usually
broke down the barrier of dislike.   Not only was he suc-
cessfully invoked by fugitives, criminal or otherwise, who
came as suppliants (ἱκέται) to clasp the knees or touch the

**Ancient
hospitality.**
beard of a host, but
even beggars (πτωχοί)
and tramps (ἀλῆται)
with no fixed home were, through
Zeus, entitled to temporary shelter and food.   Savage tribes who,
like the Thracians of Bithynia,
maltreated shipwrecked sailors
were classed as "inhospitable"
(ἄξενοι), along with the cruel
Laestrygones and the Cyclōpes of
the *Odyssey*.   Once a stranger
had been received at a foreigner's table (ὁμοτράπεζος), and par-
taken of his "bread and salt,"
he was ever after supposed to be
entitled to his host's protection.

Fig. 225.—Wayside fountain.

Athens, since the days of Peri-
cles, enjoyed a reputation for distinguished hospitality (φι-
λοξενία), in contrast to Sparta, which suffered the odium
of excluding foreigners (ξενηλασία).

**Treatment
of guests.**
Sometimes the owner of a house in lonely
districts built special apartments (ξενῶνες), in
which he received (ἐδέχετο) and entertained
(ἐξένιζε) all strangers who might come, offering them at
least shelter and fire.   If they made a long stay, they provided their own food, inviting the host to partake with

them. To his invitation, "Enter!" or "I invite you to my hospitality," the grateful answer would be, "I accept" (δέχομαι). Among the Thracians, guest and host greeted and pledged each other with wine, or sometimes they clasped hands (cf. page 182). On taking leave, which

Presents. was done in a courteous, formal manner, guest and host interchanged presents, *xenia* (ξένια), a word which was applied also to the entertainment furnished while the stay lasted. Thereafter, both host and guest stood in the relation of xenoi (ξένοι) to each other, a word

which has no exact equivalent in our language, and is best rendered by "friend" or "guest" (page 251). The xenia, which were often mere symbols, such as a signet-ring (σφραγίς, Fig. 152), were treasured as heirlooms, and were

FIG. 226.—Guest and host (Telemachus receiving parting gifts from Nestor).

brought out and displayed by the owners whenever they sought to renew the friendship.

As travel increased, this primitive hospitality was possible only among the rich or among princes like Cyrus, who

Protection of foreigners. maintained this relation with Aristippus of Thessaly and Proxenus of Boeotia. Some prominent citizen of a foreign country, therefore, was chosen by a state to protect its citizens while in that country. These persons were called *proxenoi* (πρόξενοι, page 64); they differed from modern consuls in that they were citizens of the country in which they resided and exercised their function. Thus Cimon was the proxenos of Sparta at Athens, and the first duty of a Spartan who had business to transact in Athens would be to seek him and secure his interest.

Inns.

The necessity of having regular inns soon arose. Caravansaries, which supplied shelter and a bedstead, were erected at public cost in places like Olympia,

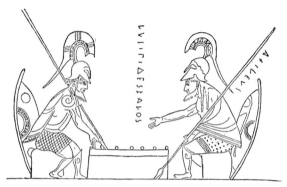

Fig. 227.—Playing draughts.

Delphi, and Delos, to which crowds flocked on the occasion of the national religious celebrations; sometimes, also, in the emporia, where merchants resorted. In the larger cities there were taverns in the modern sense, though much more primitive in character than a hotel of northern Europe or the United States. There were two

Two kinds.

kinds—the

Fig. 228.—Woman juggler.

καπηλεῖα and the πανδο-κεῖα. The first were nothing but drinking saloons and gambling resorts connected with a wine-seller's shop, pro-

viding luncheon, but no shelter for the night. They corresponded to the cheaper sort of restaurant, and were
avoided by respectable people. The second (πανδοκεῖα)
were, perhaps, a little better. They afforded both lodging
and board, and were frequented by travellers of social con-

FIG. 229.—Juggler and acrobat.

sequence, unless they
happened to enjoy the
acquaintance (ξενία) of
some one living in the
city. Inns were kept by
both men and women
(πανδοκεῖς, πανδοκεύτριαι),
who in Athens were usu-
ally metics. They some-
times tried to make their
resorts more attractive by amusements, such as dicing (κυ-
βεία). Specimens of dice (κύβοι, cf. Fig. 230), some unfairly
loaded, have come down to us. Another sport of the tavern was cock-fighting and quail-fighting; and jugglers,
tight-rope dancers, marionette-players, and keepers of wild
animals, especially mon-
keys (πίθηκοι), were all
encouraged to exhibit
here.

Tavern signs appear
not to have come into
use before Roman times.

We have considered
some of the hindrances
to travel; others will
come into view pres-

FIG. 230.—Bones used as dice.

Occasions for
travel.

ently. Aside from them, the motives to travel
were few, being confined chiefly to the desire
to further one's business—in commerce, state-
craft, or what not—or to attendance at some one of the
religious concourses. The games at the national festivals

(page 100), with the pomp of gorgeous ritual at the sanc-
tuaries ·where they were celebrated, induced many persons
every year to brave the dangers of a journey. Citizens were
sent out by the several states to represent them at these
spectacles in delegations called θεωρίαι. These were held
ordinarily (but see page 101) in the late spring or the summer, when travel, in spite of the heat, was easi-
est. Journeys were rarely undertaken in winter, especially on the water. Or again, a sick
man might take even greater risks in order to
reach some celebrated precinct where the gods
of healing were known to work wonderful cures.
On such an errand he would travel to the cave
of Trophonius in Thessaly, or to the temple of
Asclepius at Epidaurus (see page 288). Sometimes a family of women and children would
be sent away for protection during a period
of political disturbance in the city. But seldom did pleasure form the chief end in view
when a man set out from home to journey in
another country. City folk who owned estates
in the country doubtless spent their summers

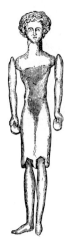

Fig. 231.
Jointed doll or
marionette.

there (cf. θερίζω, used of the Persian king in
the *Anabasis*) ; Socrates speaks of the benefits
gained by children in the country. But Greek
cities never witnessed the wholesale summer migration of
families into the country, much less to foreign lands,
which characterizes our modern civilization.

When a Greek started to go abroad (ἀποδημεῖν), he took
formal leave of his friends and relatives, offered sacrifice
and made vows for a safe journey, and con-
signed his goods and the money he did not
require to the keeping of some friend ; often
he made his will. He then dressed in his tunic, which he
girded carefully so that his legs might not be impeded,
threw his chlamys over his shoulder, and put on the broad

Preparations
for travel.

petasos to shade his head from the sun, and stout high
boots. With enough money to suffice for the journey
(ἐφόδιον), and a slave (παῖς) to attend him, he was ready to

Modes of travel.

depart. If his journey was to be overland, he
might go on foot (πεζεύω) ; but more often he
rode (ὀχοῦμαι) a horse or an ass, the latter especially if his route took him over the mountains, as in Greece
itself would general-
ly happen. On very
rough roads horses
were apt to give out
sooner than men, be-
cause horseshoes were
apparently unknown.
The Greeks under
Xenophon learned to

Fig. 232.—Peasant's cart used in the Troad to-day.

tie large cloths or bags on the fetlocks of their horses to
keep them from sinking too deeply in the snow. Wagons

The use of wagons.

(ἄμαξαι) were not used so commonly, except
when women were in the party ; it was considered effeminate of a man to drive in a wagon.
Certainly no ordinary man would show himself in a city street
in one. Chariots (ἄρματα) were used by the Greeks after
Homer only for racing, never for ordinary driving (page 98).
The wagon, *hamaxa*, was a rude board platform mounted on
four wheels, which often had no spokes, but were made of
solid pieces of wood or sometimes also of a single slab cut
from a tree trunk. The wheels were held in place on the
axles (ἄξονες) by means of a pin. A more sumptuous wagon
was the *harmamaxa* (ἁρμάμαξα). This was furnished with a
tent-like covering (σκηνή), and was much in use in Asia
Minor ; it was comparable to the Western " prairie-schooner."
Many roads were passable for wagons (ὁδοὶ ἁμαξιτοί) even in
the mountains, but we have before seen that all Greek
highways were far surpassed by the Roman roads of Italy
(page 8). Hence on special occasions, for the passage of

17

an army or a religious procession, roads had to be made over, or even new ones were constructed (ὁδοποιῶ). Nor were there any mile-stones or guide-posts, so far as we

Fɪɢ. 233.—A portion of the Themistoclean wall, with the boundary stone of the Cerameicus.

know; an occasional shrine, with its dedicatory inscription, or a boundary stone, would indicate roughly to the traveller in more populous regions his whereabouts.

Occasionally streams would have to be crossed. In most cases, except at the close of winter, when they were

Crossing a stream.

swollen by freshets, these could be forded (διαβατός). If there was no ford (πόρος), the traveller might possibly find a bridge, or else get some one living in the neighbourhood to ferry him across in a small boat or on a raft. Bridges (γέφυραι) built of permanent material seem not to have existed on the Greek mainland in classical times; the Greeks had a superstitious aversion to any device that seemed to change the face of nature or contradict the divine order of the universe. This is especially illustrated by their unwillingness to construct canals. So, in regard to bridges, they usually built only slight wooden structures, which might be easily demolished by the river-god if he so pleased. Rafts (σχεδίαι) and small boats were perhaps more commonly used for the wider rivers. Small boats were always useful; in one case we hear of dugouts (πλοῖα μονόξυλα) employed in Asia Minor.

Fɪɢ. 234.—Bridle.

When the traveller had a wagon, it was drawn by a pair of oxen or mules yoked together (cf. ζεύγη βοεικά and ἡμιονικά; also βοῦς ὑφ’ ἁμάξης). Hence the word to **Animals and** denote the **luggage.** preparation for the start is "yoke up" (ἀναζεύγνυμι), which came to be applied even when the animals were not hitched to a wagon, but carried the packs on their backs, bound by girths (δεσμοί). So the word "unyoke" (καταλύω), originally applicable to the unyoking of cattle,

Fɪɢ. 235.—Mule-cart.

was used in general for "putting up," either at night or for the midday luncheon and rest. The slave or the pack-animal (ὑποζύγιον) carried the master's bedding and wraps (στρώματα); for these also formed part of the traveller's outfit, even when he expected to find inns along the road. They made a considerable bundle, tied up in a linen sack called *stromatodesmos* (στρωματοδεσμός, page 129).

If the traveller purposed to take a sea voyage, he must

wait until he heard of some vessel going to the port nearest his destination, since there was no regular packet service. In the fifth century, and afterward, how-

Sea voyages. ever, it was easy to find some merchant vessel
(ὁλκάς) or grain-ship (πλοῖον σιταγωγόν) bound for some port
in Asia Minor or Sicily. The traveller went to the skipper
(ναύκληρος), got his consent to travel on board, and arranged
with him how much he was to
pay for his fare (ναῦλον).

Here we may notice also the
lack of any regular facilities for
despatching letters by post. A
man who had a message to com-
municate by letter sent his slave
or some other person on whom
he thought he could rely. This
method, which was the only one
available, frequently proved dangerous, as the Spartan Pausanias, when engaged in a treason-
able correspondence with Xerx-
es, and the traitorous Persian
Orontas in the *Anabasis*, found
to their cost.

Fig. 236.—Tri-form Hecaté ("Diana
of the Crossways ").

It was in such journeys across
the sea that the Greeks picked up what they knew of the

Greek knowl- language of other peoples, for they learned no
edge of other foreign languages at school (page 88). Gen-
languages. erally an interpreter (ἑρμηνεύς) was necessary
in out-of-the-way places. When these were wanting, sign
language could always be employed. Themistocles was
one of the earliest to set himself deliberately to learning
the language and the customs of the Persians. The Greeks
had quick ears and active brains, and learned a language
sufficiently for conversational purposes with little trouble.
The Greeks of different states seem to have had small dif-

ficulty in understanding one another. Thus the Arcadians, who formed the majority of Xenophon's troops, and who spoke a dialect very different from the Attic, were constantly harangued by their officers, speaking in other dialects, and yet understood them perfectly.

The protection of the gods was constantly invoked during a journey. On land, Apollo, Hermes, Hecaté, and Heracles were the special guardians of the wayfarer; on the sea, Artemis and, above all, the twin Dioscūri, Castor and Polydeuces. On reaching home safely, the traveller offered thanks in a sacrifice to one of these gods, or to Zeus the Saviour, and paid

The traveller's gods.

Fig 237.—Resting at a wayside Herm.

the vows he had made to them while abroad, often dedicating some object in the temple of the god.

CHAPTER XX

DOMESTIC RELIGION

It is impossible to grasp the full meaning of Greek private life without taking into account the deep significance **Pervading** of the popular religion, both domestic and **influence of** public, and the influence it exerted constantly **Greek** on the lives of all citizens. In every enterprise **religion.** the gods were a man's first consideration; "to begin with the gods" his first duty. To be sure, there were not wanting scoffers, like Menon in the *Anabasis*, who laughed at those who were scrupulous in matters of religion (ὅσιοι); but the universal horror caused by the mutilation of the busts of Hermes in the streets of Athens, just before the Sicilian expedition set off, shows how deep were the respect and faith that attached to the outward symbols of religion. The Greek was rare who, on undertaking any new enterprise, failed to consult a god first, and gain his consent to carry out what he had in mind. In every important act, especially if it involved a promise, the gods were called to witness.

Wherever he turned, in the street or in the house, the Greek met with some reminder of the allegiance he owed **Hermae.** to the gods of his fathers. Just in front of the main door of the house stood a pedestal surmounted with a head of Hermes (Figs. 35, 237); and a row of these Hermae was conspicuous in the agora at Athens (page 43). At the street-crossings or in the public squares were little shrines to Hecaté, and statues or symbolic representations of Apollo Agyieus, guardian of streets, were

Fig. 238.—Grand altar of Zeus the Saviour at Pergamus (restoration).

placed in dark streets; failing these, a bay-tree, sacred to Apollo, was planted instead. In the court of the house was an altar (βωμός, page 30) of Zeus Herkeios, protector of enclosures. Here the father offered sacrifice for himself and his family. A small statue of Zeus and of Apollo stood near. In the andron the hearth was itself an altar to Hestia, goddess of hearth and home; and sometimes a little clay image of Hephaestus, god of fire, stood on the shelf over the hearth. Scarcely a single room lacked its appropriate divinity. In the storerooms (ταμιεῖα) were images of those gods whose special province was to keep safe the household possessions (θεοὶ κτήσιοι); in the bedroom of the master and the mistress were placed figures of the gods of marriage (θεοὶ γαμήλιοι, θεοὶ γενέθλιοι, page 31).

House gods.

Fig. 239.
The "Praying Boy."

Every trade and handicraft looked to some special divinity for protection. The artisan generally invoked Athēna; metal-workers in particular, Hephaestus and Promētheus. Hermes was the god of commerce, and there was a whole host of minor divinities and heroes whose sanction and help were required for every form of industrial activity. A common practice was to confide one's secret cares to the earth or to the sky, in the belief that the divinities of earth or sky would hear and render aid.

Gods of trades.

The form of a prayer (εὐχή) was simple, though sometimes often repeated. The petitioner did not kneel, but stood upright, unless he was praying to the gods of the underworld, when he might knock on the ground to rouse their attention. Usually, however, he stood with outstretched hands, with palms

The form of prayer.

uppermost, and addressed by name the god or gods; if his invocation was general, so as to include them all, he would add: " Or whatever else thou art called," or " Whatever thou desirest to be called." There are many myths which illustrate the fear of omitting by chance any divinity in a prayer or sacrifice; and the altar " to the unknown god," which St. Paul found at Athens in later times, was designed to include any divine power whose existence might not already be recognized in the company of the traditional gods.

One of the commonest acts of daily life was the offering of sacrifice ($\theta v \sigma i a$), the motive of which was threefold:

Sacrifice. first, it might convey a petition, in the belief that through an offering the gods would be more inclined to grant the request; it was often accompanied with a vow or promise ($\epsilon \check{v} \chi o \mu a \iota$) to dedicate an offering if the prayer were granted, and the liver, the lobe, and other internal organs of the victim were carefully inspected to see if the omens were favourable. Such a sacrifice preceded every important step involving a serious change in the petitioner's mode of life. It was necessary before a journey. Second, it expressed thanksgiving, and was often the fulfilment of a vow ($\dot{a} \pi o \theta \acute{v} \epsilon \iota \nu$) previously made. Such were the sacrifices offered by the Greeks in the *Anabasis* for safe guidance and restoration to home. And third, it might be designed to atone for some offense: it was expiatory. To offer a sacrifice, it was by no means necessary to go to a temple; though in expiatory sacrifices a sanctuary of peculiar solemnity and holiness, like that of the Eumenides (Furies), was often felt to be more appropriate. But altars

Altars. by the wayside were sufficient (cf. Fig. 243), and merely to lay a wreath on a statue was accounted an acceptable offering. Further, the altar for burnt offerings rarely stood inside a temple, since this would have converted the sanctuary into a slaughter-house, and the smoke would have damaged many a beautiful statue or relief (page 54). Hence, altar and temple are mentioned separately by Xenophon when he tells us of the sanctuary which he built to Artemis. And if a temple was not always required, much less was a priest (ἱερεύς).

Priests. Although sacrifices occur constantly in the *Anabasis*, the word "priest" is never mentioned. Every adult male who had previously purified himself with lustral water and had put on a wreath was qualified to perform the ceremony, provided, of course, he was not under the gods' displeasure through some impious act, such as murder or profanation. The duties of a priest, which were hereditary, were confined to ministrations in some temple or at some shrine or altar of special significance, or at a festival, such as the Eleusinian mysteries.

Soothsayers. When, however, omens were to be taken from the sacrifice, a soothsayer (μάντις) was called in, and no army set out without taking at least one along. Arexion of Arcadia, Basias of Elis, Eucleides of Phlius, and Silānus of Ambracia, the last especially, figure conspicuously in the *Anabasis*. A constant attendant at a sacrifice might learn the art of divination in an amateur fashion; but when the omens were persistently unfavourable, the soothsayer was invited to conduct the sacrifice.

No man might approach the gods in prayer or sacrifice unless he was pure in their sight. A murderer must first **Religious purification.** have some one make an expiatory offering to the gods and to the spirit of his victim, before he himself could commune with a divinity. Hence, frequent purification of a whole community, sometimes attended with fasting, took place in certain festivals during the year, for fear that the displeasure of the gods might be visited on it through the presence of some transgressor. The Greeks under Xenophon, at his and the soothsayers' advice, underwent this ceremony (καθαρμός).

This ceremonial purification was accomplished in various symbolic ways, mostly by washing the hands with lus-

tral water (χέρνιψ) brought from a particular spring. When
a death occurred in the family, a vessel of water, drawn
from outside, was placed outside the door, in
Means of
purification.
order that the inmates, when they went out,
might first purify themselves of the pollution
of death before mingling with their neighbours. A bride
and groom first purified themselves in the bath (λουτρά,
page 122), that the gods might sanction the union. Fire

FIG. 240.—Ceremonial purification for murder (Orestes).

also was believed to have a purifying power. Five days
after a child was born the nurse carried him round the
hearth in the andron, followed by members of the household
(ἀμφιδρόμια, page 73). Branches of myrtle and of bay were
also symbols of ceremonial purity, and were used to sweep
the altar and the ground round it before the sacrifice began.
All the sacrificial vessels must likewise be purified. The
cup from which a libation was to be poured must be thoroughly washed, and sometimes cleaned with sulphur.

Sacrifices were either bloodless or involved the killing
(σφάττω) of a live victim. In the first, the worshipper, with

hands washed and a garland on his head, simply laid on the altar fruits or cakes. Bloodless offerings, consisting of cakes baked in animal forms, were often brought by the poor instead of an animal. Blood offerings were usually made with cattle, sheep, goats, and swine. The victims were called *hiereia* (ἱερεῖα); sometimes also *thymata* (θύματα). The kind of animal depended on the god or the occasion. Pigs were offered whenever purification—i. e., expiation—was sought, and must be entirely

Nature of the offerings.

FIG. 241.—Sacrifice.

consumed, no parts being eaten by the worshipper; this happened often to Demēter, and in the offering which Xenophon, "according to ancestral custom," made to Zeus Meilichios. Sheep and goats were perhaps the commonest offerings, but goats were not acceptable to Athēna in Athens. Bulls were frequently offered to Dionȳsus and to Zeus. Smaller creatures, like birds, especially doves, were offered by the poor, and cocks regularly to Asclepius. It was unlawful to sacrifice swine to Aphrodīte. Horses were not sacrificed by the Greeks, except perhaps in deference to the custom of other countries, as when Xenophon, while in Armenia, gave his old horse to be fattened and offered to the Sun. The Greeks did not eat horseflesh, and the taste of wild asses' meat was evidently new to Xenophon; hence such animals were considered unfit for sacrifices where the worshipper partook of the victim. Only in expiation, when the animal was always burnt entire (ὁλοκαυτῶ), were such creatures eligible, as, for instance, dogs to Hecaté.

The animal must be sound, if possible. An old animal must be set aside and especially fattened to be an acceptable sacrifice, and it was unusual to offer as victim one which

had been yoked to the plough. White animals were necessary for the gods of Olympus; black for the gods of the
The sacri- underworld. If the animal came willingly to
ficial cere- the altar, that was interpreted as a favourable
mony. omen. The ceremony began when the person
officiating as priest approached the altar, with attendants
who led the victim, while others carried the sacrificial basket (κανοῦν) in which lay the knife (μάχαιρα) used for the kill-

FIG. 242.—Sacrifice.

ing. All the participants had garlands on their heads, and
the ground about the altar and the altar itself were swept.
The head of the victim also was wreathed. Then the
lustral water (χέρνιψ), contained in a basin called the *chernibeion* (χερνιβεῖον, page 138), was passed round the assembly
from left to right, each person sprinkling his hands, head,
beard, and clothes. The priest, or whoever made the offering, after all had purified themselves in this way, called
for silence on the part of all who might be passing near the
altar and the group round it, so that no sound or word of
ill omen might reach the ear of the divinity whose presence
was believed to be near, and sprinkled barleycorns, which
he took from the basket, on the altar and the victim. He
then cut off a lock of hair from the victim's head and cast

it into the fire; this was the "consecration," or "preliminary sacrifice" (κάταργμα). Sometimes the hair was divided
among the participants, who then severally threw it into
the fire. The priest then forced the animal to kneel, and
drew its neck upward if the sacrifice were to an Olympian
divinity, downward if to the underworld gods. Then with
his knife he stabbed the animal in the neck, while an attendant held a bowl (σφαγεῖον) to catch the blood as it
spurted out; or, if a treaty were to be concluded, and the
parties desired to dip hands or swords in the blood, it might
be received in a shield. On one occasion, Xenophon tells
us, the soothsayers allowed the blood to flow into a river
between their army and the enemy, doubtless to secure
the help of the river-god.

A flute-player accompanied the ceremony with loud
notes on the flute, the object of which seems to have
been to drown the cries of the animal. The women in the
company, too, maintained a shrill ejaculation (ὀλολυγή), as
a welcome to the divinity present, and also to greet him
when the omens were favourable. In Homeric times, the
thighs were sliced separately, wrapped in two layers of fat,
and after wine had been poured over them were consumed
entirely for the benefit of the gods, who were thought to
receive the savour (κνίση) of the fat with special delight.
In later times, when temple ritual had become more elaborate, the parts of the victim that were consumed for the
gods varied with the place and the purpose of the sacrifice.

The rest of the animal was then cut up and roasted for
the benefit of the participants, who drew off their portions
with meat-hooks, being forks with five prongs (πεμπώβολα),
or with long spits (βουπόρος ὀβελίσκος). In Athens it
was the custom for a man who had sacrificed at a public
altar to carry home the meat, either to be eaten there, or
distributed as presents among his friends. In many precincts, however, it was unlawful to carry any meat away.
At Epidaurus (page 290) the worshippers were obliged to

consume it all within the precinct (περίβολος). Some of the meat left over from the state sacrifices found its way into markets, whence meat was frequently called *hiereia* (page 145); such meat caused the early Christians much embarrassment and anxious discussion (see 1 Corinthians viii).

Another form of sacrifice, very common in private life, was the libation (σπονδή), in which wine was poured, or a

The libation. few drops of it tossed, from the saucer-like cup called the *phialé* (φιάλη, page 137). This might be done in connection with a burnt sacrifice ; or it formed part of the ceremony at a banquet, when it concluded the drinking, and was followed by the singing of a paean. To some divin-

ities it was unlawful to pour wine. Honey, milk, and oil were used in libations to the Nymphs, the Muses, and the Eumenides (Furies).

All these acts of religion, happening daily in the life

Signs from the gods. of a Greek, kept him conscious of his rela-

Fig. 243.—Libation.

tions to the gods, and were the expression of his belief that he could commune with them. If that were true, then they could give signs to him, and this every Greek firmly believed. In every sacrifice the movements of the victim, the way in which the fire leaped up or died down, the colour and the condition of the inner organs, were all carefully viewed to determine the nature of the sign from the gods

Divination. which they were believed to reveal. If the omens were favourable, as interpreted by one or all of these methods of divination (μαντική), it was the signal for congratulation and exultation among all the par-

ticipants; the god was believed to favour his worshippers
by actually coming near them, and his presence was greeted
by the cries (ὀλολυγή) of the women once more. If, on the
other hand, the omens were not favourable, other victims
were tried until favourable omens were received, or until it
became obvious that none were to be expected.

There were many other ways in which, according to
universal popular belief, the gods showed signs to mortals.
Omens.   Thus, a dream was a vision sent by them,
especially by Zeus, and must be recognized by
at least a libation. Thunder and lightning also indicated
Zeus's will; a chance meeting at morning in the street, as
of a slave or an ass, was believed to have influence on the
person for the rest of the day. A sneeze was an omen,

Fig. 244.—A good omen.

always happy in import. But the most important branch
of the divining art was the watching of the flight or movements of birds; so common was this method that the word
for "bird" and "omen" is the same (ὄρνις, οἰωνός). When
Cyrus's army moved out of Ephesus an eagle was seen
perched at the right of the road; its screeching and the
fact that it was passive and not in flight were interpreted

to portend danger and glory combined. Generally, all birds seen on the right, or coming from the east, were thought to be auspicious (αἴσιος). In watching birds, the seer (μάντις) took up a station facing the north.

The will of the gods was also manifested through oracles; these were responses uttered in verse of more or less ambiguous meaning, to enquirers at some temple of special sanc-

Oracles. tity, as at Delphi, or Dodōna, or at the oracle of Zeus Ammon in Libya, or of Apollo Didymaeus near Milētus. Socrates, in spite of the fact that he was tried and put to death for alleged atheism, believed as firmly as any other Greek in their efficacy. Again, a man in doubt about any duty which he thought was owing to the gods, might consult one of the persons known as *exegētai* (ἐξηγηταί), who made a special study of ancestral customs and laws relating to religion. They gave advice, for instance, to one who had unintentionally committed homicide, telling him the proper mode of expiating the act and how to dispose of the corpse. They were frequently called in to direct funeral rites, that nothing might be omitted which was needed to gain the approbation of the gods.

We have already seen how much the great national festivals at Olympia, Delphi, Nemea, and the Isthmus contributed to the entertainment and the inspiration of Greek life (pages 100 ff.). The daily

Home festivals. occupations of all Greeks, even of women and children,

FIG. 245.—Coin of Elis (Olympia).

were constantly interrupted by other important festivals, which in Athens were celebrated with splendid processions (πρόσοδοι, πομπαί), sumptuous sacrifices at the expense of the state, beautiful accessories in the shape of temples, costly

18

vessels and robes, and general gaiety. At the beginning
of the Attic year, in the month Hekatombaion (page 241),

The Panathenaea. came the Panathenaea, with contests in singing, flute and lyre playing, and recitations of
epic poetry by the rhapsodes; in the stadion
occurred athletic and gymnastic contests rivalling those
at Olympia, in which the competitors strove for prizes of
oil made from Athēna's sacred trees (page 221) and for
painted vases—the predecessors of the modern cups—on
which the contest was figured. Conspicuous also was the
war-dance called pyrriché (πυρρίχη, page 84); and there
was a regatta, for which, however, only the ordinary vessels, and no special racing craft, were available. The
chief glory of the festival was the grand procession
(πομπή), which was marshalled in the outer and the inner
Cerameicus. From here it proceeded over a broad course
made for it in the agora till it came to a temple called the
Eleusinion, where it turned to the left, passed the north-
western slope of the Acropolis, and so on to its gates.
In the procession was borne the peplos (πέπλος, page 54),
a robe specially woven to deck the statue of Athēna;
it was spread out like a sail on the mast of a ship or
"barge" mounted on wheels. The word "carnival" is
perhaps a reminiscence of this ancient float, from the
Latin *currus navālis*.

In the winter came various celebrations in honour of
Dionȳsus, god of nature and the vine, the object of which
was to wake the sleeping spirit of generation and render
him propitious for the coming of spring and the sowing of
the crops. In the country especially the rustics made merry,
smearing their faces with wine lees, and dancing amid jokes

Festivals of Dionȳsus. and buffoonery round the altar of the god. In
the city a festival was held somewhat later,
called the Anthesteria, and also accompanied
with general merrymaking. The wine-casks were opened,
and all, even slaves, were allowed perfect holiday and lib-

erty to drink in honour of the god. The last day of the
festival was a sort of All Souls' Day, being devoted to the
gods of the underworld and the spirits of the dead. With
the coming of spring was celebrated the Greater or " City "
Dionysia, a festival revived with great pomp by the Pisistratidae, and the most important of all to us, since most of
the great tragedies were enacted there. In fact, all the
people, down to the humblest, who were supplied by the
state treasury with money to watch the spectacles (τὸ θεωρι-

FIG. 246.—The tripod, prize of the dithyrambic contest.

κόν, page 112), were treated to an imposing review of their
great literary achievements, given in the order in which
the several kinds of literary expression, epic, lyric, and
dramatic poetry, had originated. There were contests
among the rhapsodists, who recited epic poetry ; contests between choruses, consisting of fifty men or boys from each
tribe, specially trained to render lyrics composed in honour
of Dionȳsus and other gods, and called dithyrambs. The
prize, which was eagerly coveted, was a bronze tripod, after-

ward set up with an appropriate inscription in a street east
of the Acropolis leading to the theatre, called the Street
of the Tripods (page 16). Then came contests between
the comic poets, and last, between the poets of tragedy.

A curious festival, in which little girls took part, was
held in the month Mounichion in honour of Artemis. The
girls, dressed to represent bears, and actually
called " bears " (ἄρκτοι), danced in the precinct
of the goddess, offering various articles shaped
like bears to her. The women also had festivals of their
own, to which no man was admitted. One was the *Thesmophoria*, in honour of Demēter, held in the autumn at
the time when grain was sown, and accompanied with fasting and the wholesale killing of pigs to propitiate the
goddess.

The Mysteries of Eleusis, however, formed the very
centre of the worship of Demēter, to participate in which
almost every man, woman, and child in Athens
aspired. Beginning with certain local mystic
rites in the little town of Eleusis, the centre
of a grain-producing district, the festival was early appropriated by the Athenian state when Athens came to pre-
dominate over the other settlements in Attica. Although
the celebration was little known outside of the Athenian
dominion at the time of the Persian wars, by the end of
the fifth century the political power of Athens had attracted the eyes of all votaries of Demēter throughout
Greece to this festival, and from that time until the year
396 of our era, when Alaric and his Goths destroyed Eleusis
at the instance of the monks who followed him, the Eleusinian rites exerted a strong force in unifying the religious
instinct of all Greeks. Naturally, only Athenians were
eligible to initiation in the beginning; later, all Greeks
might offer themselves. Women might be received into
the rites, and also children, but only to the first grade or
degree of membership.

*Women's
festivals.*

*The
Eleusinia*

The gods who were most prominent in this worship—there were others whose names it was not lawful to mention—were Demēter, her daughter Persephoné, and the child Iacchus, who was identified with Dionȳsus. The chief festival occupied nine days in the autumn, in the month Boedromion ; but a festival of less pomp was held in the early spring in Anthesterion, not at Eleusis, but in the district Agrae, on the Ilissus, which served as a preparation to the rites of the autumn. In later times the celebration at Agrae took place at intervals of several years in the autumn, in order that strangers might not be obliged to journey to Athens twice.

The candidate for initiation presented himself to some former initiate a fortnight or more before the festival began. The person consulted became his guide **The course of the ceremony.** or *mystagōgos* (μυσταγωγός) throughout the entire ceremony. He examined the candidate to find out whether he was free from sin or other religious impediment, and advised him how to make himself acceptable to the gods by private sacrifices ; in case of doubt on this point, one of the exegētai mentioned above (page 273) was consulted. Nothing like the solemnity of a confession, in the religious sense, was required, only an affirmation or oath that the candidate was pure. In later times, therefore, the complaint arose that many mystagogues were irresponsibly helping to admit unworthy persons. A small fee was exacted in the post-classical period. Meantime the Hierophant (ἱεροφάντης), or chief priest of the Mysteries, received the names of all intending initiates, who were formally assembled in Athens on the 15th day of Boedromion, and instructed regarding the fast which they were to undergo during the succeeding nine days ; for they must abstain from all food by day, and certain viands were entirely prohibited even at night.

On the following day, the 16th, the Hierophant and his assistant, the Torch-bearer (δᾳδοῦχος), took their station in

the Painted Porch (στοὰ ποικίλη, page 43) and made a formal
proclamation (πρόρρησις), in which they warned all strangers
and murderers to keep out of the way, and ordered the
initiates (μύσται) to betake themselves to the sea, either at
the Piraeus or at two small sacred streams of salt water
(called the Ῥειτοί) which were on the way to Eleusis.
Each participant thereupon took with him a pig to be
offered the next day to Demēter, which he washed at the
same time that he bathed himself.   On the 17th the King
Archon, who represented the state on all religious occasions, offered sacrifice (hence called Σωτήρια) for the commonwealth in the temple at Athens called the Eleusinion.
At this ceremony visiting delegations from other states
(θεωροί, page 256) may have assisted.   After the public
sacrifice each initiate offered his pig to Demēter.   The 18th
was a day sacred to Asclepius, the healer, and was also the
day on which there arrived from Eleusis certain mystic
symbols—a cradle, a ball, a top, jackstones, mirror, and
fleece—which the legend referred to the childhood of
Iacchus, and which were to be carried in the procession.

In the forenoon of the 19th the procession started from
the agora, passed out of the city through the Dipylon
(page 13), and crossed the plain of the Cephīsus
by the Sacred Way.   Guarding the symbols
and the image of Iacchus, crowned and holding a torch, came the Hierophant, the Torch-bearer, the
Sacred Herald (κῆρυξ), and the attendant at the altar (ὁ ἐπὶ
βωμῷ), with many other priests and priestesses, grouped in
a kind of hierarchy, whose rank and function cannot be de-
fined with certainty in every case.   The Hierophant figured
most prominently throughout the ceremony; he was an
elderly man who held office for life, and belonged to the
ancient family of the Eumolpidae at Eleusis.   The office
of the Torch-bearer was also hereditary.   The priests wore
long raiment (στολή) and Oriental turbans or mitres, which
caused a Persian soldier at Marathon to mistake the Torch-

The procession.

bearer Callias for a king. They and their followers, the initiates, also wore wreaths of myrtle and ivy. The initiates were otherwise attired as usual, and not, as has often been supposed, in long chitons. Women were allowed to journey in wagons; but military parades did not form a conspicuous feature of the procession until later times. On the way the procession would stop at certain points to perform mystic acts, the meaning of which was explained by remote legends: there were baths at the Cephīsus; the mystai were halted to have saffron threads tied on the right wrist and right foot as a charm against the evil eye; and families who possessed hereditary priesthoods paused to perform ceremonies peculiar to their own cults. It was not strictly, to our notions, a solemn procession. The crowd gave itself up to noise and boisterous jesting, singing loudly, and shouting with acclaim the name of Iacchus, particularly when the image of the infant god reached Eleusis. In this way the whole of the 19th passed, and though the distance traversed is only a dozen miles, the arrival at Eleusis took place amid the light of torches at midnight.

What took place at Eleusis during the all-night ceremonies (παννυχίδες) which followed is known only imperfectly; for the ancient initiates were faithful to their vows of secrecy, and very little knowledge of the rites performed within the sacred enclosure (περίβολος) has transpired. A price was set on the head of a man who divulged the mysteries, and death or banishment and confiscation of property were visited on any one who travestied or profaned them in any way. Besides, it seems certain that those initiates, at least, who were admitted to the first degree understood only imperfectly the meaning of what they were permitted to see.

The The morning of the 20th was spent in sacrifices, the victims of which, we may be sure, were chiefly swine, since that animal, as we have seen in the case of the Thesmo-

The ceremonies at Eleusis.

phoria (page 276), was sacred to Demēter, and its blood was
deemed especially efficacious in expiation and propitiation
(cf. Fig. 240); furthermore, it had been the custom from
the remotest times to cut up swine's flesh and spread it
over the grain-fields, in the belief that thus the goddess
would grant fertility and an abundant harvest. Other
divinities, both gods and goddesses, were invoked in sacrifice on the 21st.

The ceremony on the night of the 22d belonged primarily to the new initiates, and constituted the initiation
($\mu\acute{\upsilon}\eta\sigma\iota\varsigma$) proper. A principal feature was the drinking of
the kykeon (cf. page 143), a mixture which consisted of
barley-meal, water, and mint. Certain relics and sacred
objects were then exposed by the Hierophant (hence his
name) to the view of the mystai assembled in the temple
of the two goddesses (the $\tau\epsilon\lambda\epsilon\sigma\tau\acute{\eta}\rho\iota o\nu$). This edifice, which
was completed after the Peloponnesian War, was of peculiar
construction, having a lower and an upper story, with an
opening in the middle of the roof to admit light. The
unusual character of the building probably tended to increase the awe of the people gathered there. The scenes
which the priests caused to be enacted were essentially
dramatic, and probably portrayed the sorrows of Demēter
as she searched the world over for her lost daughter.

A higher grade of initiates, consisting of those who
had been admitted to the first stage at least one year before,
were permitted to witness the ceremonies of the 23d day.
These were also dramatic, and probably revealed more concerning the origin of Iacchus, the mystical union of
Persephoné with Zeus, and the final joy of Demēter. The
initiate who had witnessed these last scenes ($\dot{\epsilon}\pi\acute{o}\pi\tau\eta\varsigma$, $\ddot{\epsilon}\phi o\rho o\varsigma$)
was accounted most fortunate, as having attained the full-
ness of knowledge and perfection in this world. The word
used of the ceremony, teleté ($\tau\epsilon\lambda\epsilon\tau\acute{\eta}$), signifies perfection.

In the home there frequently occurred festivals or ceremonies of a more domestic character. The father of a bride,

for instance, performed a special sacrifice before her wedding (called τὰ προγάμια or τὰ προτέλεια, page 123), to propitiate the gods of marriage ; in Athens they were Artemis, Aphrodīte, Zeus and Hēra, Peitho (Persuasion), and the Erinyes (Furies). Again, all the members of a family and its intimate friends were called in to join in the sacrifice which took place ten days after a child was born; this feast (the γενέθλια or δεκάτη, page 73), gave occasion for great merrymaking. Birthdays, however, were not observed by the Greeks, at least during the lifetime of the person. After his death there was a yearly sacrifice, held on his birthday, and called *genesia* or *eniausia*; the festival was paid for by a fund provided in his will. Still another festival which concerned the home was the Apaturia, held in October, and lasting three days. Since it involved the interests of all families belonging to a phratry, it was held in the common assembly room or house of that phratry, and not in a private house. On the last day of this festival all the children born in the families of its members since the last meeting were presented to the members (φράτερες). The member who acted as priest (ἱερεὺς τοῦ Διὸς φρατρίου) offered, on behalf of the father or guardian of the child,

Other celebrations.

FIG. 247.—Girls practising the dance for a popular festival.

a sheep called *meion* (μεῖον), i. e., lesser, in contradistinction
to the more important sacrifice called koureion (page 89),
which the father offered for a son who had attained his
majority and been admitted on that day as a regular
member of the phratry. Rhapsodic contests took place
at this festival also.

Boys in school enjoyed a special holiday on the occasion of the Hermaea and the Museia. The first was in
honour of Hermes, the protecting genius of
School festivals. palaestra and gymnasium. The boys were
dressed in their best clothes, offered sacrifices, and were permitted unrestrained liberty in games
and sports. The Museia was a school festival, to which
the parents, in the name of the boys, contributed offerings for sacrifice.

In the language of every-day converse the Greeks made
frequent reference to their gods. Oaths in the name of
"all the gods and goddesses," and mere exple-
Oaths. tives, like "By Zeus," or "By Apollo" (νὴ Δία,
ναὶ μὰ Δία, οὐ μὰ τὸν Δία), frequently began a sentence. Sometimes they were uttered in strong asseveration or even indignation, approaching in character to modern profanity; but
the Greek was always restrained from blasphemy by his
conscious personal attitude towards his deities, and the
belief that perjury (ἐπιορκία) was sure to be visited with
the lasting displeasure of the god whose name had been
taken in vain. An oath accompanied the allegation of a
plaintiff and defendant and their witnesses at the preliminary hearing (ἀνάκρισις, page 212) before a trial. When
the oath was to be especially solemn, the person swearing
it laid his hand on an altar or statue; and in concluding
a treaty between warring parties, the oath, generally sworn
in the name of three gods, was further strengthened by
dipping the hand or sword in blood. Often the swearer
invoked destruction (ἐξώλεια) upon himself and his children if he should prove to have perjured himself.

A very common habit which seems to us vindictive and hateful in the extreme was the practice of writing out curses against enemies, or against those who were supposed to exert an evil magical influence, on tablets, which were hung as amulets round the neck, or placed near some shrine. Imprecation (καταρᾶσθαι) meets one frequently in the pages of Greek literature. People took measures especially to avoid the harm wrought by the " evil eye," which they attributed to others very much as witchcraft has been ascribed to unfortunate victims in later times. An amulet with mystic signs (Fig. 248) was considered to have potency against the wicked influence.

Fig. 248.
Amulet against the " evil eye."

CHAPTER XXI

OLD AGE, SICKNESS, DEATH, BURIAL

OLD age (γῆρας) was contemplated with varying feelings in different parts of Greece. In Sparta and in Thebes, where

Popular sentiment regarding old age. the traditions of an olden time were maintained with a stricter conservatism than in Athens, and in more remote and primitive districts generally, untouched by the smart fashions set by some of the younger Athenians, the aged enjoyed the reverence and affection of the young and middle-aged alike. In such places the young readily rose and offered them places at any gathering; and in public and private their counsel was sought first and their sanction deemed indispensable for any important undertaking. Hence they were regularly selected in older times, and wherever older fashions prevailed, to represent public opinion on an embassy, so that " elders " and " envoys " were expressed in the same term, πρέσβεις. Among the Ionians, however, and even among some persons in Athens, old age was often deemed a calamity, which cut short the power to enjoy life on the material side which the luxurious desired, and the loss of which is constantly mourned in Greek poetry. But all Greeks, probably, would have prayed to be delivered from old age by an early death rather than to undergo it childless. The hope of every parent was to rear children who should comfort his or her advancing years (γηροβοσκεῖν). There is a mingled tone, half of pity, half of contempt, expressed in the interesting diminutives (found also in other languages) which Xenophon uses in reference to some forlorn old men

and women abandoned in a town along with a few sheep and
oxen (γερόντια, γράδια, "little old men," "little old women").
The cessation of a man's active physical force at the age of
sixty was recognized by the state; he was then exempt
from military duty, and became an "old man" (γέρων), who
in war, for instance, would be spurned as a hostage.

Fig. 249.—Temple of Asclepius at Epidaurus (restoration).

With all the advantages of matchless climate and constant outdoor life, at least among the free citizen class,
and in spite of the extraordinary care bestowed
Liability to disease. on the body and its systematic training in
gymnastics, the Athenians and other Greeks
of course were subject to the diseases (νόσοι) that afflict
all men. Their houses, in the first place, lacked proper
sanitary appliances. The streets were not regularly
cleaned, and people were allowed to throw offal in some of
them; for there were as yet no boards of health. The
drinking-water of Athens was not especially noted for its
healthfulness, as was that of Corinth. The apparatus avail-

able for crippled and maimed persons was of the roughest
kind—two canes instead of one, or the like. If eyes gave
out, which might happen in cases of great exposure or
unusual strain, there were no goggles or eyeglasses to relieve the sufferer.

And yet, by the middle of the fifth century, a considerable amount of skill in the treatment of disease had been

acquired, partly
Treatment of disease. from Egypt and
the Orient, part-
ly from observation and experience (ἐμπειρία). By the end
of the century the arts of surgery and medicine had been
raised to the dignity of sciences through the genius of
the Ionic physician Hippocrates. Many of the methods
of that time would not, of
course, be tolerated to-day.
Mixed with scientific knowledge was a good deal belonging to the realm of supersti-
tion and folk-lore, so that, for
example, a person suffering
pain would have young pup-
pies applied to the spot affected, in the belief that they
would absorb it themselves

FIG. 250.—Asclepius.

and thus relieve the patient. Overdosing was common.
Wine was constantly prescribed even when the sick man
was in a high fever, and Chirisophus, Xenophon's able and
trusted helper, died from an overdose of drugs while suffering a fever.

Two centuries before Hippocrates, Egypt had taught
the Greeks the use of a few primitive surgical instruments,

and both medicine and surgery were further advanced by
the Asclepiadae, an association or guild of practitioners
who professed to trace descent from Asclepius,
Medicine and the god of healing. Many of the Asclepiadae
surgery.
were priests of this god at temples which were
noted for famous cures. Later, apprentices were admitted
from families who were not akin.   Cities like Athens employed at public cost "state physicians" (ἰατροὶ
Physicians. δημόσιοι, or δημοσιεύοντες), who gave their services free to the poor.   Democēdes, a celebrated physician
who came to Aegīna from Croton, in Italy, was paid a
talent for a year's service, more than four times the pay of
the generals in the Athenian army.   At the end of the
year he was attracted to Athens by the fee of one hundred

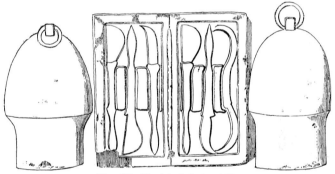

FIG. 251.—Physician's instruments.

minae, but the Athenians were in turn outbidden by Poly-
crates, tyrant of Samos, who increased his pay to two
talents. Another famous physician and writer, attached to
the court of Artaxerxes, was Ctesias, who cured the king
Social   of the wound dealt him by Cyrus at Cunaxa.
standing of   Greek physicians did not practise some one
physicians.   branch of their art as a specialty, but were
always "general practitioners," and were required to learn
the whole of both surgery and medicine.   As has been said,

the measures they took were more heroic and drastic than modern science would approve, and some were noted for ruthless cutting, bleeding, and cauterizing, as well as for administering such quantities of drugs (φάρμακα) that poisoning ensued. Hence they were often looked on with dis-

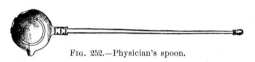

FIG. 252.—Physician's spoon.

like, and the fact that they took pay relegated them, in the opinion of

the free citizen, to the same class with tradesmen and artisans. In spite of all this, they often deserved, and in fact often received, high praise for conscientious devotion to the patient's welfare and for their dignified and cheerful bearing in the presence of the sick. Their pupils they taught with an earnestness that marked them as having the true scientific spirit.

Training of physicians.

The pupils began their course when very young, and regularly attended their masters at the patient's bedside. There they learned not only the methods of their science, but also proper deportment toward the patient and his family.

A regular corps of army surgeons seems not to have existed, but there were few armies, except perhaps those made up of mercenaries, which did not include one or two physicians drafted with other citizens or metics. In Xenophon's army eight men volunteered to act as physicians in caring for the numerous wounded during the retreat.

Besides those physicians who worked independently or in company with other Asclepiadae, there were priests belonging to the temples of the gods of healing— Apollo, Artemis, Hecaté, and later, Serāpis— who offered relief in sickness. Their methods, however, were based mainly on ritual observance and religious practice, such as the art of divination, especially through dreams. The notion was universally held that the gods who caused the affliction could, when properly ap-

Health resorts.

FIG. 253.—Interior of the temple at Epidaurus (restoration).

19

proached with sacrifice, indicate the cure by signs and dreams. Hence, both in Athens and elsewhere, and especially in the fourth century at Epidaurus, the precinct of Asclepius became a kind of sanatorium, thronged with patients who devoutly lay at night in or near the temple waiting for the dream that should give them the directions required. Having got it, they told it to the priest, who interpreted it in hard cases. The grateful convalescents then made offerings to the god, which generally consisted of small images of the hand, leg, or whatever part of the body had been diseased. These images, made of marble, clay, wax, or the precious metals, were then hung up in the temple, with an inscription recording the name of the patient, a description of the disease, and the manner of its cure.

Dream cures.

Fig. 254.—Votive eye.

The temples of Asclepius (᾿Ασκληπιεῖα) usually stood in healthful regions, sometimes near mineral springs ; and though the cure was always regarded as the miraculous intervention of the " kindly " god, it was doubtless furthered by wise prescriptions given by the priest in regard to diet, fresh air, exercise, and legitimate amusements. The votive tablets, also, constituted in course of time a record of large experience which could be relied on for similar cases in the future.

Within the domestic circle the methods of cure for slight ailments were more primitive and superstitious. Among them, magic incantations (ἐπῳδαί) ranked chief in importance. These were generally crooned by old women called in to exorcise the evil spirit which was thought to possess the patient. Amulets were thought to be an efficient preventive and remedy on the same theory of a possessing demon. There were male quacks (γόητες), too, who were ready to apply their drugs at lower prices and to befool patients with their pompous magic. In the market were druggists (φαρμακοπῶλαι)

Home cures.

through whom many might avoid the employment of the more expensive, if more enlightened, physicians.

If the patient felt that recovery was hopeless, he made his will (διαθήκη). In Athens this was a privilege not al-

Last sickness. lowed to women or minors. The last wishes might be expressed orally (ἐπισκήπτω) or in writing. The testator began with a pious formula, such as, "It shall be well; but if aught happen, this is the disposition of his goods" (ἔσται μὲν εὖ· ἐὰν δέ τι συμβαίνῃ, τάδε

διέθετο); or else the phrase, "Be it entrust-ed to good fortune" (τύχῃ ἀγαθῇ), preced-ed. Then followed the phrase, "This is the disposition I make of my effects" (τάδε διατίθεμαι περὶ τῶν κατ᾽ ἐμαυτόν). The be-quests, with the ex-ception of a legacy here and there to a friend, or a special gift to a son, were limited in certain

Fig. 255.—Votive tresses.

Restrictions governing wills. ways by the law. The testator was obliged to respect the ties of kindred, and since every citizen was a member of a clan or γένος, the prior rights of that clan over outsiders must be considered. If a man had legitimate sons (παῖδες γνήσιοι), by which, as we saw (pages 61, 74), were meant those born of parents who could trace descent on both sides through a genuine line of

Adoption. Attic citizens, his property went directly to those sons. A son could not be disinherited. If the dying man had no sons, he might designate a young man to be his adopted son, under the condition that the young man marry the daughter of the house, if there were any. Adoption was a prerequisite to inheritance for a male not sprung from the testator. The children of the adopted son were regarded as descendants of the adopting father, and therefore preserved his ancestral worship and paid homage at his tomb; for the primary object of adoption was to obtain what descendants alone could insure, a regular maintenance of the family cult and worship of the family's ancestors. After these arrangements had been specified in the will, it then set forth directions about freeing favourite slaves, about presents (δωρεαί) to friends, votive offerings (ἀναθήματα) to the gods, and finally it contained minute directions about the burial and disposition of the corpse, concluding with an imprecation against any who might neglect or violate its provisions. The contents of the will were kept secret until after death, but were read just

Provisions of the will.

Fig. 256.—Bronze dog (votive offering).

before the last rites (τὰ νομιζόμενα) were begun. It was signed and sealed in the presence of witnesses chosen from the family or intimate friends, and deposited in the care of some citizen or public officer, or in a temple. Sometimes several copies were made and stored in different places. The chief archon had jurisdiction in all testamentary disputes. The will was not valid if the testator's mind was unbalanced or if undue influence could be proved.

Religious importance attaching to burial rites. The burial customs of the Greeks were remarkable for the scrupulous care with which every detail, enjoined as it was by religion, was carried out. Without burial, it was believed that the unfortunate spirit of the dead must wander in eternal unrest, visiting with reproach his neglectful kinsmen. To the corpse that lacked proper burial Charon

would refuse passage over the Styx. If the body of a man
were lost in shipwreck or in battle, his friends were bound
to erect an "empty monument" or cenotaph (κενοτάφιον)
and perform all the other rites as they would had they recovered the body. If a traveller came upon an unburied
corpse and failed to give at least symbolic burial by throwing over it three handfuls of earth, he was looked upon as
accursed, and as one who would be haunted by the spirit of
the dead. Hence, after a battle, a herald was always sent

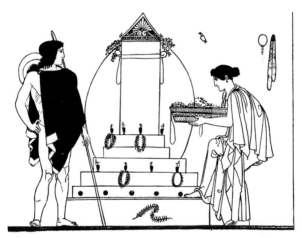

Fig. 257.—At the tomb.

out with his staff (κηρύκειον), answering to the modern flag
of truce, to arrange for the privilege of picking up the
bodies of the dead.

Character of the Greek burial ceremony. Thus it is easy to see that when a man died
his family felt bound by the strictest commands
of religion to execute the last rites as he would
have wished them to be performed. The names
given to these rites, "that which is right," "that which
is customary," or "incumbent" (τὰ δίκαια, τὰ νομιζόμενα,
or τὰ προσήκοντα), show the obligation that was felt to be

imposed. While the loud wailing of mourners hired to sing ancient and half-intelligible dirges (θρῆνοι) may perhaps seem to us undignified, yet there were influences which tended to make the funeral ceremonies a pious and solemn act of great impressiveness. Among these influences were first the laws restraining excessive demonstrations of grief and the extravagant expenditure of money for the burial. Further, the Eleusinian Mysteries and the belief in a life after death, which was derived from the Egyptians, lent further dignity to the rites of mourning, though all Greeks, of course, did not share in the Mysteries.

The women of the family first washed the body carefully, anointed it with perfumed unguents, and dressed it in clean chiton and himation. The garments of the dead were white (in Homer of linen), either plain or ornamented with embroidery or coloured stripes. The lips and eyes were closed, and a wreath was placed on the head, of laurel, olive, or parsley. During the day immediately following the death the body thus lay in state on a couch (κλίνη), which was decked with garlands

Care of the dead body.

Fig. 258.—The prothesis.

given by relatives and friends. The laying out of the body was called the *prothesis* (πρόθεσις). On the floor round the couch stood the pitchers (λήκυθοι) that were to be buried with the deceased. All this day the women stood near singing the dirge, to which the men added a refrain. Solon

forbade the extravagances we read of in Homer, such as
tearing the cheeks with the finger-nails, violently beating
the breast, and rending the chiton. But in funeral customs
the habits of people are rigid, and, in spite of his laws, extreme modes of showing grief persisted.

On the following day the procession (ἐκφορά) and the
burial took place. This always happened before sunrise,

The proces-
sion to the
grave.
because religion taught that the light of the
sun was polluted by the sight of a corpse.
The same feeling that death was a pollu-
tion prompted the custom in Athens of interring bodies
outside the limits of the city. In primitive Athens this
had not been observed, and
the Spartans retained their
ancient habit of burying inside the city. In the country persons were buried on
their own estates. The body
was borne on the same couch
on which it had lain during
the prothesis, and the garlands and pitchers were carried with it to the grave.
Sometimes the head of the
deceased was crowned with a
chaplet of gold leaf for the
progress to the grave ; remains of these gold chaplets
have been found in graves
recently excavated. The
body-bearers (νεκροφόροι) were
friends or family slaves ; but

Fig. 259.—Group from a funeral
monument.

professionals could also be hired for this office. The procession started with a signal given on the flute, which then
accompanied the song of mourning as the funeral party left
the house. In front of the bier (κλίνη) marched the male

relatives in the order of relationship down to the sons of cousins; these were followed by the male friends of the dead. Behind the bier the female relatives, extending to the same degree of relationship, closed the short and modest procession. All other women, whether related or not, were excluded, except distant kinswomen over sixty years of age. All the mourners wore dark clothes, either black or gray. The men had their hair shorn close.

If the deceased came of a wealthy family, the interment or cremation, whichever had been decided on, took place on a highroad or near some resort frequented by the living. The suburb called the Outer Cerameicus, just beyond the Dipylon, became a beautiful burying-ground filled with splendid and tasteful monuments (page 9). For the poorer classes there were public burial-places, where corpses were interred either singly or in numbers (νεκροπόλεις). Cremation (κατακαίεσθαι) was costlier than simple burial (κατορύττεσθαι), and therefore generally confined to the rich, except in the event of a plague, such as that which afflicted Athens in the early years of the Peloponnesian War. Those who died in battle or in foreign lands were cremated, if possible; in the latter case, that the ashes of the dead might be carried home and buried in their native soil. If it were possible, the body of a man struck by lightning was buried on the spot where he fell, since it was felt that he had met with a special visitation of Zeus; the corpse, as being something sacred (ἱερός) to the god, must not be removed.

After calling three times on the spirit of the dead, the mourners placed the remains, if they had been burnt, in an urn of clay or bronze; if the corpse was to be buried merely, it was laid in a coffin, *soros* (σορός), usually of cypress wood or earthenware, sometimes of metal. Stone or marble sarcophagi did not come into use until Roman times. The coffin was then lowered into the grave, which was frequently excavated in the rock. This made a natural coffin called *thēké* (θήκη), and the soros was then sometimes dispensed with. Again, the body, whether it had been placed in a coffin or not, might be laid out in a tomb or vault (τάφος); only in extraordinary cases, probably, was a body put into an earth grave (βόθρος) without a coffin. The Athenians buried their dead with the head lying toward the west, the feet toward the east. Beside the dead were placed the pitchers (λήκυθοι), which had surrounded his couch during the prothesis, and various other articles which had been connected with the dead during his lifetime, or were thought necessary for

Fig. 260.—Charon's boat.

his long journey—money, ornaments, tools, toys, food, and drink—according to age, sex, and calling. The money (usually an obol) was often placed in the mouth of the deceased; we have seen that people carried it thus in their daily marketing. The obol was thought to be the price (ναῦλον) of Charon's ferrying over the Styx.

Funeral monuments. Beside the mound (τύμβος, χῶμα, σῆμα) a monument was ordinarily reared. In earlier times, before the Persian wars, it was customary to erect a huge stone urn (λήκυθος) over the grave. The urn survived in later times, but it became more usual to place a slab of stone or marble (στήλη), sculptured in relief, with a life-size portrait of the dead. The name of the dead and sometimes of the friend who erected the memorial

FIG. 261.—Monument to Dexileus.

were inscribed near the relief. Sometimes Doric or Ionic columns (κίονες) were erected in place of these stē̆lai. These were surmounted by some figure, such as an eagle or siren. The stēlé later developed, by the addition of columns on the sides, into a miniature façade, showing pillars, architrave, and pediment. This served as a frame for elaborate portraits, in sculpture, of the deceased and his family. Many of these, depicting some pleasant scene out of the home life of the departed still remain to testify to the kindlier and more affectionate traits of the Greek character.

Returning from the grave, the mourners set about purifying themselves and their house, on the theory, as before explained, that death brought pollution in the sight of the gods. The water for purification was brought in a special vessel (ἀρδάνιον) from another house, and kept at the front door. Three days were then spent in fasting, which was broken by the funeral banquet (περίδειπνον). At this a place was set for the dead, as if he were the host, and his good qualities were set forth while the mourners strove to comfort one another, and to eat and drink once more. On the ninth or tenth day a sacrifice was offered at the tomb, which was

Mourning customs.

decorated with ribbons and chaplets. The period of public mourning ended finally on the thirtieth day, when another sacrifice and another banquet were held. Citizens who fell in battle were buried at public expense (δημοσίᾳ) with special honours, notably with a eulogy pronounced by some eminent man ; such eulogies were not customary at a private burial before Roman times. The missing dead were given a symbolic burial, in that an empty couch (κλίνη κενή) was borne for them in the procession, and a cenotaph was erected to their memory.

Graves were everywhere cherished with thoughtful piety. The stēlai were anointed with oil, and decorated with ribbons and wreaths. In their vicinity were planted shade

Fig. 262.—The funeral banquet.

trees, especially cypress and poplars, and flowers, notably the asphodel, with large thick white leaves and yellow, white, and bluish flower. Into this garden, which often contained fountains, friends came in the belief that their presence was helpful to the dead, whose spirit would be there to note their coming. Especially were the dead remembered in the festival of the Anthesteria (page 274) and at the *Nekysia* (νεκύσια), a day devoted to them in the month Boedromion.

From the tomb the modern explorer has gathered some

FIG. 263.—The so-called "mourning Athēna."

of his most instructive material for composing the picture of ancient life. The grave of the Mycenaean warrior, the last resting-places (κοιμητήρια) of the early Christian, alike prove to be sources of intimate knowledge concerning Greek life. The seeker finds arms and armour, ornaments of silver, gold, and copper, the toys that were dear to the child, the objects of household use cherished by the adult, coins and vases which bear contemporary witness to the life they adorned, and form, as it were, a picture within a picture. Out of the grave rises the spirit of ancient Hellas to-day, and offers lessons of simplicity, faith, and beauty that may not be forgotten.

SUPPLEMENTARY MATTERS

1. LIST OF THE ATHENIAN MAGISTRATES

THE general term for magistrates is *archontes* (ἄρχοντες);
for public office, *arché* (ἀρχή). Election or sortition, the latter
being employed for all offices except the generalship and a few
others, took place in the spring, allowing time for the public
scrutiny (δοκιμασία, cf. p. 206) of each officer, since office was
held from the 1st of Hekatombaion. White and black beans
were used in the election by lot (hence the phrase ἀπὸ κυάμου).
All but the military offices were annual, and all underwent an
examination (εὔθυνα) at the close of service.

ADMINISTRATIVE

The Nine Archons, also called collectively *Thesmothetai*
(οἱ ἐννέα ἄρχοντες, θεσμοθέται). For a long period the Thētes were
ineligible to the office. At the end of their service the archons
became members of the Council of the Areopagus (p. 42).

The first archon (ὁ ἄρχων *par excellence*) is sometimes called
in modern books the Archon Eponymous, because his name
was used in dating records (p. 242). His office was in the Prytaneium, where he was assisted by two aids (πάρεδροι) appointed
by himself. In the courts he presided at cases which concerned
family interests, the protection of orphans, the apportioning of
orphan heiresses, the appointment of guardians, and divorce.
He managed the City Dionysia (pp. 113, 275). He conducted
the expiatory rites at the Thargelia (p. 310).

The second archon was called the King (ὁ βασιλεύς). His
office was in the King's Portico (p. 43). With the name, he
also retained the religious duties of the ancient Attic kings, and
had general oversight over temples and altars. He represented
the state in the celebration of the Mysteries (p. 276), conducted

301

the Lenaea (p. 113), and managed the torch races (λαμπαδη-
δρομίαι) at all festivals where they occurred. In the courts he
had jurisdiction in all cases that pertained to religion, and
therefore presided over the Areopagus when it convened to
try murderers, since bloodshed involved religious uncleanness.
His wife took a conspicuous part in the Anthesteria, when she
was symbolically married to Dionȳsus.

The third archon was called the Polemarch (ὁ πολέμαρχος).
As his name signifies, he originally was commander-in-chief,
but was superseded by the generals (p. 197). He offered the
state sacrifices to Artemis Agrotera and Enyalius (both divinities of war) at the festival of Marathon (p. 306), and also the
sacrifice for dead warriors (ἐπιτάφια, p. 307) and for Harmodius
and Aristogeiton. In the courts he had jurisdiction where foreigners, particularly metics, were concerned.

The other six archons, styled Thesmothetai, attended to the
revision of the laws, and when conflicts were discovered, recommended to the Council the repeal of old laws, or the passing
of new ones. They presided at the examination of public officers; in certain cases of *endeixis*, where information of mis-
demeanour had been laid before them; impeachment (εἰσαγγε-
λία); and in cases brought on by the proposing of some unconstitutional measure (γραφὴ παρανόμων); in general, they took
charge of all cases that did not belong to some other magistrate.
They decided when a case should be heard and assigned the
court-rooms to the several magistrates.

The Eleven (οἱ ἕνδεκα), an executive board. These superintended the prisons and executed the death penalty by administering poison (κώνειον, "hemlock").

The Astynomoi (οἱ ἀστυνόμοι), ten in number, five for Athens,
five for the Piraeus (see pp. 16, 20).

The Agoranomoi (οἱ ἀγορανόμοι), distributed like the Astynomoi (see pp. 20, 34).

The Metronomoi (see p. 242).

The Commissioners of Grain (οἱ σιτοφύλακες). They were ten
in number until the latter half of the fourth century, when
twenty were chosen for Athens, fifteen for the Piraeus. They
noted the amount of grain imported, exercised control over the
importers and the retailers of breadstuffs, and enforced a legal
standard of weight and price.

The purchasers of grain (οἱ σιτῶναι), specially chosen in times of famine to buy grain for distribution to the poor.

Overseers of the Port (ἐπιμεληταὶ ἐμπορίου), ten in number, who had functions allied to those of the grain commissioners. Athenian law, in order to insure a sufficient supply of grain (cf. p. 220), required that two-thirds of all grain coming to the Piraeus should be landed and sold in Athens.

Superintendent of the Springs (ὁ ἐπὶ τὰς κρήνας). This was an important office which required experts, and therefore was filled by election, not by lot. The officer chosen repaired spring-houses and water conduits.

Repairers of the Roads (ὁδοποιοί), five in number, road commissioners.

Repairers of the Temples (οἱ ἱερῶν ἐπισκευασταί). To these were appropriated annually thirty minae for the repair of Athenian shrines.

Superintendents of Public Works (ἐπιστάται τῶν δημοσίων ἔργων) were elected as occasion arose.

Purchasers of Oxen (βοῶναι) were distinguished citizens elected to the honorary office of buying oxen for the sacrifices.

Athlothetai (ἀθλοθέται) managed the Greater Panathenaea held every four years. They retained office for the unusual term of four years.

FINANCIAL

The Apodektai (οἱ ἀποδέκται), ten in number, were general treasurers, receiving war-taxes, market and other tolls, and all debts due the state, which were determined by a list given to them by a commissioner (δημόσιος) of the council.

The Kolakretai (οἱ κωλακρέται) were an ancient board, number unknown, which managed the public dinners (σίτησις ἐν πρυτανείῳ, p. 63) and paid the jurymen. In the sixth century they seem to have had higher functions, but in the fifth many of their powers were transferred to the Apodektai.

The Polētai (οἱ πωληταί) were ten officers who had charge of the collection of state dues. They leased the mines, farmed out the taxes to tax-gatherers for a lump sum, and made contracts for public works. They sold confiscated property, especially of those whose war-taxes had not been paid, or of metics who had not paid their market tolls or procured a patron (p. 65).

The Praktores (οἱ πράκτορες) were collecting agents, probably ten in number, who secured the payment of fines imposed by the courts.

Comptroller of the Treasury (ἀντιγραφεὺς τῆς διοικήσεως) had charge of the money paid into the treasury at the Prytaneion by the Apodektai. He rendered an account during each prytany (p. 207).

Stewards of the Funds of Athēna (ταμίαι τῶν ἱερῶν χρημάτων τῆς Ἀθηναίας). These were ten men chosen only from the Pentakosiomedimni. They had the keeping of the temple or temples of Athēna and of Niké, with all the treasures of the Acropolis.

Stewards of the other Gods (ταμίαι τῶν ἄλλων θεῶν). These had charge, under the preceding, of the treasures of other divinities, which were transferred in 454-3 B. C. to the temple of Athēna Polias on the Acropolis.

Stewards of the Greeks (ἑλληνοταμίαι) were treasurers of the Confederacy of Delos. They originally had their office in Delos, and represented the several states which formed the league. Later the treasury was removed to Athens, and only Athenians were chosen to the office, one from each tribe. They received the tribute of the dependent allies, which was paid each year at the time of the Greater Dionysia. This fund was kept separate from all others, though one-sixtieth was devoted as an offering (ἀπαρχή) to Athēna. Payments from this fund, which was appropriated for public buildings and military enterprises, were controlled by them.

The Syndics (οἱ σύνδικοι) were a temporary board chosen at the restoration of the democracy in 403 B. C. to recover, so far as possible, money and property illegally appropriated by the Thirty Tyrants.

The following magistrates are mentioned chiefly in the records of the fourth century :

The Treasurer of the People (ταμίας τοῦ δήμου) controlled money used in erecting and restoring records of legislative decrees. He paid travelling expenses of ambassadors and the expenses of making honorary crowns (p. 63).

Treasurers of the Theoric Fund (οἱ ἐπὶ τὸ θεωρικόν, p. 112), instituted by Eubūlus between 354-339. Eubūlus brought about a decree by which all balances of money in the state treasury should be given to the people to enable them to take part in the state festivals.   These treasurers held office from one Panathenaea to the next following.

Treasurer of the Military Funds (ταμίας τῶν στρατιωτικῶν), established at the instance of Demosthenes on the abolition of the system of Eubūlus in 339.   He dispensed the balances which were formerly in the hands entirely of the theoric officials.

Late in the fourth century a single official, called ὁ ἐπὶ τῇ διοικήσει, took the place of the Apodektai, and in conjunction with the Polētai saw to the contracts for public works, the making of honorary crowns and statues, and paid the expenses involved in setting up the decrees of the people in stone or bronze.

MILITARY

The Generals (στρατηγοί, p. 197).   At the beginning, one was elected (by show of hands, χειροτονία) from each tribe; later, all the ten were elected from the whole body of citizens. Five had special duties: the first (ὁ ἐπὶ τοὺς ὁπλίτας) took command in foreign campaigns; the second (ὁ ἐπὶ τὴν χώραν) conducted defensive operations at home; the third (ὁ ἐπὶ τὴν Μουνιχίαν) and the fourth (ὁ ἐπὶ τὴν Ἀκτήν) maintained the defense of the ports; the fifth (ὁ ἐπὶ τὰς συμμορίας) managed the trierarchies and conducted legal procedure concerning them when necessary.   Theoretically all the generals had equal power; practically the chief command might be assigned by the ecclesia to one or more of them, or as agreed on by the others; sometimes also each took command in turn.   They had diplomatic as well as military functions, made treaties, and in general conducted foreign affairs.

The Taxiarchs (οἱ ταξίαρχοι) were ten officers, each commanding the hoplites of a single tribe.

The Captains (οἱ λοχαγοί) commanded small detachments under the Taxiarchs.

The Hipparchs (οἱ ἵππαρχοι) were two cavalry officers.   Under them were the phylarchs, ten in all, one for each tribe.

Captains of Ten (οἱ δεκάδαρχοι) were cavalry officers appointed by the Hipparchs.

20

2. ATTIC HOLY DAYS AND FESTIVALS (ἑορταί)

METAGEITNION

12th. The Kronia (τὰ Κρόνια). Originally a rural festival, sacred to Kronos and Rhea. Masters and slaves ate together. It was deemed old-fashioned in Aristophanes's time.

16th. The Synoikia (τὰ ξυνοίκια). In honour of Athēna and Hestia. It celebrated Theseus's consolidation of Attica. Bloodless offerings were made for peace.

21st–29th. The Panathenaea (παναθήναια, p. 274). The Lesser Panathenaea (τὰ μικρά or τὰ κατ᾽ ἐνιαυτόν) were held annually ; the Greater (τὰ μεγάλα), every four years, in the third year of each Olympiad.

> 21st–22d–23d. Musical contests.
> 24th–25th. Gymnastic contests.
> 26th. Horse-racing and chariot-racing.
> 27th. The pyrriché (p. 84).
> 28th. Torch-race at night.

The great procession (πομπή), with sacrifice of cattle and sheep to Athēna, followed by general feasting.

> 29th. Boat-race.

In this month (or when the sun was in *Virgo*) occurred also the Heracleia (τὰ Ἡράκλεια), in honour of Heracles, and the Adonia (τὰ Ἀδώνια), celebrated especially by women. The first day was given over to the lament for the disappearance (ἀφανισμός) of Adōnis ; the second, to the symbolic search for his body. Plants that grew and faded quickly were set before the street door and the entrance to the temple of Adōnis.

BOEDROMION

3d. Celebration of the victory at Plataea (479 B. C.).

5th. The Genesia (τὰ γενέσια, τὰ νεκύσια, or τὰ νεμέσια, p. 299). A day devoted to the dead ; the Erinyes were believed to be abroad on this day, ready to avenge the neglect of departed spirits.

6th. Holiday in celebration of the victory at Marathon (490 B. C.). Sacrifice, conducted by the polemarch, of 500 goats to Artemis Agrotera and to Enyalius.

12th. The Charisteria (τὰ χαριστήρια ἐλευθερίας). Thanksgiving for the fall of the Thirty Tyrants (403 B. C.).

15th–23d. The Eleusinia (τὰ Ἐλευσίνια, see pp. 276 ff.).

PYANOPSION

7th. The Pyanopsia (τὰ πυανόψια); literally, the Feast of Beans. A festival in honour of Apollo and the Hōrai, attended with offerings of beans, pease, lentils, and other products of the earth. A conspicuous feature was the branch (εἰρεσιώνη) of olive or laurel, which was decorated, much like a Christmas tree, with white and purple tufts of wool and with fruits and cakes, and carried by a young lad, specially chosen for the honour, to the temple of Apollo. There it remained until the next year.

7th. The Oschophoria (τὰ ὀσχοφόρια). Two young men from each tribe carried, as they raced with one another, branches loaded with grapes from the temple of Dionȳsus, near the theatre, to the temple of Athēna Skiras at Phalēron.

8th–11th. The Theseia (τὰ Θήσεια) was celebrated with splendid offerings to Theseus and Aegeus, at which the poor were fed free.

9th. Contests of trumpeters and heralds.

10th. Torch-race and gymnastic contests.

11th. Horse-race.

12th. The Epitaphia (τὰ ἐπιτάφια). Public burial of dead warriors. Empty couches or coffins of cypress wood were carried for those whose bodies had not been recovered. An oration (λόγος ἐπιτάφιος) was delivered in the Cerameicus.

About this time also was held the Apaturia (τὰ ἀπατούρια, pp. 74, 281), which lasted three days. At the beginning of the first day, i. e., at evening, the members of a phratry supped at the assembly room of the phratry; this day was called the *dorpia* (δορπία). The second day (called the ἀνάρρυσις) was devoted to the gods, notably Zeus and Athēna, or any other divinity who was the object of a phratry's special devotion. The third day (κουρεῶτις) was occupied chiefly with the registration of infants and young men in the register of the phratry, as described on page 74.

10th–14th. The Thesmophoria (τὰ θεσμοφόρια, p. 276), a festival of the women of Attic birth in honour of Demēter.

10th. The Stenia (τὰ στήνια), attended with much scurrilous jesting, during which the women went from Athens to Halimus, at Cape Colias, and there spent the night.

11th. At Halimus were celebrated Aphrodīte and her attendant spirits, the Genetyllides.

12th. The return (ἄνοδος) of the women to Demēter's temple in Athens.

13th. The Nesteia (νηστεία), a very strict fast.

14th. The Kalligeneia (τὰ καλλιγένεια), a day of rejoicing after the fast, in which Demēter was extolled as the mother of a beautiful child (Persephoné).

POSEIDEON

19th. The rural Dionysia (τὰ κατ᾽ ἀγροὺς Διονύσια). This was the rustic celebration of Dionỹsus in the several demes, attended sometimes with scenic performances, as at Acharnae, Aixoné, Eleusis, Icaria, Piraeus, Salamis, and Thoricus. The head man of the deme, or demarch, conducted the festival, the expenses of which were paid by each deme. Besides other rustic sports, the *askoliasmos* (p. 77) was especially prominent.

The Haloia (τὰ Ἁλῷα) was a festival held in Athens and Eleusis in honour of Demēter and Dionỹsus. No blood offerings were allowed.

GAMELION

12th. The Lenaea (τὰ Λήναια, or ὁ ἐπὶ Ληναίῳ ἀγών, p. 113). A festival in honour of Dionỹsus of the wine-vat, attended with the broaching of the new wine, just fermented. A procession and scenic contests marked the festival. The Theogamia (τὰ θεογάμια, or ἱερὸς γάμος) celebrated the marriage of the gods, particularly Zeus and Hēra, and the conception of Hephaestus.

ANTHESTERION

11th–13th. The Anthesteria (τὰ Ἀνθεστήρια, p. 274). A festival to Dionỹsus, which bore many resemblances to the Roman Saturnalia and the modern Christmas.

11th. The Opening of the Wine-casks (τὰ πιθοίγια).

12th. The Feast of Pitchers, or *choës* day (χόες). There was a procession, with a mystic marriage of the wife of the king archon to Dionỹsus. With this has been compared the marriage of the Doges of Venice with the sea. A drinking contest gave occasion for extraordinary license and merry-making.

13th. The Feast of Pots (χύτροι). Vegetables were offered in pots to the dead, to whom the day was devoted.

18th–21st. The Lesser Mysteries (τὰ ἐν Ἄγρας). In later times these were also held in the autumn (see p. 277). Demē-ter, Koré, and Dionȳsus were celebrated at Agrae, on the Ilis-sus. A "truce of God" was proclaimed to insure the protection of the celebrants.

23d. The Diasia (τὰ Διάσια). A solemn propitiatory cere-mony to Zeus Meilichios, with holocausts of swine. For these the poor were allowed to substitute images of animals made of dough.

ELAPHEBOLION

8th–13th. The Greater, or City, Dionysia (Διονύσια τὰ ἐν ἄστει, or Διονύσια τὰ μεγάλα, pp. 113, 275).

8th. The Proagon. This embraced a formal announce-ment, in lieu of written programmes, of the lyric and the dramatic contests which were to ensue. Chorēgi, actors, and choruses appeared in the theatre in holiday, but not theatri-cal, attire.

9th. A procession, in which the image of Dionȳsus was carried from his ancient temple (the Lenaion) to the theatre, marched through the Cerameicus, attended with singing, dancing, and revel (κῶμος).

10th. Lyric contests of the choruses of boys and men.

11th–13th. Dramatic contests.

MOUNICHION

6th. Supplication of Apollo at the Delphinion (τὰ Δελφίνια?), on the coast, in memory of the rescue of Theseus and the seven youths and seven maidens from the Minotaur.

16th. The Mounichia (τὰ Μουνίχια). The Aianteia (τὰ Αἰάν-τεια), in memory of Ajax, son of Telamon. The Brauronia (τὰ Βραυρώνια), a purificatory ceremony, in which Artemis and the sacrifice of Iphigeneia at Aulis were commemorated. Rhap-sodes recited the *Iliad*. Women and girls (dressed as bears, p. 276) made offerings to Artemis.

19th (?). The Olympieia (τὰ ᾿Ολυμπίεια), in honour of the Olympian Zeus, whose precinct was near the Ilissus.

THARGELION

6th. Sacrifice of a ram (κριός) to Demēter Chloé.

6th–7th. The Thargelia (τὰ Θαργήλια). A solemn purificatory festival to Apollo and Artemis, to avert pestilence. Scape-
goats (φαρμακοί) were driven forth to remove the sins of the
people. An offering was made of the first fruits of the year.

6th–7th. The Delia (τὰ Δήλια). A festival held at Delos, but
restored and managed chiefly by the Athenians. A sacred
vessel (θεωρίς) was despatched from Athens, during which no
public executions were allowed, since the city was to be purified
of all guilt.

19–21st. These days were devoted to cleansing certain
shrines. The Kallynteria, held on the 19th, was a purification
of the Erechtheion. The Plynteria, a dread and solemn rite,
was devoted to Athēna, and was attended with the formal
cleaning of the image of Athēna Polias in the sea at Phalēron.

On the 19th and 20th occurred the Bendideia, established
during the Peloponnesian War in honour of the Thracian goddess Bendis. Besides a procession, there was a relay race on
horseback, the riders striving to carry a lighted torch to the
goal.

SKIROPHORION

12th. The Skira (τὰ Σκίρα), a festival of agricultural significance, was celebrated by a procession to the suburb Skira in
honour of Athēna Skiras, and with the spreading of gypsum or
lime (σκίρα) on the earth.

The Arrephoria (ἡ Ἀρρηφορία) was an offering made by girls
in a cavern in the gardens of Aphrodīte (p. 11). The offerings
were of a secret nature, intended to secure fruitfulness.

14th. The Dipolia (τὰ Διπόλια, or βουφόνια). an ancient and
curious ceremony in honour of Zeus Polieus. The slayer of
the bull used at the sacrifice struck the animal with an axe as
if in anger and fled. The axe was then tried for the murder
and thrown beyond the border.

3. BIBLIOGRAPHY

The best works in English are cited first in alphabetical
order; then follow others which are sometimes still useful,
though now in part antiquated. French and German works

are given last, but all of them are important for an understanding of details and the study of controverted questions, and many are indispensable on account of the lack of similar treatises in English. Other pertinent works are cited among the sources of the illustrations.

(a) GENERAL

1. American Journal of Archaeology: the journal of the Archaeological Institute of America, from 1885. New series, from 1897. New York.
2. P. Gardner and F. B. Jevons. A Manual of Greek Antiquities. London and New York, 1895.
3. P. Gardner. Classical Archaeology in Schools. Oxford, 1902.
4. Journal of Hellenic Studies: published by the Society for the Promotion of Hellenic Studies. London, from 1880.
5. J. P. Mahaffy. A Survey of Greek Civilization. Meadville, Pa., 1896.
6. J. P. Mahaffy. Social Life in Greece from Homer to Menander, 3d edition. London, 1875.
7. J. P. Mahaffy. Greek Life and Thought from the Age of Alexander to the Roman Conquest, 2d edition. London, 1896.
8. Nettleship and Sandys. A Dictionary of Classical Antiquities, Mythology, Religion, Literature, and Art. Based on No. 34. 3d edition. London, 1895.
9. T. Schreiber's Atlas of Classical Antiquities. Edited for English use by W. C. F. Anderson, with a preface by Percy Gardner. London, 1895. Same as No. 33.
10. W. Smith, W. Wayte, and G. E. Marindin. A Dictionary of Greek and Roman Antiquities, 3d edition, 2 vols. London, 1890–1891.
11. Alice Zimmern. The Home Life of the Ancient Greeks; a translation of No. 21. London, 1895.
12. W. A. Becker. Charicles; translated by Rev. F. Metcalfe, 4th edition. See No. 20. London, 1874.
13. W. H. Browne. Greece and Rome; a translation of No. 23. New York, 1882.
14. C. C. Felton. Lectures on Greece, Ancient and Modern, 2 vols. 1867.

15. Guhl and Koner's Life of the Greeks and Romans, described from antique monuments. Translated from the 3d German edition by F. Hueffer. New York, 1875. See No. 28.

16. J. P. Mahaffy. Old Greek Life. London, 1876 ; New York, 1888.

17. A. Rich. A Dictionary of Roman and Greek Antiquities, 5th edition. London, 1890.

18. J. A. St. John. The Hellenes, 2 vols. London, 1844.

19. A. Baumeister. Denkmäler des klassischen Altertums, 3 vols. Munich, 1884–1888.

20. W. A. Becker. Charikles ; neu bearbeitet von H. Göll, 3 vols. Berlin, 1877–1878.

21. H. Blümner. Leben und Sitten der Griechen. Leipzig, 1887.

22. C. Daremberg et E. Saglio. Dictionnaire des antiquités grecques et romaines d'après les textes et les monuments. Paris, from 1873.

23. J. von Falke. Hellas und Rom ; eine Kulturgeschichte des klassischen Altertums, 2d edition. Stuttgart, 1878–1880.

24. A. Forbiger. Hellas und Rom ; populäre Darstellung des öffentlichen und häuslichen Lebens der Griechen und Römer. Leipzig, 1876.

25. G. Fougères. La vie publique et privée des Grecs et der Romains. Paris, 1894.

26. P. Giraud. La vie privée et la vie publique des Grecs. Paris, 1890.

27. H. Göll. Kulturbilder aus Hellas und Rom, 2 vols., 3d edition. Leipzig and Berlin, 1880.

28. Guhl and Koner. Das Leben der Griechen und Römer, 6th edition by R. Engelmann. Berlin, 1893.

29. K. F. Hermann. Lehrbuch der griechischen Privataltertümer, 3d edition by H. Blümner. Freiburg, 1882.

30. R. Ménard et C. Sauvageot. La vie privée des anciens. Paris, 1880–1883.

31. I. v. Müller. Die griechischen Privataltertümer. Munich, 1893.

32. R. Opitz. Das häusliche Leben der Griechen und Römer. Leipzig, 1894. Vol. vi of Seemann's Kulturbilder aus dem klassischen Altertume.

33. Theodor Schreiber. Kulturhistorischer Bilderatlas; Part I, Altertum, 2d edition. Leipzig, 1888. With text by K. Bernhardi.
34. O. Seyffert. Lexikon der klassischen Altertumskunde. Leipzig, 1882.
35. K. L. Weisser. Bilderatlas zur Weltgeschichte, 2d edition. Stuttgart, 1881–1882.

(*b*) SPECIAL

To CHAPTER I.—E. Abbott. History of Greece, chap. i.

K. Baedeker. Greece. A Handbook for Travellers. English 2d edition, 1893.

S. J. Barrows. The Isles and Shrines of Greece. Boston, 1898.

C. Diehl. Excursions in Greece. Translated by E. R. Perkins. London, 1894.

E. A. Freeman. Studies of Travel in Greece and Italy, 2 vols. New York, 1894.

H. Kiepert. Manual of Ancient Geography. English translation. London, 1881.

J. P. Mahaffy. Rambles and Studies in Greece, 3d edition. London, 1887.

H. F. Tozer. Lectures on the Geography of Greece. 1873.

H. F. Tozer. A History of Ancient Geography. Cambridge, 1897.

C. Wordsworth. Greece, Pictorial, Descriptive, and Historical. Revised by H. F. Tozer. London, 1882.

Bursian. Geographie von Griechenland, 2 vols. 1862–1868.

Lolling. Topographie von Griechenland, in vol. iii of I. v. Müller's Handbuch der klassischen Altertumswissenschaft.

Neumann and Partsch. Physikalische Geographie von Griechenland. 1885.

A. Philippson. Der Peloponnes. Berlin, 1892.

To CHAPTER II.—Encyclopædia Britannica, s. v. *Athens.*

T. H. Dyer. Ancient Athens. London, 1873.

J. G. Frazer. Pausanias, Description of Greece. London, 1898.

Harrison and Verrall. Mythology and Monuments of Ancient Athens. London, 1890; New York, 1894.

Johnson's Universal Cyclopædia, s. v. *Athens.*

Smith's Dictionary of Antiquities, s. v. *Agora, Agoranomi, Astynomi, Sycophantes.*

E. Curtius and J. A. Kaupert. Karten von Attika. Berlin, 1897.

E. Curtius. Die Stadtgeschichte von Athen. Berlin, 1891.

Guides-Joanne, vol. i. Athènes et ses environs. Paris, 1890.

C. Wachsmuth. Die Stadt Athen im Altertum. 1874–1890.

To CHAPTER III.—E. Gardner. Journal of Hellenic Studies, xxi, 1901, pp. 293 ff.

Gardner and Jevons (No. 2), pp. 21–45.

P. Gardner. New Chapters in Greek History, chap. iv. (on the palace at Tiryns).

J. L. Myres. Journal of Hellenic Studies, xx, 1900, pp. 128 ff. (on the Homeric house).

Smith's Dictionary (No. 10), s. v. *Andron, Antae, Aula, Clavis, Domus, Focus, Paries, Peristylium, Scalae, Tapites, Tegula.*

Baumeister (No. 19), s. v. *Haus, Heizung, Thüren.*

Becker-Göll (No. 20). Excursus I to Scene III.

Bulletin de correspondance hellénique, 1895, pp. 485–546.

Daremberg et Saglio (No. 22), s. v. *Domus.*

K. Lange. Haus und Halle. Leipzig, 1885.

P. Gardner. New Chapters in Greek History, chap. viii.

To CHAPTER IV.—Harrison and Verrall, pp. 343 ff.

Baumeister, s. v. *Pergamon.*

A. Boetticher. Die Akropolis von Athen. 1888.

O. Jahn and A. Michaelis. Arx Athenarum a Pausania Descripta in usum Scholarum. Bonn, 1901.

To CHAPTER V.—Gardner and Jevons, pp. 454–463; 611–629.

G. Gilbert. The Constitutional Antiquities of Sparta and Athens, translated by E. J. Brooks and T. Nicklin. London, 1895.

Smith's Dictionary, s. v. *Civitas, Servus, Libertus.*

Schoemann. The Antiquities of Greece, translated by E. G. Hardy and J. S. Mann. London, 1880.

A. Boeckh. Die Staatshaushaltung der Athener, 3d edition by Max Fränkel. 1886.

Büchsenschütz. Besitz und Erwerb. Halle, 1869.

BIBLIOGRAPHY

G. Busolt. Die griechischen Staats- und Rechts-Altertümer. Munich, 1892.

Fustel de Coulange. La cité antique. Paris, 1898.

K. F. Hermann's Lehrbuch der griechischen Staats-Altertümer, by V. Thumser. 1889.

G. F. Schoemann. Griechische Altertümer, 4th edition by J. H. Lipsius. Berlin, 1896.

To CHAPTER VI: Smith's Dictionary of Antiquities, s. v. *Incunabula, Amphidromia, Nomen, Vannus, Paedagogus, Aeora, Apodidraskinda, Basilinda, Chelidonia, Myinda, Ostracinda, Pila, Pupa, Trochus, Turbo.*

L. Grasberger. Erziehung und Unterricht im klassischen Altertum. Würzburg, 1864–1881.

L. Grasberger. Stichnamen. 2d edition, 1883.

J. L. Ussing. Erziehung und Unterricht bei den Griechen und Römern. Berlin, 1885.

To CHAPTER VII.—E. Abbott. Hellenica, pp. 67 ff. (The Theory of Education in Plato's Republic, by R. L. Nettleship.)

J. P. Mahaffy. Old Greek Education. New York, 1882.

W. L. Newman. The Politics of Aristotle, vol. iii, pp. xxxix ff. Oxford, 1902.

Smith's Dictionary of Antiquities, s. v. *Ludus litterarius, Abacus, Arithmetica, Atramentum, Buxum, Calamus, Capistrum, Libellus, Liber, Stilus, Tabulae, Lyra, Syrinx, Tibia.*

Baumeister's Denkmäler, s. v. *Musik, Flöten, Saiten-Instrumente.*

T. Birt. Antikes Buchwesen.

K. Dziatzko. Untersuchungen über ausgewählte Kapitel des antiken Buchwesens. Leipzig, 1900.

P. Girard. L'Éducation athénienne, 2d edition. Paris, 1891.

To CHAPTER VIII.—P. Gardner. New Chapters in Greek History, chap. ix.

S. P. Lambros and N. G. Polites. The Olympic Games, B. C. 776–A. D. 1896. Athens and London, 1896.

Smith's Dictionary, s. v. *Athletae, Cursus, Discus, Halteres, Lampadephoria, Lucta, Palaestra, Pancratium, Pentathlum, Pugilatus.*

F. G. Kenyon. The Palaeography of Greek Papyri, especially chapters i–ii, pp. 1–33. Oxford, 1899.

J. H. Putnam. Authors and their Public in Ancient Times. New York, 1894.

Sir E. M. Thompson. Handbook of Greek and Latin Palaeography, 1893.

H. N. Fowler. A History of Ancient Greek Literature, pp. 179–266. New York, 1902.

A. Haigh. The Attic Theatre, 2d edition. Oxford, 1898.

Smith's Dictionary, s. v. *Theatrum, Tragoedia, Comoedia.*

K. F. Hermann's Lehrbuch der griechischen Bühnenaltertümer, by A. Müller. Freiburg, 1886.

W. Dörpfeld and E. Reisch. Das griechische Theater. Athens, 1896.

J. Bintz. Die Gymnastik der Hellenen. Gütersloh, 1878.

A. Boetticher. Olympia. Berlin, 1886.

O. H. Jäger. Die Gymnastik der Hellenen. Stuttgart, 1881.

J. H. Krause. Die Gymnastik und Agonistik der Hellenen, 2 vols. Leipzig, 1841.

To CHAPTER IX.—Contemporary Review. July, 1878, and March, 1879.

C. C. Felton. Greece, Ancient and Modern, i, pp. 343 ff.

Guhl and Koner, pp. 185–195.

H. W. Hayley. The Social and Domestic Position of Women in Aristophanes (in Harvard Studies in Classical Philology), vol. i, 1890, pp. 159–186.

J. P. Mahaffy. Social Life, pp. 52, 142, 274 ff.

Smith's Dictionary, s. v. *Dos, Gamelia.*

St. John's Hellenes, i, 401–424; ii, 1–49.

Baumeister's Denkmäler, s. v. *Hochzeit, Spinnen, Weberei, Sticken.*

To CHAPTER X.—S. Birch. History of Ancient Pottery. London, 1873.

Collignon. Manual of Archaeology. Translated by J. H. Wright, pp. 261–324.

Von Falke. Greece and Rome, pp. 89–91.

Smith's Dictionary, s. v. *Amphora, Ampulla, Arca, Aryballus, Calathus, Calix, Calpis, Candelabrum, Cantharus, Carchesium, Cathedra, Cista, Cotyle, Crater, Cyathus,*

Dolium, Fax, Hydria, Lanterna, Lectus, Lucerna, Mensa, Patera, Psycter, Pulvinus, Pyxis, Rhyton, Scyphus, Sella, Speculum, Stamnus, Taeda, Thronus, Vas.
J. M. Miller. Die Beleuchtung im Altertum. Würzburg, 1885.
H. Weiss. Kostümkunde. Stuttgart, 1881, pp. 368–398.
To CHAPTER XI.—A. de Candolle. Origin of Cultivated Plants. New York, 1885.
T. D. Seymour. Homeric Viands (in Proceedings of the American Philological Association, vol. xxx, 1899, p. xxvi).
Smith's Dictionary, s. v. *Opson, Vinum, Cena.*
Baumeister's Denkmäler, s. v. *Bäckerei, Brot, Mahlzeiten, Löffel.*
V. Hehn. Kulturpflanzen und Hausthiere, 6th edition. Berlin, 1894.
O. Keller, Thiere des classischen Alterthums. Innsbruck, 1887.
To CHAPTER XII.—Lady M. M. Evans. Chapters on Greek Dress. London, 1893.
Gardner and Jevons, pp. 49–67.
T. Hope. The Costume of the Ancients. London, 1875.
Smith's Dictionary, s. v. *Calceus, Crepida, Embas, Endromis, Pera, Soccus, Solea, Cothurnus, Tunica, Palla, Pallium, Amictus, Exomis, Tribon, Vestis, Cingulum, Strophium, Pilleus.*
Zimmern. Home Life, pp. 2–77.
Baumeister's Denkmäler, s. v. *Kleidung, Chiton, Chlamys, Himation, Gürtel, Fussbekleidung, Schuhmacher.*
J. Boehlau. Quaestiones de re vestiaria Graecorum. Weimar, 1884.
F. Studniczka. Beiträge zur Geschichte der altgriechischen Tracht. Vienna, 1886.
H. Weiss. Kostümkunde. Stuttgart, 1881, i, 302–337.
To CHAPTER XIII.—F. W. Nicolson. Greek and Roman Barbers (in Harvard Studies in Classical Philology), vol. ii, 1891, pp. 41–56.
Smith's Dictionary, s. v. *Barba, Coma, Culter, Forfex, Mustax, Pecten, Volsella.*
Baumeister's Denkmäler, s. v. *Haartracht, Barttracht, Barbiere, Scheren, Nadeln, Kämme.*
Bintz. Gymnastik der Hellenen, pp. 70–74.

To Chapter XIV.—H. W. Hayley. The κότταβος κατακτός in the Light of Recent Investigations (in Harvard Studies in Classical Philology), vol. v, 1894, pp. 73–82.

Smith's Dictionary, s. v. *Aenigma, Corona, Cottabus, Mappa, Erani, Parasiti, Symposium, Micare digitis, Nuces, Par impar ludere, Tali, Tessara.*

St. John's Hellenes, ii, pp. 125–219.

Baumeister's Denkmäler, s. v. *Symposion, Kränze, Kottabos, Gaukler, Komos.*

Becq de Fouquières. Les jeux des anciens. Paris, 1869.

Anastasios N. Maltos. Περὶ τῶν συμποσίων τῶν παλαιῶν ἑλλήνων ἐναίσιμος διατριβή. Athens, 1880.

Ohlert. Rätsel und Gesellschaftsspiele. Berlin, 1885.

C. Sittl. Gebärden und Gesten der Griechen und Römer. Leipzig, 1890.

To Chapter XV.—S. P. Bunting. Res nautica apud antiquos. Oxford, 1897.

G. C. V. Holmes. Ancient and Modern Ships. London, 1900, pp. 27–38.

Smith's Dictionary, s. v. *Clipeus, Exercitus, Gladius, Hasta, Navis, Pelta, Strategus.*

C. Torr. Ancient Ships. Cambridge, 1894.

A. Bauer. Die griechischen Kriegsaltertümer (in I. v. Müller's Handbuch), 2d edition. Munich, 1892.

Baumeister's Denkmäler, s. v. *Seewesen.*

A. Breusing. Die Nautik der Alten. Bremen, 1886. .

A. Breusing. Die Lösung des Trierenrätsels. Bremen, 1889.

A. Cartault. La trière athénienne. Paris, 1880.

H. Droysen. Heerwesen und Kriegsführung. 1889.

R. Eins. Das Rudern bei den Alten. Danzig, 1896.

M. Fickelscherer. Das Kriegswesen der Alten. Leipzig, 1888.

Graser. De veterum re navali. Berlin, 1864.

R. Haack. Ueber attische Trieren, in Zeitschrift des Vereines deutscher Ingenieure, xxxix. 1895.

J. Kopecky. Die attischen Trieren. Leipzig, 1890.

H. Liers. Das Kriegswesen der Alten. Breslau, 1895.

E. Luebeck. Das Seewesen der Griechen und Römer. Hamburg, 1890.

R. Stahlecker. Ueber verschiedene Versuche der Rekonstruktion der attischen Triere. Ravensburg, 1897.

H. Weiss. Kostümkunde, pp. 337–355.

To CHAPTER XVI.—Gardner and Jevons, pp. 630–661.

Gilbert. The Constitutional Antiquities of Sparta and Athens, pp. 265–310, 391–416.

A. H. J. Greenidge. A Handbook of Greek Constitutional History. London, 1896.

B. E. Hammond. The Political Institutions of the Ancient Greeks. London, 1895.

Smith's Dictionary, s. v. *Boulé, Cheirotonia, Dokimasia, Ecclesia, Psephus, Prytaneium.*

K. F. Hermann's Lehrbuch der griechischen Rechtsaltertümer, by T. Thalheim. Freiburg, 1884.

Meier and Schoemann. Der attische Process, new edition by J. H. Lipsius. Berlin, 1883–1887.

To CHAPTER XVII.—Smith's Dictionary, s. v. *Agricultura.*

H. Blümner. Kunstgewerbe im Altertum. Leipzig and Prague.

H. Blümner. Technologie und Terminologie der Gewerbe und Künste bei Griechen und Römern, 4 vols. Leipsig, 1875–1887.

Büchsenschütz. Besitz und Erwerb.

W. Richter. Handel und Verkehr, in Seemann's Kulturbilder aus dem klassischen Altertume. Leipzig, 1886.

To CHAPTER XVIII.—Smith's Dictionary, s. v. *Artifices, Fullo, Mola.*

Catalogue of Greek Coins of the British Museum.

P. Gardner. The Types of Greek Coins. Cambridge, 1883.

G. F. Hill. Handbook of Greek and Roman Coins. London, 1899.

W. Ridgeway. The Origin of Metallic Currency and Weight Standards. Cambridge, 1892.

F. Hultsch. Metrologie, revised edition. Berlin, 1882.

To CHAPTER XIX.—Smith's Dictionary, s. v. *Caupona, Currus, Hospitium, Jugum, Plaustrum.*

Baumeister, s. v. *Wirtshäuser.*

320   THE LIFE OF THE ANCIENT GREEKS

To CHAPTER XX.—Gardner and Jevons, pp. 235–286.
Smith's Dictionary, s. v. *Eisiteria, Exodia, Eleusinia, Sacri-
ficium, Thesmophoria.*
Bouché-Leclercq.   Histoire de la divination dans l'antiquité.
Paris, 1880.
A. Mommsen.   Die Feste der Stadt Athen in Altertum.   Leip-
zig, 1898.
C. Petersen.   Der Hausgottesdienst der alten Griechen.   Cas-
sel, 1851.
Preuner.   Hestia-Vesta.   Tübingen, 1864.
O. Seemann.   Die gottesdienstlichen Gebräuche der Griechen
und Römer.

To CHAPTER XXI.—Century Magazine.   April, 1882.
P. Gardner.   New Chapters in Greek History, chaps. x, xi, xii.
J. P. Mahaffy.   Social Life, pp. 290 ff.
Smith's Dictionary, s. v. *Chirurgia, Diaetetica, Medicina,
Medicus, Pharmacopola, Superstitio, Ardanion, Cenota-
phius, Funus, Mausoleum, Sepulchrum, Stele.*
Baumeister's Denkmäler, s. v. *Aerzte, Apotheken, Asklepios,
Hippokrates.*
P. Kavvadias.   Fouilles d'Épidaure.   Athens, 1891.
F. G. Welcker.   Kleine Schriften, iii, 1 ff.

4. PASSAGES IN XENOPHON'S ANABASIS ILLUSTRATING THE TEXT

(a) ARRANGED ACCORDING TO BOOKS

BOOK I	PAGE OF THE TEXT	BOOK I	PAGE OF THE TEXT	BOOK I	PAGE OF THE TEXT
1, 9	246	2, 27	67	5, 6	244, 246, 248
1, 10	253	3, 17	200	5, 7	219
2, 7	12, 99, 100	3, 21	246, 249	5, 8	162, 167
2, 8	83	4, 6	235, 236, 260	5, 10	151, 219, 259
2, 10	80, 104	4, 9	147	5, 12	223
2, 16	163, 192, 257	4, 10	12	6, 1	81
2, 17	260	4, 13	246	6, 7	282
2, 18	236	4, 18	258	6, 10	182
2, 21	257	5, 1	149	7, 1	240
2, 22	148	5, 2	147, 268	7, 3	72
2, 24	254	5, 5	219, 220	7, 4	190

21

PASSAGES IN XENOPHON'S ANABASIS 325

PASSAGES IN XENOPHON'S ANABASIS   329

5. SOURCES OF THE ILLUSTRATIONS

22

6. INDEX TO THE ILLUSTRATIONS

7. INDEX OF GREEK WORDS

INDEX OF GREEK WORDS 353

23

8. GENERAL INDEX

Hydria, 19, 135, 250.
Hymettus, 10, 11, 150, 224.

Ilissus, 10, 11, 18.
Illiteracy, 87.
Illumination, 15, 34, 108, 139.
Imprecation, 283.
Incantation, 290.
Incense, 140.
Inhabitants of Athens, 60 ff.
Ink, 85.
Inns, 254.
Interment, 295.
Interpreters, 260.
Ionic columns, 50, 298.
Irrigation, 217.
Isthmia, 100.

Jars for water, 19, 135.
Javelins, 99, 196.
Javelin throwing, 94.
Jerkins, 161.
Jewel-caskets, 131.
Jewellers, 230.
Jumping, 80, 94.

Kalathos, 141.
Kalpis, 135.
Kantharos, 137.
Karchesion, 137.
Keramia, 134.
Kerchiefs, 167.
Kettles, 136.
Keys, 29 f.
King's Portico, 42, 43.
Kitchen, 31, 36.
Koppatias, 98.
Kothōn, 138.
Kotylé or kotylos, 138.
Koureion, 89.

Krater, 136 ff.
Kyathos, 137.
Kykeon, 143, 280.

Labourers, 233.
Laconian key, 30.
Lamps, 34, 35, 108, 139.
Languages, 260.
Lanterns, 141.
Law courts, 211 ff.
Leaping, 80, 94.
Lebes, 136.
Lekythos, 135.
Lenaea, 113.
Lentils, 149.
Lettuce, 147.
Libations, 182, 271.
Libraries, 57, 108.
Lighting, 15, 34, 108, 139.
Liturgia, 62, 66.
Lofts, 33.
Long walls, 8.
Loutra, 122.
Lucky days, 122.
Luxury, 127, 144.
Lycabettus, 8, 11.
Lycēum, 59, 91.
Lyre, 82, 123.

Magistrates, 14, 20, 301 ff.
Maidens' Porch, 55.
Majority, age of, 89.
Mantles, 129, 158 ff.
Manufacturers, 166, 227 ff.
Marble quarries, 2, 8, 10.
Market, 13, 14, 40, 58, 236 ff.
Marriage, 31, 61, 119 ff.
Marsyas, 83.
Masks, 115.
Masons, 196, 231.

Masts, 203.
Mathematics, 87.
Mats, 129.
Measures, 243 ff.
Meat, 143, 145.
Media, wall of, 23.
Medicine, 286.
Men, life of, 40.
    occupations of young, 91 ff.
    demeanour of, 158–160.
Mespila, wall of, 23.
Metals, 10.
Metics, 64 ff., 170, 228.
Metopes, 47.
Metrŏon, 42.
Military training, 81, 90, 190 ff.
Milk, 144, 150.
Millet, 148.
Mills, 220, 228.
Mina, 98, 129, 246.
Mines, 10, 68, 230.
Mints, 247.
Mirrors, 132.
Money, 245 ff., 303.
Months, 240 ff., 306 ff.
Moriai, 221.
Mountains, 1, 10, 11.
Music, 79, 82, 123, 185.
Mycēnae, 5, 17.
Myrrh, 175.
Mysteries of Eleusis, 276 ff., 294.

Name day, 73.
Naos, 44 ff.
Navy, 199 ff.
Necklaces, 167 ff.
Nemea, 100 f.
Nicknames, 74.
Niké, 50, 55 ff.
    24

Nurses, 75 f.
Nuts, 148.

Oars, 201.
Oaths, 90, 282.
Obol, 246.
Occupations, 188 ff.
Odeium, 108.
Odes on athletic victories, 104.
Oikiai, 33.
Oil, 133, 139, 147, 148, 150, 174, 220 ff.
Old age, 284.
Olives, 2, 144.
Olympiads, 105.
Olympic games, 97, 100 ff.
Omens, 272.
Onions, 147, 149.
Opson, 146.
Oracles, 273.
Orchestra, 113.
Ornamentation in dress, 162, 163.
Ornaments, 162, 167 ff., 178.
Orphans, 72, 74, 88.
Ovens, 32.
Owls, 24.

Painters, 3.
Palaestra, 80, 92, 135.
Panathenaea, 51, 62, 100, 104, 274.
Pankration, 95, 103, 105.
Pantomimes, 186, 218.
Paper, 109.
Papyrus, 85, 108.
Parasols, 170.
Parastas, 28, 46.
Parks, 11 f.
Parthenon, 51 ff.

Pastas, 28, 30, 36.
Pasturage, 223.
Pavements, 8, 15, 34, 36, 37.
Pears, 148.
Peas, 147.
Pedagogues, 67, 77, 78.
Pediments, 47.
Pens, 85.
Pentakosiomedimnoi, 61, 301.
Pentathlon, 95, 102.
Pentelicus, 10, 18.
Peplos, 54, 56, 274.
Perfumes, 175.
Pergamus, 23, 57.
Pericles, 16, 64, 108, 118, 121.
Peristyle, 28, 36, 37.
Petasos, 100, 166, 257.
Peusinioi, 20.
Phialé, 137.
Phidias, 51, 53.
Phratry, 74, 89, 124, 281.
Physical characteristics, of
    Greece, 1 ff.
    of the Greeks, 171 ff.
Physicians, 27, 286 ff.
Pigs, 145, 268.
Pillows, 129.
Pilots, 203.
Pinakothēké, 50.
Pins, 167 ff.
Piraeus, 16, 64.
Pitchers, 135 ff.
Pithos, 133.
Platters, 141.
Plays, 113 ff.
Ploughs, 218.
Poets, 103, 104, 234.
Police, 16, 19.
Polītai, 60.
Pomegranates, 144.

Popular assembly, 63, 208 ff.
Population of Attica, 60 ff.
Poros, 2.
Porridge, 145, 147.
Porters, 26, 36, 67.
Porticoes, 14, 28, 42, 43, 57, 237.
Poseidon, 101.
Potters, 3.
Pottery, 10 f., 232.
Poultry, 27, 146.
Prayers, 264.
Prices, 248.
Priēné, 32, 37, 38.
Priests, 30, 89, 266.
Prizes, 103.
Processions, 8 f., 16, 123, 278,
    295.
Pronaos, 46 ff.
Propylaea, 48 ff.
Prothesis, 294.
Proxenos, 64, 253.
Prytaneium, 42, 63, 104, 301.
Prytanes, 42, 43, 63, 207.
Purification, 266, 298.
Purple, 4.
Pyrrhus, 24.
Pyrriché, 84, 274.
Pythia, 100 f.

Quinces, 144.

Radishes, 147.
Raisins, 148.
Reading, 79, 85, 108, 179.
Reaping, 219.
Refuse, 16, 17.
Religion, 262 ff., 292.
Rhapsodes, 107.
Rhyton, 138.
Riding, 97.

Rings, 167 ff.
Rivers of Greece, 2 f.
Roads, 7.
Roofs, 24.
Rooms, 28 f.
Rotunda, 42.
Rowing, 201.
Rugs, 128, 129.
Running, 80, 101, 102.

Sacks, 142.
Sacred springs, 11, 18.
Sacred Way, 8, 13.
Sacrifices, 89, 123, 265 ff.
Sailors, 166, 202.
Salesrooms, 27.
Salt, 149.
Salutation, 181.
Salves, 148, 175.
Samphoras, 98.
Sandals, 75, 164.
Sauces, 149.
Sausages, 146.
Scales, 244.
Schools, 79 ff., 282.
Seasoning, 149.
Sesame, 122, 149.
Sewers, 17 f.
Sewing, 125.
Sheep, 145.
Shepherds, 10.
Shields, 193.
Ships, 199, 260.
Shoemakers, 229.
Shoes, 164 ff.
Shops, 14, 27, 36.
Sickness, 125, 285 ff.
Sidewalks, 9, 15.
Silphium, 150.
Silver, 10.

Singing, 82, 123, 185.
Sisyra, 162.
Skené, 114.
Skins, 129, 142, 166.
Slaves, 26, 27, 66 ff., 125, 126.
Sleeping-rooms, 29.
Sleeves, 156.
Slings, 99, 195 ff.
Soap, 174.
Socrates, 28, 105, 172.
Soldiers, 190 ff.
Solonian division of the citizens, 61.
Soothsayers, 266.
Sophists, 105.
Soup, 144, 182.
Sowing, 218 f.
Sparta, 22, 164, 100, 173.
Spears, 99, 194.
Spear-throwing, 80, 94.
Speech-writers, 213, 214.
Spelt, 148.
Spices, 149, 150.
Spinach, 147.
Spinning, 125 f.
Spits, 146.
Sponges, 4.
Springs, 11, 18.
Stadion, 93, 102.
Stairs, 32, 35.
Stamnos, 134.
Stilus, 85, 111.
Storerooms, 29.
Strainers, 136, 151.
Strangers, 251.
Straps, 19, 78, 95.
Streets, 12, 15, 16, 20, 62, 70, 227.
Strigils, 80, 81.
Stromata, 129.
Suburbs, 11.

Water-supply, 18, 33, 285.
Weapons, 192 ff.
Weaving, 125.
Weddings, 119 ff., 141.
Weights and measures, 43, 242 ff.
Wheat, 143, 148.
Wicks, 139.
Wills, 291.
Windows, 24, 33.
Wine, 133, 143, 144, 150 ff., 183, 220 f., 286.
Witnesses, 213.
Women, 28, 30, 35, 68, 70, 119 ff., 156 ff., 186, 236, 279, 294.

Woodenware, 131, 132.
Workshops, 27, 36.
Wreaths, 103.
Wrestling, 80, 92, 101, 102.
Writing, 79, 85.
Writing-tablets, 85, 111.

Xystis, 160.

Year, 241.
Yeast, 149.

Zeugītai, 61.
Zeus, 30, 57, 100, 208, 252, 261, 264, 282.

THE END